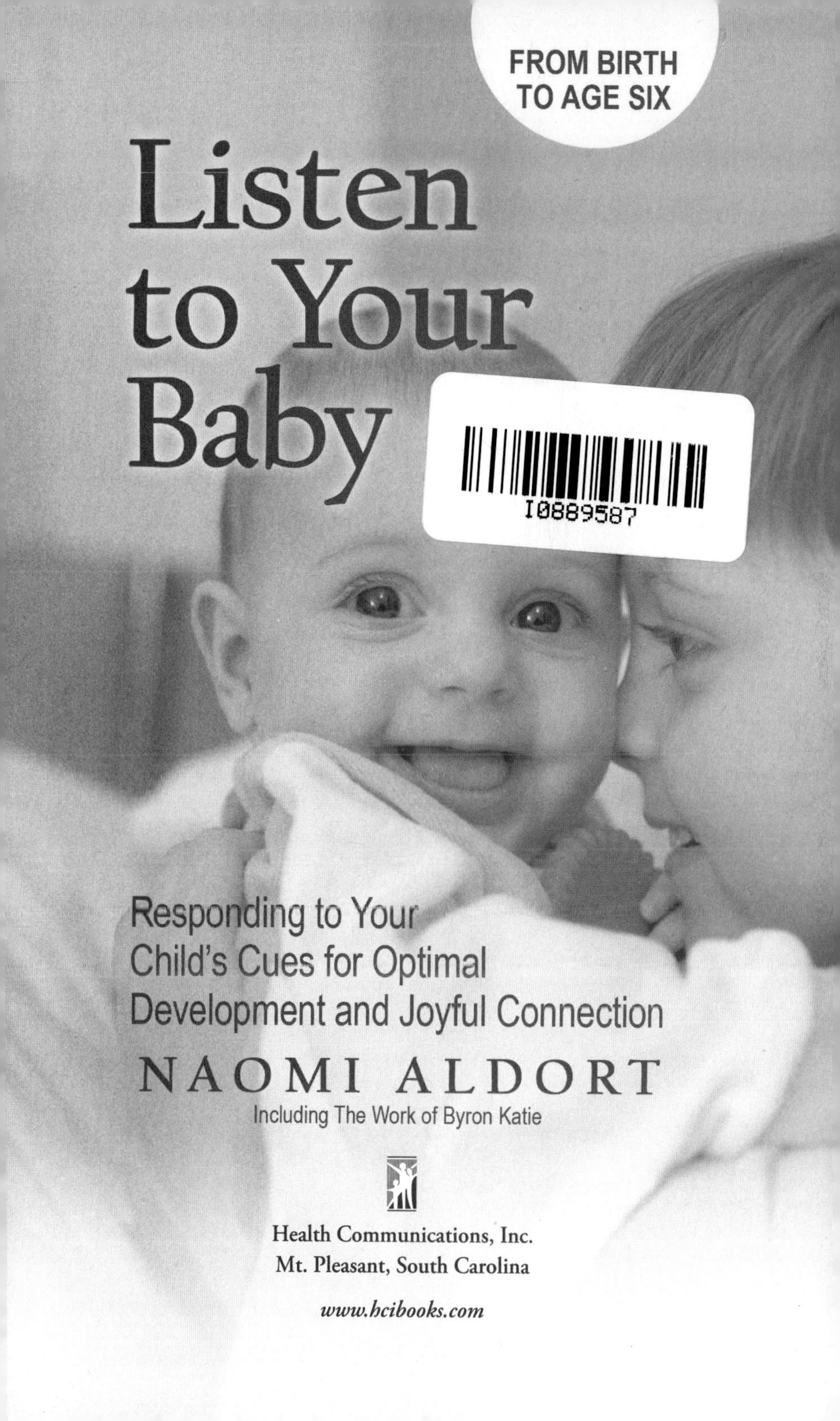

FROM BIRTH TO AGE SIX

Listen to Your Baby

Responding to Your Child's Cues for Optimal Development and Joyful Connection

NAOMI ALDORT

Including The Work of Byron Katie

Health Communications, Inc.
Mt. Pleasant, South Carolina

www.hcibooks.com

Library of Congress Cataloging-in-Publication Data
is available through the Library of Congress

ISBN-13: 978-07573-2604-2 (Paperback)
ISBN-10: 07573-2604-8 (Paperback)
ISBN-13: 978-07573-2605-9 (ePub)
ISBN-10: 07573-2605-6 (ePub)

Publisher: Health Communications, Inc.
1240 Winnowing Way, Suite 102
Mt. Pleasant, SC 29466

Editing by Carol Rosenberg and Christine Belleris.
Cover, interior design, and formatting by Larissa Hise Henoch.

Contents

Introduction

Whether this is your first or third baby and whether your child is a newborn or toddler, you have likely come to this book for fresh insight into parenting your child—maybe even to undo some of the confusion you have about parenting. You have most likely been bombarded with advice ever since (and even before) your baby's birth:

Hold her, put her down, nurse her on cue, nurse at even intervals, don't nurse, give him a pacifier, don't give him a pacifier, put him to sleep by himself, keep him in your bed, carry her on your body, put her in a stroller, let her cry it out to sleep, nurse her to sleep, don't nurse her to sleep, let him cry, don't let him cry, feed him, give her a bottle, only nurse till three months, wean at nine months, wean at three years, don't wean, don't nurse, go back to work, don't go back to work, toilet train, don't toilet train, use elimination communication, feed by spoon, give only finger food, breastfeed only. . . .

By the time you've heard it all, there isn't one issue about which you didn't receive conflicting advice. So, how do you know what's best? It's as simple as *listen to your baby.*

Think of this book as a translation of the manual that came with your baby to a language you can understand so that you can do what is best for his or her development, inner power, and joy. Indeed, our babies have all the answers if only we learn to read their signals.

The greatest difficulty is not figuring out what your baby is telling you; it is clearing your mind from the noise of all the opinions and expectations that have complicated parenting and made the obvious invisible. Once your mind is clear, you will not only hear and understand your baby but also trust her rather than be swayed against her by the many voices in your head and around you. Here's an example: You may understand that your baby is unhappy when you put her in a crib, but you don't find a solution, because your mind is full of ideas that obscure the obvious. You try to stay next to her, to leave, to give a pacifier, to keep the light on, to sing, to rub the baby's feet, to make noises, to rock, to hold, to put back down, and so on.

The simple solution that your baby is asking for may perhaps not be present in your consciousness, because it is outside the accepted paradigm and requires that we *trust* ourselves and, most importantly, the baby. The majority of us have been trained by our caretakers, teachers, and the media not to trust ourselves and to do whatever authority figures tell us is the correct thing to do. We've learned to ignore our own inner yearning and, instead, surrender to the dictates of other voices and seek their approval. We do our best to do the "right thing" according to the ideas passed on to us by those we think are "in the know." In doing so, we often forget to check with ourselves—not realizing how wise we already are in the depth of our being.

Your natural wisdom is as clear as daylight, but, as is the case for most of us, it may be covered up by an endless barrage of cultural and well-intended but misguided expectations. Most of us have been trained and habituated to seek external approval and dismiss our own inner guide. This book is about going back to trusting your own deep and reliable wisdom. It is about becoming who you already are in caring for your child. It is about learning to listen to your child and trusting the way of nature. Although you will learn how to read your baby's cues and elicit your own wisdom, I also offer specific ideas and solutions throughout this book for your consideration. You will learn to apply the principles of inquiry as presented in this book to any idea that does not feel peaceful to you.

Parenting gives rise to our fallibilities, our own childhood issues, and our emotional limitations. In this book, you will find tools for discovering loving answers within yourself, as well as guidance based on my experience with thousands of parents worldwide. You will learn to question your assumptions and habitual thoughts using a process of self-inquiry known as The Work of Byron Katie to gain clarity and confidence in caring for your child from infancy through the early years and all subjects of being alive.

To best benefit from this work, make sure to first read Chapter 1. In it, you will find clear examples and instructions on how to benefit from the rest of the book so that it becomes not just a set of ideas but a collection of tools you can use daily. When you use these tools, you will be able to awaken your own wisdom and enable yourself to be the loving parent you want to be for your beloved child.

Avoid turning what you read in this book into yet another external rule to follow. Keep your child in front of you as your main guide, and keep your heart open and free; otherwise, the whole point of the book would be missed. Although you will learn new ideas, the main purpose of this book is for you to gain emotional freedom so that you can really hear and see and feel your child. The guiding principle is keeping unconditional love awake and present.

Please note that although this book's many real-life examples are mostly with married mothers in a two-parent home, it is equally valuable for all types of parents and family setups. If you take away the principles rather than the particular circumstances, you will be able to use these tools in any situation with your unique child, no matter his or her age. This book can also be read by extended family, friends, your doctor, and others who support you in bringing up your child or children. Throughout the book, I often use the words "baby," "toddler," and "child" interchangeably. What you read here can be applied to children of any age in your life right now.

My wish is that you enjoy the reading and mostly that you become skillful at finding loving solutions for raising your child with clarity and joy so he or she can become a confident, compassionate, and resilient human being.

A note about gender: I alternate between male and female pronouns when referring to your child throughout the book.

Chapter 1

Eliminate Mind Chatter and Access Your Parental Wisdom

Sometimes, we mistakenly believe we are following our own guidance. This occurs when the thoughts that were imprinted on our minds are so deeply engraved and our self-doubt so ingrained that we believe these thoughts to be our own. And, as humans, we believe these thoughts to actually be who we are. Yet, thoughts are not you. The illusion that they are you is powerful and therefore confusing. When you obey your thoughts without inquiry, then the thoughts have you rather than you having thoughts. *Once you learn to use your thoughts rather than be used by them, you can become the being who is in charge and can freely choose which thoughts serve you and your baby and which do not.*

Who would you be if different thoughts had been planted in your mind? Who are you really when you are free to respond to life from within, without the voices of others, and without needing to impress anyone or fit into their convictions? Who are you—to your baby and to yourself—when your mind is still and you are fully present to reality?

My intention throughout this book is to help you recognize your own wisdom, which comes from observing reality, and distinguishing it from all the other mind chatter you erroneously believe to be yours so that you can be the kind and loving parent you are by nature. When you aren't confused by a jumble of thoughts that aren't your own, it is simple to respond to your baby from love.

Thoughts are learned and recorded over all the years of our lives. No thought can be true, simply because it is a thought as opposed to reality. A thought can, however, match reality. When it does, it feels peaceful, and when it doesn't, it hurts and feels stressful. Thoughts from any source can provide guidance if we inquire into them until we find the one that brings peace and joy to the situation. When you respond from love to what is real in the moment—that is, your baby's cues—caring for your baby comes naturally.

Forgive Yourself So You Can Move On

One of the common emotional reactions to learning something new about parenting is regretting the mistakes we may have made. Fortunately, humans were designed to be raised by imperfect parents who learn "on the job." However, we tend to forget that and turn our regret for our mistakes into guilt and self-judgment.

Guilt means applying a courthouse to your own humanity. The idea of being at fault can cause all sorts of reactions—from blaming the book for making you feel bad to dismissing the idea that this can be a valuable approach. Try to be kind to yourself if you have these thoughts; they can get in the way of considering helpful information. There is no risk if you simply keep reading and decide for yourself if this is a route you are ready to take.

In this book, you will learn how to deal with discouraging thoughts as well as many other parenting ideas that block you from being the parent you truly wish to be. You will learn to peel off the layers of habits and automated reactions that obstruct your loving self from showing up.

Guilt, shame, and fault are different from regrets and from taking responsibility for learning. In responsibility, there is no courthouse; there is just forgiveness and a moving on: "Oh, I see, this way I was treating my little one was actually causing more difficulties." Such awareness leads to positive action and change: "This new way touches my heart and is worth trying."

Trying something new does not mean you were doing a terrible job before. It only means that you are committed to keep learning, growing, and improving your ways of responding to your baby or child. Welcome to being human. Forgive yourself for any mistakes you feel you have made as a parent and move on.

Question Preconceived Notions

We see the world through our own lens, and we project our own image onto others. If we cannot trust our inner guidance, we cannot trust the baby to give us the "right" cues. We then tend to see the baby as having the "wrong" will inside her, just like we do. We think that what she wants is often wrong or misguided so we must train her to do what is considered "right." This is a projection of our own self-mistrust.

For example, we often don't trust the baby when she wants to breastfeed very frequently. We believe our own thoughts that she shouldn't be hungry so soon. We doubt the toddler's idea of when and where to sleep and designate firm nap times and bedtime. We believe the baby should sleep through the night and that the less the baby wakes at night, the better, so we struggle through nighttime wakings, feeling resentful. We may think that the sooner she sleeps in her own bed, the more independent she will become, so we push the idea of being a "big girl" for sleeping in her own bed.

All our efforts that go against what the child is doing naturally are based on thoughts—not reality—and, therefore, not truth nor what is best for the baby. In this book, you are encouraged to question all these misguided notions and come back to your senses.

Your baby gives you cues, and you can learn to read these cues and to trust yourself and trust your baby. Nature doesn't give a baby the "wrong" idea of how to survive. Training babies and toddlers to ignore or oppose what they feel and need is difficult, painful, and harmful to the child's development of self-reliance. Meanwhile, understanding and trusting the baby's true primal needs are joyous and peaceful, and such connection enables optimal development. We are still the guides, but even if we cannot provide something in the moment, we can make sure that the baby knows her inclination is valid and we care and are doing what we can.

Rethink Following "Majority Rules"

Can a whole culture be wrong? Of course it can. Humanity has been wrong before and will keep being convinced of one idea or approach only to discover new ideas that demolish those previous convictions. Humanity, like children, is always learning in this evolutionary manner.

History is full of examples. Whole cultures believed the Earth was flat; whole cultures killed and tortured people for supposedly being witches; whole cultures believed the sun revolved around the Earth; whole cultures believed it was right to beat up women and children or cut off parts of sexual organs (and some still do); and whole cultures treated women as lesser than men (and some still do). The examples are endless.

A society can easily be on a wrong path and eventually look back with dismay. Majority agreement does not mean right or best. "Majority" only means that no one is thinking for himself or herself and everyone follows the mythical "others." A majority opinion does not make something right for your baby; in fact, it can be contradictory to his well-being and to the future of a peaceful and thriving society. That's why we are starting in this book from ground zero.

How would you care for your baby without all the cultural noise and without your mind's noise that comes from others' voices?

While this book does not assume anything about the teachings of any particular culture, I am not suggesting that we abandon our history and knowledge. On the contrary, if we raise children who are cared for optimally, based on their inner guidance, they will be better able to join society, learn its culture, and make a positive contribution.

If you dare to question the notions passed on to you from other sources, you can determine what is best for the individual child in your care. In the process, you will find that you already know how to be the best parent for your child. You will rediscover your innate wisdom that's been covered up with all the confusing thoughts you inherited from others. You will start your own path of healing from past hurts in your own upbringing, which will free you to respond to your baby with innate wisdom and based on her cues.

Be Guided by Reality

We idealize thinking because the mind is indeed amazing. But thoughts can often lead us astray. Reality, by contrast, is a much more reliable source of guidance. Throughout this book, you'll discover that answers to common questions are often found in "reading your baby's lips."

Each question has a few possible answers, shedding light on your child's signals and cues. Once you consider them, you can do the inquiry as explained later in this chapter to see whether a certain answer is a fit for your baby's situation or whether your baby requires something else to bring her peace. This requires you to tune in to your baby and your own loving heart. Due to the many subtle and significant differences among human beings, each baby is a world unfolding, and your goal is to learn this one specific world and respond to this young being on his terms. This results in a confident, connected, and caring child and later a human being who acts with compassion and is responsive to and respectful of all living beings.

Recognizing and understanding your baby's signals will become easy once you have implemented what you read in this book. Even if your baby's particular cues are not represented in any of these pages, you will still become skillful at reading your baby like a book, trusting him and yourself.

Clear Yourself of Obstructive Thoughts

As you continue reading this book, your mind may rebel because of the thoughts you have inherited from others. Remember, those thoughts are not yours. Knowing this will help you to not take the thoughts so seriously or personally. They are not you. You just have these particular ones in your mind's reel. Here are two pieces of proof that your thoughts aren't truly yours:

1. If you had grown up in a different culture from the one in which you were raised, you would have developed a different set of thoughts and beliefs from those you currently have. If thoughts are determined by the environment in which you were raised, then those thoughts cannot have originated with you. In fact, all thoughts are recycled through society.
2. If your thoughts don't bring peace to you and your child, they cannot be true. The struggle is proof of their falseness; the very nature of struggle is to go against the stream, against what is real and true. The cause of stress is the action of choosing to oppose reality—in this case, to oppose your baby's direction.

To get the most out of this book and become tuned in to your child, it's crucial to clear yourself of obstructive thoughts, creating a mental space in which you can see your baby directly and not through filtering dogmas.

See with your eyes, hear with your ears, and feel with your being—not with the stories in your mind.

You can become an expert on your baby just by removing obstructing concepts. The following are some common concepts that sway us away from responding to a baby on his terms and prevent us from caring for him in a way that is best for his development and emotional competence (you may have others to add to the list):

My baby will be spoiled if I respond to all her cues as she wishes.

She will never learn to . . . (for example, sleep, be independent, have structure).

She must stop . . . (for example, crying, demanding, screaming, throwing tantrums, staying awake).

He must be trained to . . . (for example, sleep, eat, be clean, not cry, get out of diapers).

A baby should sleep through the night.

My toddler should do as I say.

My parents, friends, and/or pediatricians know better than I do.

She won't grow up well if I don't control her.

She will control me if I give in to what she wants.

He will never get used to . . . unless I force him to do it.

Babies don't know what they need (for example, to sleep, to eat, to be only with Mom).

I cannot trust my baby to know her own needs correctly.

If I always give my baby what she needs, my friends will say I am a bad parent.

What the baby wants is not what she really needs.

My baby should be happy all the time.

My baby should learn to fall asleep by herself.

My baby should sleep in her own bed.

If she doesn't sleep by herself now, she will never be able to.

If she doesn't learn to obey, she will be out of hand when she gets older.
I need to control the situation involving my child.
She should take a nap.
The baby is tired but doesn't know it.
The baby needs routine.
My toddler should understand that the baby comes first.
My toddler should be quiet when the baby is asleep.
My toddler should get whatever she wants in order to feel loved.
My value is measured by how my child behaves.

Look for more thoughts that do not feel authentic or responsive to your heart and to your baby. Notice how these types of thoughts control you by taking away your freedom. You'll find guidance on questioning your thoughts later in this chapter, but for now, just start noticing. Without these thoughts, you are free to love and respond to your baby or child based on the way she is.

Without your thoughts, there is no struggle—your baby is right, and your inner wisdom and need to respond to her flow easily and with joy.

Your mind might be rebelling right now. Yes, it is true that sometimes a toddler wants something that they shouldn't have and shouldn't be provided. Rest assured, when you are connected to your authentic wisdom, you will know when that is the case and how to communicate it in a way that fosters connection, cooperation, and trust. You will find more on this topic later.

How to Free Yourself from Stressful Thoughts

When you are experiencing stress or conflict with regard to your parenting choices, write each of your thoughts down. Look at each thought, and question its validity. The process of self-inquiry designed to identify and question stressful thought known as The Work of Byron Katie is an excellent guide for this process. Byron Katie is the author of *Loving What Is* and other books that teach how to free oneself from the grip of thoughts that get in the way of peace and of loving action. Below are the four questions as Byron Katie presents them, followed by the turnaround of the original thought. To use it effectively, you must first write down the thought that gives you stress or disconnects you from the child (examples will follow). The mind is easily fooled by thoughts. Once they are written down and you look at them, it is much easier to not identify with them, have a clear view, and see the thought for what it is and what it is not.

Once the thought is written down, ask four questions and then do a turnaround as follows:

1. Is it true?
2. Can you absolutely know that it's true?
3. How do you react, what happens, when you believe this thought?
4. Who would you be without the thought?

After asking these questions, step 5 is to turn the original thought around in a few ways. We'll get to that part shortly. Here are additional questions to help you dig deeper as you are learning the process:

1. Can you know the thought is true?
2. Can you absolutely know and be sure?
3. Can the thought be more valid than your natural responsiveness to your baby's cues?
4. You were designed by Mother Nature (and/or God if that resonates) to know and respond to your child. Can Nature/God be wrong?
5. Whose thought is it really?
6. When you believe this thought, do you feel peace or stress?
7. Who would you be without this thought or when not believing it?

Write down any thoughts that bring you anxiety about your baby or toddler; focus on thoughts that arise with a sense of stress or confusion. Stress means that the thought does not match reality. Here are some possible thoughts to apply the questions to:

The baby is not breastfeeding enough.

She is overfeeding.

She cries a lot; something is wrong.

She should sleep more at night.

Should the baby start turning by now?

Her poop shouldn't be runny.

I should be able to put my baby down off my body.

My toddler isn't eating enough.

My baby is crying too much.

He should learn to walk by now.

He shouldn't have a diaper rash.

I shouldn't have to hold my toddler all the time.

My baby should not cry while I change his diaper.

Some thoughts may feel natural due to habit, but it's worth looking deeper in your inner being. Does the thought bring you stress or peace? If it brings stress, it tells you that you are going against your own truth and integrity and against reality. Indeed, your inauthentic, stressful thoughts create anxiety and confusion, causing you to struggle. They prevent you from trusting your baby and yourself and from finding your own wisdom and peace.

When considering who you would be without the thought, take your time. The automated response tends to take some people out of presence. Close your eyes and, with a still mind, imagine the same scenario or issue. If your mind didn't have the idea or if you didn't believe it, who would you be with your baby in that same situation?

Recall times when you went against your wisdom and you followed thoughts that were not yours or useful for you. The resulting stress and regrets can help you scrutinize the current thoughts. Then recall times when your wisdom rose above the voices in your head—and how clear and peaceful you felt. You are already there; just remove the blinders. Remind yourself of those things and that, no matter what relatives or the so-called authorities say, you are going to stay true to your path of following your baby's direction.

Without stressful thoughts, you will respond to your baby or toddler with no fear of losing control and without concern that she will never learn, that your relatives won't approve, that your baby will be spoiled, and all the other unfounded worries. Once you answered what is true and how you feel with and without a stressful thought, you will experience freedom to explore the opposite of your thought, thereby opening your mind and loosening up its grip on you. This is when you do the *turnaround* of your thought.

Take the original thought and inquire to see whether the opposite isn't as true or truer (there may be more than one opposite), and you can also turn it around by putting it on yourself as demonstrated next.

Example 1: "I'll spoil my baby if I hold her all the time."

Ariana shared in her Zoom session with me that she believes she would spoil her baby if she holds her almost all the time. I prompted Ariana to answer the four questions:

Ariana wrote down the thought: *"If I hold the baby most of the time, she will be spoiled."*

Naomi: Is this thought true?

Ariana: Yes.

Naomi: Can you absolutely know that it's true?

Ariana: No. I believe what people say to me.

Naomi: *"If you hold your baby most of the time, she will be spoiled."* How do you react when you believe this thought and your baby wants to be held?

Ariana: I deny her wish. After I have held her for a while, I put her down and she cries, so I try to soothe her or give her a pacifier.

Naomi: That must be painful.

Ariana: It is.

Naomi: How else do you react?

Ariana: I struggle. I want to hold her. I love her. I wish to respond naturally. I am afraid to harm her, so I don't let myself connect with her.

Naomi: Yes. This is the nature of going against your child, against yourself, believing thoughts that aren't yours and aren't even true and that, to obey them, you must disconnect from love, from yourself, and from your baby. Who would you be, with your baby wanting to be held most of the time, without this thought that she would be spoiled if you hold her all the time?

Ariana (sobbing): I would hold my baby.

Naomi: So, *with* the thought, you create distance and you feel fearful. Without the thought . . .

Ariana: Without the thought, just joy to hold her as much as she and I want.

Naomi: "*If I hold the baby all the time, she will be spoiled.*" Turn it around to the opposite.

Ariana: If I hold my baby all the time, she will thrive.

Naomi: Is this thought as true or truer than the original thought?

Ariana: It is truer. She would feel good about herself when I respond with love and ease.

Naomi: Yes. When do you fulfill your motherly heart more—when you are feeling good about yourself or when you are anxious and doubting yourself?

Ariana: When I feel good. Yes, I see that she would be better off when I fully respond to her. She will learn from me to be responsive, and she will be satisfied rather than needy and anxious.

Naomi: Yes. Isn't that simple? How does this opposite thought feel inside you?

Ariana: Such a relief.

Naomi: Take the thought and turn it around to yourself.

Ariana: If I hold myself back, my baby will be harmed.

Naomi: Can you find the truth in this?

Ariana: Oh, yes. If I hold back my love and affection, then she will be harmed—not the other way around.

This inquiry left Ariana open to discover what is real. She can see with her own eyes, hear with her own ears, and feel with her own heart rather than through a bunch of recorded concepts.

Will her baby be harmed by being held as much as she wants and truly needs? Not possible.

As Ariana continued to explore her thoughts, she got greater clarity. She inquired into the thought, "What babies want isn't really what is best for them," and discovered that babies know best what they need, and they communicate it. If we dare to listen and respond, we will be the parent we wish to be and that the baby needs.

Is It *Always* Best to Follow Your Child's Signals?

The answer is always yes when it comes to your child's primal basic needs—that's what reality teaches us. Of course, sometimes toddlers want to pick up a bee, eat candy all day, walk on their own into the ocean, and so on. In these times, we say yes to the toddler's intent while responding to her big-picture desire to stay alive and well. It is a yes to the yearning and a no to the bee or to a jump into the ocean.

Therefore, the response can be a yes to the intent, "You like to get in the water" or "This bug is pretty" and you pick the child up saying, "You wish to hold the bug. The bug doesn't like to be touched, and so it can hurt you when you hold it." We are saying yes to the child's interest while, of course, responding by keeping her well and safe.

Similarly, in addition to natural dangers, we want to protect the baby from human-made things or intruders that do harm. Babies do not on their own develop a need for gadgets, sugar, or other artificial stimulation. Introducing such artificial stimulants to the young mind impacts its wants outside of primal needs. These are the intruders we protect the baby from as much as possible.

When thinking about responding to your baby's cues, I mostly mean primal, basic needs that are nature's design for the baby's optimal development: the need for holding, breastfeeding, sleeping, motion, body contact, elimination, nourishment, affection, and connection. These are all primal and "programmed" in the baby from birth for optimal development.

When responding to these primal needs, you not only allow the baby to thrive, but you also create a bond of trust between the two of you. With such trust, the toddler follows your guidance when you remove her from the street or take her away from unsafe situations.

Example 2: "It is important to swaddle the baby."

Swaddling or giving your baby a pacifier may stop your baby from crying, but does this mean that it is a real and healthy need of the baby? Not necessarily. These methods may suppress the baby's physical or emotional expression or other real needs or prevent us from noticing a different need that has to be met (more likely for suckling or motion than for being tied up). Learning each baby's nature occurs through a connection that is not hindered by dogma.

Questioning your thoughts on this issue is quick and simple. Patty called for a session simply because she was confused by too much well-intended advice. Here is Patty's inquiry about swaddling:

Patty: *"My baby needs to be swaddled."*

Naomi: Is that true?

Patty: I am not sure. Everyone says it's good for the baby.

Naomi: Can you absolutely know that it would be best for him to be swaddled?

Patty: No.

Naomi: How do you react when you believe this thought?

Patty: Confused. I swaddle the baby even when he resists.

Naomi: How would you be without this thought?

Patty: I would connect and find out what is the real need and respond accordingly.

Naomi: Turn it around.

Patty: *"My baby does not need to be swaddled."*

Naomi: Find proof for that.

Patty: He doesn't want to. He wants to move. He wants something else. He wants me to rock him. These are healthy neurological developmental motions.

Naomi: Can you find another turnaround?

Patty: *"My thoughts need to be swaddled—to be restrained by questioning them. Or perhaps I actually need some rest in a motionless state."*

Naomi: Maybe while caring for your baby isn't the best time for it, but recognizing the need is a useful realization too.

Patty: I have another turnaround: *"He often needs to be able to move freely."*

A discussion on swaddling comes later in the book. Suffice to say here that listening to your baby is likely the optimal response. There are a few tricks to get a baby to be what appears calmer. Is that what is best or what the baby needs? Let's keep exploring.

Heal Your Triggers

It is useful to notice your emotional reactions so you can best catch yourself and bring healing to your own pain and put your attention back on your child. Feeling triggered is noticing not only the stressful thought but also the pain and reactions from your past that accompany that thought. The inquiry is designed to help you identify the buried emotions, allow them to be, and notice that the thoughts that trigger them are not valid in this moment.

Not being triggered is not about teaching your baby (or anyone, for that matter) to accommodate your emotional issues, but about healing yourself so your baby can be free to be herself—something over which she has no control.

Perhaps the baby cries, and you notice that you get angry or scared. What happened to you when you cried as a child? Or is there another pain being triggered? Use the inquiry as demonstrated earlier to heal your own triggers. Each time you do an inquiry, you answer the question, "How do I feel when I believe the thought?" The thought may be that the baby shouldn't cry, that she should use the pacifier, that she should sleep by herself, that the toddler shouldn't bite, and so on.

When you inquire into each thought, you often discover that your emotional reaction to the thought is rooted in past experiences. Doing the inquiry not only clears the mind but also heals the pain that comes to the surface.

Here are some of the answers parents give to the question, "How do you react when you believe this thought?" (You may have some of your own.)

1. *I get annoyed by the baby.*
2. *I feel stressed out.*
3. *I feel helpless; I don't know what to do when she cries.*
4. *I feel lost and resigned.*
5. *I think that I am a terrible mother/father.*
6. *I think something is terribly wrong with my baby.*
7. *I feel anxious and want to cry.*

When you identify the feelings, and ideally the memory attached to it, feel it with your body and heart. Some parents complain that Byron Katie's inquiry is harsh and dry. It is not. It touches your depth, not as a pity party with yourself but as you being a compassionate witness to reality. It turns into laughter often, because the next questions to ask yourself are "Who would I be without this thought?" and "How would I react to my baby if I did not believe these thoughts (or didn't even have them)?"

1. *I would just respond to my baby with no worry.*
2. *I would feel peaceful and see myself as a capable mother/father.*
3. *I would pick up my baby in my arms and do whatever she needs based on her cues.*
4. *I would be free to notice my child and respond from my heart.*
5. *I don't know who I am without all these opinions, so I will feel new and ready to discover.*

Without the conversations in your head, you can discover some freedom to notice your baby directly without anyone's interpretations, expectations, or predictions and without your triggered emotions from the past.

In being present for your child without obstructing dogma and ideas, you find healing for yourself:

1. *I trust myself rather than depend on others' opinions.*
2. *I learn to cry.*
3. *I become unconditionally loving.*
4. *I become independent in my parenting.*
5. *I notice that I have a long way to go to have such a level of trust in my child and in myself.*
6. *I have an opportunity to face my fear of the expression of intense emotions.*

7. *I gain more and more emotional freedom.*
8. *I stay connected with my baby, toddler, or child.*
9. *I become resilient by releasing old pain that is not relevant to my baby.*

And much more.

You can add your own responses to the previous thoughts and find out what is valid and useful for you. The common thread is that, at each turn with your baby (and later, toddler), you can choose between changing his direction to fit your emotional comfort or breaking through your limitations and expanding who you are by allowing yourself to be guided by your baby on your path to self-realization and maturity.

CONCLUSION

The path of parenting a new being is not one of shaping but of responding with a mind that does not know but is wide-open to discover the new being. A baby is an unfolding new world we have never encountered before. To allow this magic to manifest itself optimally, we have to serve while getting ourselves out of the way. Guide without controlling the actual being; this is the nature of true leadership.

Naturally, you learn from others' discoveries and errors. Of course, you want to learn and find value and guidance in other people's experience. But, ultimately, select only the ideas that are right for your child by responding to her cues. Examine each idea to see whether it fits your baby's cues. No one knows her better than she and you. To do that, notice when you struggle, write your thought down, and do the inquiry.

The coming chapters cover many common and less common issues parents struggle with in caring for babies, toddlers, and young children. You will read other parents' questions and stories and follow their inquiry toward kind and liberating solutions. When you read an inquiry, I suggest that you do it yourself on the same or related thoughts. In this way, you will give yourself a chance to practice, gain clarity, and resolve your particular issues with your child.

Chapter 2

Feeding Your Baby: Breastfeeding and Healthy Alternatives When Needed

Most often, your baby comes into the world with a clean slate of vibrant health. She is also equipped with a healthy instinct of hunger and the ability to breastfeed. For most mothers, nature provides the baby's food through breast milk, which is the best and easiest for both you and your baby. But mothers sometimes adopt a baby or have difficulty or circumstances that require an alternative. In this chapter, you will learn mostly about breastfeeding, but the principles of breastfeeding are just as useful when you bottle-feed. Responding to your baby, holding her in your arms, and other factors are relevant to all ways of feeding. This chapter is not about breastfeeding techniques or technical difficulties, but about reading your baby's cues for timing, night and day nursing, bonding, health, and optimal development.

Breastfeeding

A mother's milk is the optimal baby food. Not only is it the healthiest food for the baby's brain and physical growth, but breastfeeding is important for the development of the bond between mother and baby. It is also most convenient for mothers, since this perfect food is always ready and at a perfect temperature and freshness. If you have to bottle-feed, you will learn about the best alternatives in this chapter; outside of that, follow the guidance for breastfeeding.

"How often should my baby breastfeed?"

Your mom, your dad, your doctor, your relatives, and your friends may tell you to breastfeed every specific number of hours. Or you hear from others that once the baby is fed, she should be satisfied for a couple of hours. Then, one day, you feed your little one for forty minutes, and she seems full and happy. Twenty minutes of joy go by, and then she signals for the breast again and feeds for a long time. Again, she is happy, but ten minutes later, she is ready for more.

If your mind is already set to believe that she does not need to feed so soon, you assume her squirming is for something else. You try to distract her with a toy, or you sing, soothe, and rock, or you give a pacifier. At this point, the baby is fully crying. Despite all your caring effort, your baby is still hungry.

As long as you believe the thought that she shouldn't feed yet, you cannot see that your baby is hungry or that she may need to suckle for emotional reasons. Failing to get the breast, she becomes frustrated and even scared: *Will Mom give me the breast again? Can she understand me?* The baby feels helpless and is failing to communicate her needs. Such anxiety around primal needs has an impact on the child's emotional makeup and sense of self. She is learning that *the world is not safe or friendly; survival can be a struggle, requiring crying and screaming; and even Mama isn't always responsive.*

If you do not think her need to suckle is valid, or if you believe the thought that it is not good for her to feed so soon, then you may innocently miss your baby's cue. Not only must she feed or suckle based on her body signals (for both biological and emotional needs), but she also must succeed in her communication with you to build self-reliance and confidence.

Believing the above thoughts prevents you from believing your baby and from giving her the best care in that moment, and it causes unnecessary anxiety and distress for both you and your baby. It is a learning curve of trial and error. No parent can be perfect or read all the cues accurately. Your baby can handle your imperfections, so there is no need to panic about long-term harm. She senses the love and the intention to care as long as most of the time she gets the needed responses to her cues. Yet we all want to do our best to ease her passage into life. Hopefully this guidance allows you to tune in accurately more and more often and make it easier for both you and your baby.

A powerful question to ask is: "Who would I be with my baby who is hungry or needing to suckle if I didn't have or believe these thoughts about how often she should breastfeed?"

To develop trust, imagine being told how often you should be hungry or tired. Feel how this would thwart your trust in yourself.

Imagine your partner coming over and taking your food away, saying, "Oh no, sweetheart, you shouldn't be hungry yet." Babies are as clear as adults on their own biological needs. And the way they can get these needs met is only through you, communicating with facial expressions, movements, little sounds, and when failing, with crying.

If you listen and trust the baby, then when she nudges toward your breast, you will give it to her without looking at the clock or doubting her. She is unlikely to cry because you are right there, holding her, ready to respond to her cues. She will learn that she is able to communicate and that she is worthy of a prompt response to her needs and is deserving of care. She also learns that she does not need to make a grand commotion to get her needs met. And eating does not become associated with hardship or scarcity. Best of all, by learning that she can get her needs met without crying, your baby will develop into a child who tends to ask for things calmly.

The following is an inquiry about frequent breastfeeding that Sharon did in one of my parenting workshops:

Sharon: *"She couldn't be hungry again."*

Naomi: Is that true?

Sharon: No. Not if I ask the baby.

Naomi: How do you react when you believe this thought?

Sharon: I feel confused, and I deprive the baby of her need.

Naomi: How would you be and feel without this thought?

Sharon: I would breastfeed my baby with delight in response to her cues. Gosh. Such a relief.

Naomi: Feel it. (Sharon closes her eyes and enjoys the ease.) Now, turn it around.

Sharon: *"My baby should be hungry again or need to suckle as often as she does. Because she is growing. Because she knows best what her body needs. Because she is the only one who can know what is the need inside her body."*

When you trust the baby's cues, the baby learns to communicate gently—"I don't need to cry, whine, or throw a tantrum to get what I need." When you respond on her terms, she also learns to honor herself and thereby, later on, to honor you and others.

"Shouldn't I follow my pediatrician's guidance on how often to breastfeed?"

Only your baby knows how often she needs to breastfeed. Life is simple and kind. There is no need for struggle against the flow, no need to consult with books, lab research, or statistics. You can relax and enjoy the dance of love between baby and mother, the way of this unique baby. All advice is given with good intentions, but "they" don't know your baby.

The doctor doesn't know your baby.

Grandma doesn't know your baby.

The author of this book doesn't know your baby.

The magazine writers don't know your baby.

The teachers don't know your baby.

Your friend doesn't know your baby.

Other parents don't know your baby.

Again, only your baby knows. The instructions, you might say, are from Mother Nature. Listen, connect with your baby, respect her, and cooperate with her. She counts on you. When you listen to her, you become the one who also knows, and she grows to trust you and herself.

Nurture Self-Trust

Your baby counts on you to respond to her cues and to shield her from the words of other adults who don't really know her. It is not your duty to impress anyone through complying with their parenting approaches. You are here to represent your baby's needs and be her guardian angel.

Your baby is right. There is no need to pull her out of her habits or out of her needs and developmental stages. Teach peace by responding peacefully and loving her path and her timing. There is no right or wrong, only a loving response to the baby's cues on her terms.

She will be the peaceful being that she already is because she will experience life as flowing at ease. And she will develop confidence because she will experience life as responding to her inner voice and will therefore trust herself. Self-trust is confidence and emotional resilience.

The most cooperative and content children are those who have not been trained to struggle and rage to get their needs met. Such children don't mind when, occasionally, things don't go their way because they are generally content and trust their parents' guidance.

Most babies nurse many times a day. As they become toddlers, the frequency goes down, but if allowed, breastfeeding can continue for a few years. There is no benefit to putting them on a schedule or deciding for them the duration for which they should nurse. How does a mother know? By responding to the baby's basic needs. Life is so much simpler when we realize that, in terms of primal needs, what the baby wants is what's best for her. This trust of nature is the end of struggle and the end of self-doubt and the difficult behaviors that result from the denial of the baby's basic needs.

A first-time mother, Becky, was grappling with the question of frequency of breastfeeding.

Becky: *"There should be a limit to frequency of breastfeeding."*

Naomi: Is that true?

Becky: Not in reality. So, no.

Naomi: How do you react when you believe this thought?

Becky: Stressed and less responsive to my baby.

Naomi: How would you be without this thought?

Becky: Peaceful. I would just breastfeed in response to the baby, which feels kind and joyful.

Naomi: Turn it around.

Becky: *"There should not be a schedule or limit to the frequency of breastfeeding; it should be unlimited."*

Unless the mother has a special biological limitation, nature's program works; respond to the baby. It's a dance of two, with you being the adult at the steering wheel, responding to the baby's cues.

Not only is breastfeeding best for your baby but also for your own health. According to the National Library of Medicine, a collaborative analysis of data from forty-seven epidemiological studies conducted in thirty countries, the risk of breast cancer dropped by 4.3 percent for every twelve months of breastfeeding, in addition to a 7 percent reduction for each birth.[1]

"How do I handle my self-doubt about breastfeeding?"

When you doubt yourself and your ability to know what's best for your baby, consider what is going on inside you that is clouding your self-confidence. Your self-trust may have been eroded by a childhood where your feelings and choices were denied or you felt unsafe to follow your own inner voice. Your baby is now giving you a chance to recover your self-reliance and heal your own hurts through trust.

You are not alone; the stories we hear throughout our lives often obstruct our authentic knowing. The way to distinguish obstructing thoughts from your true, loving wisdom is through inquiry. When the many voices in your head are so loud and overwhelming that you cannot find your own authentic voice, be sure to write these confusing thoughts down, put them under the scrutiny of the four questions, and then turn them around. Any doubt or anxiety you have deserves your loving care through questioning your thoughts. If your mind says, "But it is only feelings, no thoughts," keep tuning in to find the thoughts, memories, and conclusions associated with the emotions you feel. Every feeling has words connected to it.

Does believing the thought make you and your baby's lives more peaceful and connected or more stressful? If it makes life more stressful, it cannot be true, because stress is the manifestation of going against what simply "is." Flowing with reality feels kind. If you find the thought stressful, you are following ideas that are not yours, are not true, and get in the way of your and your child's well-being.

How would you treat your baby without the thoughts that have been placed there by society? If you lived on a deserted island, never hearing any breastfeeding "guidelines," would you deny your baby milk when she asks for it? No. So, the opposite thought is indeed truer: *"She should feed as often as she does."* Learn by observing, listening, and responding, not by believing unexamined rules from external sources.

How I know what the baby needs
is by observing the baby with my own eyes and
listening with my own ears and heart.

If you still feel doubtful after questioning your thoughts, it is of course totally fine to seek support to help you regain clarity. There is no one answer that fits all. Your baby will teach you who she is and how to care for her while you trust your loving self to protect and guide her on her path.

I have listened to thousands of mothers, and I repeatedly hear that when they breastfeed freely in response to the baby's cues, things flow smoothly with the least stress and minimal crying. In addition, in order to be responsive, mothers who keep the baby in arms in a baby wrap/snugly often report most peaceful babies because the baby has no need to cry to get her needs met; mothers quickly learn to recognize gentle signals, and the baby learns that gentle communication works. (Colic and crying babies even in arms will be covered later.)

"Is it possible to confuse my baby when it comes to breastfeeding?"

Yes, it is possible for a baby or a toddler to adjust herself to the way parents present themselves or to their emotional expressions. But when it comes to breastfeeding frequency, it is rare to confuse a baby, although there are exceptions.

One exception is when the mother holds her baby only when breastfeeding and the father and other caregivers hold him at all other times or he is put down away from a human body. In such a situation, a smart baby concludes that, to stay in Mama's arms, he should breastfeed. The solution to this is simple and obvious: The mother should hold the baby when not breastfeeding.

Another exception is when a mother keeps offering her breast more than the baby asks for. Even an infant can sense that they are expected to obey Mama's "guidance." Again, the simple solution is to trust the baby and respond to her cues when needing the breast and for all her needs.

"How do I respond to all the breastfeeding advice people offer me?"

Treat people's advice the same way as you are learning to treat your own thoughts. Say, "Thank you." Appreciate the love and good intention of each person, and let her or him know that you do value their care. Hear their thoughts and let your heart decide which of them helps you listen to your baby. If their advice brings you doubt, write it down and do the inquiry.

Once you are clear, it will be simple to do what the baby is communicating. She is the only one who knows. She was born able to take care of herself, with the natural premise of having parents who respond to her cues.

If they ask you why you breastfeed your baby so often, you can say, "Because she asks for it," "Because she is hungry," or "Because that's what I do." What she wants is what she needs, both emotionally and biologically.

Bring the inner war to an end and trust creation. Without seeking approval of whoever is advising you, what they say is harmless. It doesn't have to take you away from responding to your baby, who is giving you the real valid cues.

Nature never intended for the baby to want the wrong things or for parents to deny her needs and cause her distress.

We do not need to struggle against nature's amazing design. We only need to respond. (As you will see later, this does not mean that the baby gets whatever she wants; wants are not always primal needs.)

"What if I have no breast milk?"

Although breastfeeding is the optimal and most natural way to nourish and nurture a child, babies can grow up well with other feeding situations. However, before we look at other loving options of nursing a baby, I invite you to question even the seemingly factual detail "I have no milk." Unless your baby is adopted (and even then, some mothers succeed in stimulating the mammary glands and get at least some milk) or you have special health problems, most lactation issues can be solved with guidance and information from skilled midwifes, La Leche League leaders, Attachment Parenting leaders, Grandma, and other lactation guides.

Separation of the baby from mother right after birth may send the hormones the wrong message. You may then have a slow start, but don't give up; breastfeeding stimulates the production of milk. And, if you are reading these words before the birth of your baby, make sure to put her/him to the breast upon being born and let the feeding awaken the colostrum production and later the milk.

It is not within the scope of this work to go into details of herbal and food support for lactation or the emotional and nutritional and dietary reasons that inhibit breast milk production. If you want to breastfeed, take it upon yourself to research how to have an abundance of milk. It is nature's way and most often is available and plentiful.

If, however, your situation is clearly such that you *cannot* breastfeed, find the best alternative for your baby, and do with the bottle what you would have done with the breast: *Feed in the mother's arms and with affectionate contact.* One of the greatest benefits of breastfeeding is the hormonal and biological impact on the mother-child bond through touch. Do your best to establish the same connection as though you were breastfeeding. Bottle-feed in arms with the same eye contact and affection as you would if you breastfed.

From my studies and experience with thousands of families, I came to conclude that the best substitute to mother's milk is raw organic milk from grass-fed goats, sheep, or cows. Some parents are not comfortable with raw dairy due to government warnings, pediatricians, and friends. In this book, you are learning to do your own research and make your own choices. If you decide to try raw milk, you can get it in health food stores or directly from local organic regenerative farmers. Raw milk from such healthy organic sources is by far safer than industrially produced milk, which must be pasteurized due to the cows being so filthy, crowded, and often sick.

I recommend against any formula, even organic, as it is highly processed and is made of dubious ingredients such as corn syrup, sugar, artificial vitamins, and soy, which has growth-inhibiting enzymes, toxic phytic acid, lectins, and other antinutrients. Again, it is your choice. The industry is supported by the FDA's recommendations, but those too are to be inquired about rather than believed. You can also make your own substitute from real food such as eggs, liver, or coconut, but raw goat milk or milk from other mammals is the closest to mother's milk and is, in my experience and research, the best substitute for mother's milk.

"Until what age should I breastfeed?"

If you get caught in this question, it must be because of common cultural beliefs. What does everyone tell you? They usually prescribe a time limit, anywhere from six months to a few years. What? Did I say *years*? Yes, I did. Some stay-at-home moms breastfeed until age two or three, and often even later, but not all mothers can do that. In Chapter 14, you will find some suggestions for mothers who have to return to work.

Obviously mothers may have varied circumstances that could limit the duration of breastfeeding. However, I have known working mothers who express milk for bottle-feeding when they are not home and continue to breastfeed when they are. Many mothers work part-time, work from home, or find other creative solutions. This section is about meeting the baby's needs on her terms when the conditions are possible or when mothers create solutions to be with their baby most of the time. If allowed to choose, most toddlers, if not using a bottle or a pacifier, would continue with breastfeeding a couple of times a day for a few years.

You may know adults who nursed as young children. It doesn't show on their face. No nipples grow on their tongues. They don't keep moving their mouths in a suction motion. They are normal, mature, and loving people. They didn't experience a struggle against their natural and healthy inclination, and they often carry this peaceful experience into the rest of their lives.

Instead of prescribing a time limit for breastfeeding, I am suggesting you simply respond to your child. This book is about clearing your mind from dogma and reading your child like a book so you can respond to her in a dance of care and love.

Why have a time limit? Did someone tell you that you must be done with sex by age thirty-nine or that you must be done with learning by age twenty-five? Why the imposed timetable? How can one person know for another when they are done with any phase of their growth or relationship? Does nature ever create a nursing teenager? What's the fear?

In one of my workshops, a mother did an inquiry on weaning age. She was breastfeeding her fifteen-month-old.

Sheila: *"My baby shouldn't breastfeed beyond the first year."*

Naomi: Is it true that your baby shouldn't nurse beyond the first year?

Sheila: Well, many children nurse till ages that range from one to four or longer. But I am not sure. I still believe it.

Naomi: Can you absolutely know that your baby shouldn't nurse beyond the first year?

Sheila: No. Indeed, I cannot know that my baby shouldn't keep nursing much longer than one year.

Naomi: How do you react when you believe this thought that your baby should wean by age one?

Sheila: When I breastfeed her while believing this thought, I feel anxious. I tell myself that she is too old and should wean. I feel stressed and worried, wondering if I am causing damage and fearing the judgment of the people close to me.

Naomi: How do you *act* when you believe this thought?

Sheila: As I feed her, I try to pull away and wish she would stop. I sometimes refuse her and push her away, and she cries. I cry inside too.

Naomi: How would you be without this thought?

Sheila: When I breastfeed without the thought about age limits, I enjoy it fully and my baby can sense my peace and feeds in my unconditionally loving embrace.

Naomi: So, *with* the thought, stress and disconnection, and *without* it, joy, peace, and connection. Try turning it around now.

Sheila: "*My baby should breastfeed beyond the first year. This is more true because she passed her first birthday three months ago. My baby should breastfeed for as many years as she needs; that seems kind. I don't have to fight her now; that's a relief. At least for another year.*"

Naomi: Can you find another turnaround?

Sheila: *"I shouldn't pamper this limiting thought that flows through my mind blindly."*

Naomi: Yes, if the thought brings you stress and disconnection. Any other turnaround?

Sheila: *"I shouldn't feed myself other people's ideas without questioning them."*

At this point, Sheila realized that she was worried about others' judgments, about looking good, about preserving her breasts, and about having more physical freedom. I encouraged her to write down all these considerations and study the subject to find what would bring her and her baby peace and connection.

After some research, she learned that breast health is enhanced by longer breastfeeding and that she gains freedom in many ways by flowing with her child's needs for breastfeeding—no bottles when going out, easy nights, and a content, well-bonded baby who has fewer colds.

Does it mean that weaning is only child-led? No. But stress is *not* the leader. Seeking approval is *not* the leader. It's a dance of two—a dance of love and nurturance.

"Should my child decide when to wean?"

Many mothers are afraid of continuing with breastfeeding because they think it will never end or go on for years. However, when I advise clients to respond to the baby and not to dogma or relatives, I do not mean another dogma. Child-led weaning can become another dogma, indeed, and it is best to question it as well. Is it true that the child should breastfeed as long as he wants? Wild animals do push their pups away after a while. For humans, it's a two-person dance that mostly ends smoothly and differently for each child-mother duo.

The thought often becomes stressful as the child grows older. One mother told me that she feels like a "gas station" when her toddler would come by for a sip and run off. After questioning her thought about it, she realized that she has a say on how her toddler treats her body. She then established a routine that her toddler comes to breastfeed only when he is hungry enough to cuddle and breastfeed for a full duration. The toddler responded. He just needed guidance. As a result, she didn't wish to wean him anymore.

Free of dogma and aware of the child's needs, a mother can be responsive to her toddler's cues while taking into account her own responsibilities, health, and the needs of the rest of the family. Such leadership creates gentle weaning in the best time, ensuring a sense of completion and readiness to move on for both mother and child.

Consider being responsive to the child and to yourself. Your body tells you when it feels violated rather than nurturing. Watching animals, we do notice mothers refusing and even pushing away their young. Humans can speak, so there is no need to push—only to sense and respond as a leader attuned to the child.

Free of the opinion of others, what is your child telling you? And what is your body saying? Weaning a three-year-old is obviously more complex than doing so when the child is less aware. However, at that age and beyond, children mostly breastfeed only at night to go to sleep and occasionally for a nap or for comfort and connection.

If you are expecting another baby and don't wish to tandem nurse, that could be a reason to gradually wean (there's more on tandem nursing on page 49). Each mother-child pair must take into account the needs of both themselves and of the whole family. A toddler can handle weaning and doesn't benefit from being the only one in charge.

Sometimes a younger child uses the breast longer just to possess Mommy, especially when there is an older sibling close in age. Other times, a child continues beyond needing it out of boredom and as a way to get Mommy to be with her.

Such nuances can be noticed by aware parents. For boredom, nurture the child's interests and needs for engagements socially and through play and activities. For the attention-getter, gradually shift to spending time with Mother without breastfeeding. If the child gets plenty of Mommy time, using the breast to get her attention will naturally subside.

There are many other dynamics that would drive a child to stop or to continue with breastfeeding beyond a primal need. Babies who use a pacifier often stop breastfeeding much sooner, usually too soon for their own good. On the other hand, babies who regularly use the breast as a pacifier for upsets may continue beyond a real biological need and create an emotional crutch rather than a healthy bond.

Each relationship is unique, and as a mother, you are in the leadership position with the duty to be aware and to respond to the child with full understanding of the need and well-being of both of you and the rest of the family.

Sit down with your thought, a pen, and paper so you can inquire and discard the deceptive thoughts that get in the way and see clearly what is needed.

"Will my breasts sag if I breastfeed?"

Some women worry about the impact of breastfeeding on the shape of their breasts. I have not done research or studied statistics, but my personal experience and my knowledge of female relatives and close friends tells me that breastfeeding is *not* the cause of sagging breasts. Aging is, combined with an unhealthy diet, lack of exercise, and heredity. Each woman is different. More important, beauty is in the eyes of the one who loves you.

Your loving partner reflects your view of yourself, and a thriving partnership does not depend on such factors. Sound relationships grow and change with our bodies. No one stays young. Love yourself in all the many forms that your body must go through as a woman and as a mother. Don't let your love of your own beauty fade, and you will embrace all the changes ahead—and so will your partner.

Most mothers remember breastfeeding as one of the greatest experiences of their lives. I notice that when a woman is comfortable with her own body through the many natural and healthy changes it goes through, men are more likely to be just as appreciative.

Nature directs men and women to select traits that secure the survival of the species—looks that represent health and vitality. Healthy and peaceful people are beautiful at all ages, and emotionally healthy people enjoy aging. I invite you to question the following ideas:

"My breasts will sag more if I breastfeed longer."

"I look better/sexier with girlish breasts than with womanly/motherly breasts."

"My husband/partner will not be attracted to my breasts after years of breastfeeding."

Add to these your own personal concerns, and find if they are true. Notice how believing them robs you of some of the greatest joys of life. Can you really miss this incredible, heavenly joy of breastfeeding, for what? Some arbitrary, untrue idea?

Do you really want to compromise what is best for your baby for some illusion about eternal youth that is pushed by a greedy industry?

You cannot know what the future will bring. Depriving yourself of joy and your baby of a primal need and loving nurturing based on unfounded fear and for the sake of an unknown mind's made-up concept becomes your and your child's loss. Instead, you have the choice to enjoy what comes your way to its fullest; your baby will thank you, and so will your own body and soul.

"How much should I breastfeed at night?"

Overnight, your prolactin level—the hormone designed to support milk production—is at its highest, showing that your baby needs lots of nutrients at night. Research shows that breast milk nutrients change all the time in response to the needs and health of your baby, the temperature, and the time of day. For most mothers, at night, breast milk will gradually increase in fat content to support the baby's growth, provide calming nutrients at night, and if sick, more nutrients to support healing and even antibodies for the specific pathogen. During the evening, your milk has the most fat, as well as tryptophan, which in turn aids your baby in making melatonin, helping him sleep and gradually respond to the circadian cycles.

To learn more about the physiological and emotional impact of breast milk on the baby's health, intelligence, sleep, and emotional well-being, I recommend the bestseller *The Breastfeeding Book* by pediatric experts Martha Sears, RN, and William Sears, MD. The changes, including color changes of breast milk and its composition, have been scientifically proven by many studies, including those by International Milk Genomics Consortium, and the findings have been published far and wide, including in parenting magazines such as *Mothering* and *Today's Parent.*

"When will my baby sleep through the night without breastfeeding?"

This might be one of the most stress-producing thoughts ever invented. Just imagine not having that thought. Imagine not having the thought that you, yourself, must have an uninterrupted whole night's sleep. If you just let life tell you how it all works simply by watching the way it is, how would you be then?

Because babies do wake up at night, the thought that they should sleep through the night can only bring stress and disconnection. Bettina called for a session saying that her baby is not sleeping through the night. I suggested that she write down her thought and question it:

Bettina: *"My thirteen-month-old baby should sleep through the night."*

Naomi: Is that true?

Bettina: Yes. He did once or twice.

Naomi: Can you absolutely know that it's true that he should sleep through the night? Truth is reality. What is the fact?

Bettina: No. I cannot know that for sure.

Naomi: When your baby wakes up at night, how do you react when you believe this thought?

Bettina: With annoyance. I feel stressed, tired, and I resist the interruption.

Naomi: How would you be, when he wakes up, without this thought. Take your time to imagine that moment, he wakes up, needing to breastfeed . . . without believing this idea of yours, how would you react?

Bettina (closing her eyes and imagining it): I would be fine, just like I was a few months ago.

Naomi: So, with the thought, annoyance and stress. Same baby, same middle of the night, but without the thought you are fine. So this has nothing to do with the baby.

Bettina (smiling): I can see that.

Naomi: Turn the thought around.

Bettina: *"My baby should not sleep through the night."*

Naomi: Is that as true or truer?

Bettina: Well, it is more true, as in reality, he does wake up. So, he should wake up as often as he needs. That feels so good.

Without this thought, a mother flows with the baby's rhythms of waking and sleeping with no resistance. It is not always safe for the baby to sleep through the night. You don't need to sleep uninterrupted either because that's how parenting a baby goes. Nothing is wrong and nothing has to be fixed about babies and how they sleep. Instead, find the kindest way to accommodate the baby's need to breastfeed and to be close to you during the night.

Nature didn't make a mistake; it is all perfect when you let it be. A baby is often hungry at night. She also needs to wake up to regulate her own breathing and to make sure you are next to her—all perfectly the way it should be. Again, there are no mistakes here to fix or fight against. Instead, when you question your convictions about uninterrupted sleep, you are more likely to feel at peace or perhaps even look forward to your baby waking up and latching on to your breast and to your heart's joy. You get to feel your baby and smell and sense her tenderly, all in the quiet of the night, with no one and nothing interrupting this precious experience, which will pass all too soon.

The turnaround to needing sleep with no interruption is: *"Both the baby and I need to wake up often at night to connect, breastfeed, change her diaper, and snuggle. I cherish each wake-up with joy."*

Tandem Nursing

Breastfeeding twins is unavoidable. But nursing a baby and a toddler is a choice that can be either a worthwhile challenge or a huge difficulty. It depends on three humans, which makes the decision complex and the outcome hard to predict.

Mothers who consult with me report from both camps. There are those who love tandem nursing, and their children bond and thrive with it, and those who tear their hair out with frustration, pain, discomfort, and children fighting, pushing, and biting. There are also cases with a happy child and baby, but Mom's nipples are very painful.

Yes, there is a lot a mother can do to make tandem nursing a success, but there is also a lot over which the mother has no control, including the two children's personalities, age differences, level of jealousy, habits, and emotional needs, as well as the number of adult caregivers available. These and other factors can make tandem nursing either heavenly or a peacebreaker.

In my personal experience of over thirty years, I find many more parents who struggle with tandem nursing than those who find it nurturing. It doesn't mean you cannot do it, but I suggest you consider your older child's nature and try to plan accordingly. In many families, I find that the older child does much better when not tandem nursing.

That said, a young toddler's benefit from continuing to breastfeed may outweigh the challenges. For example, if the difference is only a year or so, tandem nursing can feel similar to the experience of nursing twins. It is also more likely to work well for a while.

Since the benefits are obvious, I will address only the reasons to wean the older toddler before the birth of the new baby. I am not saying you must wean your older child; I only suggest you consider it and be aware of possible challenges. Again, writing your thoughts down and inquiring is the best way I know of to gain clarity on the subject. Obviously, one would have to then face reality in time, and perhaps you may need more inquiry to know how or whether to continue with tandem nursing.

"I am tandem nursing, and it is painful. What should I do?"

It can be more difficult to interrupt tandem nursing peacefully than to avoid it in the first place. I therefore stress the importance of making the decision a few months before the birth.

When mothers tell me that it is too painful and difficult to keep breastfeeding their older child, I often focus on trying to help with the pain, finding ways to reduce the toddler's frequency of breastfeeding, and planning to wean him gradually. Certainly, weaning the older one when the baby is already present can introduce a stronger sense of deprivation and jealousy in the older child and therefore may not be as easy to do.

Most toddlers respond well to honest communication about it being painful for Mommy and needing to reduce the frequency and duration for her sake.

However, it is possible to wean the older toddler gently. Every child is different and responds to a different approach. I have seen mothers wean the older child overnight with a benign attitude and taking their child's cooperation for granted. With other children, a gradual process seems to fit better. You know your child best. To do it gradually, read the section on weaning a toddler on page 53. If you think your child is responsive to abrupt simplicity, go for it.

Question the thought: "It would be difficult to wean my child." You don't know that. Without that thought, you are open for anything and may be surprised. The opposite is as likely to be true. Your child may be waiting for your leadership and may even feel relieved.

Some mothers manage to do the total wean simply by telling the child one day something like, "Now you are done with the booby." In these cases, most mothers report that the child responded with something like "Ah" and was happy and accepting of the change. One mother said, "It seemed like he was relieved and just waited for me to finally show up as a leader and say the obvious."

This is not necessarily as simple for everyone, depending on age, the child's nature, and your relationship with him. I just want you to also consider the easy way of showing confident leadership.

One mother whose child didn't respond with relief said that it took three days of persistent, compassionate, clear leadership for the child to recover. Another mother reported, "After talking about it for a week in advance, when the day came to wean, my child started crying and saying that she is a baby, too. I held her and let her cry for as long as she needed. Then she got up and went to play. Come the evening, she wanted to breastfeed. I reminded her that breastfeeding was over. She had a tantrum this time. Again, I validated without drama. I said, 'I know you would like to continue with the booby.'"

This mother then called me for guidance. After the session, she did The Work with the little one. The next day, when the child again asked for booby and didn't get it and whined, her mother asked, "How do you feel when you want the booby and you don't get it?"

The child demonstrated her feeling by kicking and said, "Bad Mommy."

The mother responded, "So when you don't get the booby you think Mommy is bad or doesn't love you?" The child burst out laughing. This did not make sense to her as she knows Mommy loves her.

The mother then asked her child how she would feel without the thought, but she adjusted it for the child, saying, "Funny. Without wanting the booby, you know that Mommy loves you." They jumped up and down together, cracking up with laughter, and then hugged.

This was pretty much the end of it. The mother reported a few more of the child's attempts to evoke guilt by complaining but without much emotion—more like trying to keep a dead thought from fading. By the fourth day, the subject was not mentioned again, and the child was happy and free.

The way of this mother above may not seem as peaceful, and it may not be your choice. I am including it just to let you know that it is possible and, when done with such honesty, does not do harm, because all emotional expression occurs in the open and the connection is alive.

It is easier if you plan in advance, but if the plan is to tandem nurse and it turns out not to be harmonious, know that the stress of such disharmony is likely more harmful than weaning the older child even after a period of tandem nursing. Children are resilient; when we show up with clarity and confidence, they respond well and are able to move on, even if it takes some time to adjust.

The Benefits of Weaning the Older Child Before the Birth of the Younger

This section is not intended to cancel the possibility of tandem nursing, but to guide you if you are considering weaning the older child before the birth.

An older toddler can benefit emotionally from weaning before the birth of a sibling. Depending on his age and character, he could be less likely to compare himself to the baby. He tends to embrace an idea: "I am not a baby; I am big and have my own independent life," and he is more likely to see himself as someone who wishes to care for the baby rather than to compete for attention. This could mean less jealousy and therefore less aggression toward the little one. Embracing "maturity" and freedom can make things more harmonious. Obviously, as mentioned earlier, this is hard to predict in advance, but it is worth considering.

Maternal age is also a factor. I was forty-four when my third child was born. The middle child was three-plus when the third baby was born. I gently weaned him while pregnant, both for his sake and to avoid overtaxing my body or depriving the baby of the high-quality breast milk he would need. This proved to be a good choice for all.

Bottle-Feeding

Although the breast is clearly best, there are situations when a mother cannot breastfeed. Whether the baby is adopted or for other health reasons, she may have to use bottle-feeding in place of the breast. The bottle substitutes for the breast but not for the love and cuddles.

If you introduce a bottle, treat it like it was the breast. Your baby is getting the bottle *instead* of the breast, so you want his experience to be as close to being breastfed as possible—in your arms, with eye contact and loving touch. Even if a toddler who uses a bottle doesn't mind holding the bottle, maximize in-arms drinking if the child wants it.

Being held in arms and using a high-quality nipple that does the least harm to the mouth and teeth structure are both crucial. MomLovesBest.com is just one of a few sources for most fitting nipples.

Most important is what you put in that bottle. Feed your baby with something as close to mother's milk as possible; although not easy, if you can find another mother's milk, that would be amazing. In replacing mother's milk, consider a healthy, organic, unprocessed, noncommercial liquid, not human made, but nature made.

Mother's milk is nutritionally dense and high in protein and cholesterol, which is crucial for brain development. In regard to the baby's brain and body development, check Dr. Shawn Baker's book *The Carnivore Diet* and Sam Dillard's *Keto Kids.* You can also learn a lot from other medical doctor's videos about the importance of cholesterol for the child's brain development—Dr. Chaffee, Dr. Ken Berry, Dr. Paul Mason, and others. Fruit juice is not recommended;

it is not the same as eating fruit. It is mostly sugar and can do harm to future teeth and create dependency on sugar; plus, it lacks the nutrients the baby needs most. Even fruit is best minimized as the baby needs animal proteins and fats.

When I was a child, bottle-fed babies were given milk from cows or goats—often raw if available and safely produced—a practice that still continues in many countries today, where the babies are thriving now just as they had then. The narrative against raw milk is financially and politically motivated. Please do your own research and make the decision that is best for your baby. As mentioned earlier, you can also use eggs, liver, and milk combined to create a nutritionally dense "milk."

"When do I wean my baby off the bottle?"

Read back on how long a baby should nurse, and you will be back to trusting your baby and yourself. If she were not using the bottle, she would have been breastfeeding. We are not gods to decide how long a child needs to breastfeed or use a substitute, just like we don't decide how long before they are born or when they walk or talk. It has already been decided and is programmed into the child's brain. She lets you know. There is no need to worry that she will never stop: I have never encountered a teenager drinking from a baby bottle.

Breastfeeding or bottle-feeding for as long as she needs will prevent your child from being stuck in an incomplete oral need to suckle. Such lack can create thumb-sucking, nail-biting, and other mouth-related compulsions. You don't want to go against your child's needs just to satisfy the opinions of your relatives or anyone else. On the contrary, armed with your own self-confidence and assertiveness, relieve yourself of believing the thoughts that sway you to please others instead of caring for your child. You don't have to say anything to anybody. You can even validate their concerns without following their advice (read the mock scenario about co-sleeping on page 323). Follow your child; she is your highest priority and the source of her true nature.

CONCLUSION

Breastfeeding creates a healthy bond and trust between mother and child. It also positively impacts brain development and intelligence. As discussed in this chapter, breast milk is the optimal food for your baby's growth, overall health, and brain and emotional development. Breastfeeding comes naturally to mothers and babies and is amazingly convenient. Most mothers need no help, but sometimes, the baby may initially have some problems latching on, or the mother may have positioning or other technical challenges. In such instances, a La Leche League professional or a midwife can be of great help. Bottle-feeding can be used when breastfeeding is not an option but should be done in arms and with affection and responsiveness.

Responding to the baby on her terms, timing, and quantity is the most loving and healthy way to create this new relationship and meet the baby's needs optimally. And when the time comes, weaning is a dance of two between mother and child, with mother in the responsive role of a leader.

Chapter 3

Health and Food in the Early Years

This is not a food or health book, but raising children demands of us to learn and research which foods are crucial for the child's health and development. Although the goal of this book is for you to follow your baby's cues, today's food is often a great departure from nature. If we offer modern foods, even organic and natural ones, to a baby, the response will not be natural but formed by what we offer. Therefore, in this chapter, I will temporarily depart from the guidance to follow your baby's cues and offer some facts for you to consider. When you offer real food, your child's cues are more likely to indicate true need and not habits and addictions.

Don't take my word for it. Do your own research, not with dogma or ideology but with scientific facts and with your child's biological and mental needs in mind.

Questioning the Need for a Doctor

Although today's parents are encouraged to have regular contact with a pediatrician, this trend is quite new and, in many countries, not the norm; it can actually get in the way of your child's health. In his book *How to Raise a Healthy Child in Spite of Your Doctor,* Robert Mendelsohn, MD, gives very clear guidance on benefiting from conventional medicine while avoiding the harm. It's an eye-opening read that will help you make informed medical decisions.

My own children were born and raised in the United States, and we, for example, did not have a doctor; we rarely used medical services, and only when they were truly needed. I gave birth at home (in my late thirties and mid-forties), and the babies cued us for what they needed. Simple. Likewise, I grew up without such a concept of having a family doctor. A doctor was called only for serious illness, not for a flu, cold, or all the childhood diseases we experienced with no issue and with no doctors (before vaccines).

Sharing this point of view is only intended to create a bit of space or freedom around the subject; it's a historical perspective. When you trust yourself and your baby, you will know when you need medical help. Obviously, it will be your choice whether to have a regular doctor for your baby.

My own three children had colds, flu, strep throat, injuries, chickenpox, whooping cough, and rubella. We sometimes used homeopathy and once used medical services for an injury that required stitches. At another time we went to a naturopath for a blood test to check whether our oldest had nutritional deficiencies. Mostly, we let the body heal itself with rest, chicken soup, water, and love, and we fed our children organic whole food while ensuring they got plenty of sunshine. Without suppressing the body's healing work (fever, runny nose, rash, and so on), the children's flu and strep throat never returned.

In current times, parents do not trust nature or their own senses. We have been indoctrinated to rely on "experts" and rush to the doctor or ER for little things that would otherwise cure themselves with time and home care or that require dietary adjustment, which most doctors don't know much about anyway. Modern medicine excels at emergencies. We went to a clinic when my son fell off his bike and needed stitches. But when sick, we preferred to let the body practice its immune system, which strengthens it.

The nutrients in food are required to keep your child's immune system functioning and play key roles in all the body's functions. So do your research, trust your instincts, and consider advice, but don't rely on it.

Foods to Introduce to Your Baby and Toddler

What we did to stay healthy was avoid sugar and simple carbs, because they suppress the immune system and slowly harm the child's metabolism. When one child got sick, our whole family became even more committed to eating only healthy, whole foods to prepare our immune systems for possible defense.

Sugar or anything that turns to sugar in the body paralyzes the immune system for up to a couple of hours. No wonder Halloween inaugurates the colds season!

In his book *The Common Cold and Common Sense*, Dale Alexander demonstrates with many studies the way sugar depresses the immune system. And the National Library of Medicine quotes ninety studies about the connection between elevated glucose levels and a suppressed immune system. It is widely recognized that sugar is generally detrimental to human health.

Food is a big theme that, in today's world, is rather emotional and political and evokes passions and even aggressive reactions. Since I will not cover the topic fully here, I recommend that, after reading my suggestions, you do your own research in books and, carefully, online. (Check who financed each study and inquire into commonly believed thoughts.) There are many physicians today advocating the direction I offer.

Make an informed choice that isn't about your ideals, your diet, or the environment but is about your child's best. When done this way, your baby and the planet will be healthier.

Considering the strong opinions and convictions out there, I hope you can have the humility to consider less popular options without taking these suggestions personally, knowing you are free to disagree and that exploring other options doesn't threaten your choices.

Our philosophy and choice about food should not be imposed on our children without thorough inquiry. They may or may not benefit from our ideals and could even be harmed long-term if we feed them in a way that doesn't fit their anatomy and nutritional needs.

Let me start with some general information that can change the whole way we think about food:

- Just because a certain food has certain nutrients does not mean the specific, individual baby/person's body is able to assimilate them, regardless of skilled food combinations, soaking, and cooking.

- Just because a certain food has certain nutrients does not cancel the impact its antinutrients, carbs, and natural toxins may have, some of which can deplete the body's nutrients and contribute to a toxic load.
- Consider thinking about food without envisioning a supermarket. By nature, food has no list of ingredients. Instead, each ingredient is a whole food. For optimal health, consider feeding your child whole, organic, real, nutritionally dense foods that require no "making" it into anything, and require no added human-made supplements.
- Whatever you hear about nutrition from your doctor or others, check who paid for the studies. The food industry is eager to addict your child to carbs and processed foods. Beware of instructions to give your child unlimited access to sweet foods.

There is no need to add foods or water in the first year or so, although most babies can enjoy some solid food around six months or later, depending on the presence of teeth and hand-mouth coordination.

Interest in food arises when enough teeth have grown in the baby's mouth and/or she is able to direct things from her hand to her mouth. Nature knows. A baby may be seated with you or in your arms at mealtimes. She may become curious and grab foods off your plate. If your food isn't safe for her, keep it at safe distance. When there are safe foods for a baby on your plate and on the table, consider letting her play with it, smear it, and let her put it in her mouth, ears, or hair. This is the learning process.

It is best not to feed the baby by spoon. Let the baby find the way. Babies fed by spoon are often still dependent on an adult feeding them at a few years of age. This is neither good for them nor necessary. If the baby cannot eat a certain food on her own, she doesn't need it.

Our primal mothers sometimes chewed food in their own mouths and gave it to their babies. That's fine but not a necessity most of the time.

Breast milk is nutritionally complete for babies and can tell us what they need and what they can assimilate. Breast milk is an animal-based, predigested, complete protein with other needed nutrients and fats in the most bioavailable form, and it keeps the baby ketogenic, which means running on fats and not on carbs. Best first foods are animal fats (butter, lard, tallow, suet), ground beef or lamb, and soft egg yolks.

A study available through the National Library of Medicine discusses a 1930 study by Dr. Clara David, in which they let small children self-select their diets, offering them a variety of foods, including organ meats. The kids naturally chose animal foods: meat, liver, kidney, eggs, and muscle meats. No child in this study opted for modern pediatric-recommended foods such as milk with cereal and fruit. Not one. Instead, they went for the foods we are hardwired to eat as humans: meats and very little fruit. (Today's fruit, however, has been bred to be, by far, sweeter than it used to be, and it can end up being lots of sugar and even more so when juiced.)

However, once a child does try processed sweets and carbs or even too much fruit, the same mixed plate will elicit choosing carbs. The food industry preys on children. They teach your pediatrician to tell you to "prevent eating disorders" (fear-based) by putting a bit of everything, including lots of sweet stuff, on your child's plate and letting her choose. Eventually, the child "chooses" mostly sweet foods and carbs, which addicts her further and harms her metabolism. Children are very happy with one savory whole food at a time, in its whole original form, and it is much healthier.

We should attempt to provide foods that have similar nutrients to those in mother's milk without adding lots of flavors and complexities. Humans have been mostly hunters for millions of years. In only a tiny fraction of our history have humans eaten grains and plants as a main course. The results of these changes are far from optimal.

Babies in natural tribes are known to chew on raw meat fat to alleviate teething discomfort and gradually eat the meat itself. Egg yolks and meats are wonderful starters with full nutrition. This means—and I apologize to all the plant-based advocates; I used to be one—that it is best to save plant food for when the child's digestive tract is much more developed and able to handle natural plant toxins and roughage. Some humans can never handle those, so be alert to how your child responds to foods.

My personal experience may be useful here because I went the wrong way. I was vegan for many years. I was vegan when I got pregnant with my first son and initially raised him vegan. By the time my second pregnancy occurred, I was already damaged by my own vegan eating. Like most vegans, I believed it was the best, and so, while my health was deteriorating, I failed to realize that my food choices were the cause.

I miscarried my second pregnancy as a result of irritable bowel syndrome (IBS) caused by plant foods. Despite all my correct combinations, supplements (which are highly processed and a proof that I was eating a depleted diet), and knowledge, my health was falling apart, and my body couldn't keep the second embryo. To recover from IBS-induced miscarriage, I added eggs back to my diet. This helped a lot, and I did have my second child healthfully. However, even the vegetarian food was not and is not fit for children, and it wasn't healing me, either.

Growth and brain development depend on cholesterol and predigested fats, protein, and other nutrients, which means an animal-based diet. Animal food contains natural, bioavailable (and not processed) nutrients including iron, B12, all amino acids, EPA, DHA, and other healthy fats. I didn't know that. Such foods also contain numerous amino acids and types of fats that are completely nonexistent in plants.

Even nutrients that are in plants are not bioavailable to the human body, especially babies and young children. In fact, many of today's researchers and doctors suspect that eating plant food with meat or eggs seriously hinders the assimilation of the proteins and nutrients from the meat. This opposes the food industry's profit goals and has therefore not been sufficiently proven. It is worth keeping your mind open to investigating.

In my own experience with thousands of families, children's behavior and focus are highly affected by what they eat. Books such as *Food and Behavior* by Barbara Reed Stitt and *Gut and Psychology Syndrome* by Dr. McBride, MS, are helpful resources.

If you eat only plant-based foods, you may skip the rest of this section. It is not meant to convince you, only to share certain knowledge. You are free to do things your way.

Here are two lists. The first list is of nutrients in animal-based foods that your child needs and cannot acquire from plants. The second list is of those nutrients that are minimally present in plants but not in sufficient quantities and not in a bioavailable form.

Nutrients that are found only in animal-based foods:

- Vitamin D3
- Vitamin B12
- Vitamin A (Retinol)
- Creatine
- Carnitine
- Carnosine
- Heme iron
- Docosahexaenoic acid (DHA)
- Eicosapentaenoic acid (EPA)
- Taurine

Nutrients found, minimally and not in bioavailable form, in plants that are best assimilated from animal foods:

- Biotin
- Castine
- Zinc
- Methionine
- Lysine
- Leucine
- Carnosine
- Creatine
- Carnitine
- Copper
- Iron

To continue with my personal journey: By age seven, my first-born wasn't well. I caught it in time by just seeing the number of his allergies, the dark circles under his eyes, and his volatile temper.

This was one of the rare cases I considered professional medical help. Still, I didn't go to an MD. I took my child to a naturopath (a vegetarian one) to do a blood test. To my dismay, the blood test showed my child as malnourished, lacking in iron, B12, proteins, and other nutrients. The naturopath explained that my child, like all children and most humans, cannot assimilate proteins and other nutrients from plants and that plants also lack many nutrients and plants can bind and leach minerals, proteins, and nutrients out of his body. He noticed my resistance as a longstanding vegan/vegetarian. But he insisted that my son needed red meat on a daily basis. He promised, "You will see a new child in three days." Indeed, that is what happened. In three days, the rings under our son's eyes vanished, pink cheeks showed up, and he calmed down and looked amazing.

At that point, we introduced animal foods to the whole family. Through my third pregnancy, I ate meats of all kinds. It was, at age forty-four, by far my healthiest pregnancy and birth.

The more I learn, the more I am dismayed at history. The studies show clearly that the agricultural revolution was the greatest blunder for human health and, to my utter surprise, for the environment too. It introduced diseases that never existed before—cancer, diabetes, other autoimmune diseases, IBS, sun sensitivity, and weak muscle tone, as well as cavities, tooth loss with age, smaller brains, shorter stature, and so on. Lots of food for thought that I won't get into here; you can do your own research if you are interested.

It is worth mentioning that the myth that we live longer now is simply not true. Hunter-gatherers' (who were mostly hunters) average length of life is the wrong statistic to consider when discussing their longevity and health. Being eaten by wild animals, falling off cliffs or trees, being bitten by snakes, suffering infected injuries, and newborn/infant mortality all skew the average to seem short. But those who did stay alive often lived to over a hundred, had practically no diseases, died with all their teeth intact, and were healthy. Their lifespan was longer, not shorter.

In addition, today we count people as "living" when medicine keeps them alive with drugs and procedures, machines, injections, and other maintenance "treatments." Being alive does not always mean living. Longevity since the agricultural revolution gradually but significantly decreased, and so did stature and brain size. Recently, thanks to improved hygiene and medical interventions, life expectancy has increased relative its historical low levels, but it still does not match the lifespans experienced by hunter-gatherer societies (when not killed by animals, snakes, fires, or floods).

Knowing that people frequently bring up these alleged "facts" about longevity, I had to mention the above. Again, food is a subject that deserves thorough exploration. I am not a medical professional, only an experienced mother who hears the stories of thousands of families and has studied medicine and food for forty years on my own. Even the environmental impact of animal agriculture has been full of lies, and in fact, grazing cows can solve environmental problems created by plant agriculture. Read articles and books and listen to talks by experts such as Dr. Paul Mason (www.youtube.com/@lowcarbdownunder), Dr. Anthony Chaffee (www.howtocarnivore.com), Professor Ben Bikman, Professor Bart Kay, and Dr. Ken Berry. (See the resources for books by researchers and physicians on this fascinating subject.)

I am also certain that I cannot know anything for sure as we are always learning and discovering. Different people, with different genetics, may do differently. Yet, in my experience and to my scientifically informed knowledge, the growing human depends on animal proteins and fats.

If you feel you must attempt veganism with your child, go big on fats such as avocado and coconut oil (although coconut oil is processed food) and avoid the most toxic: beans, grains, seed oils, bitter greens (oxalates), and any kind of sugar, including minimizing fruit. Again, if my take on food triggers you, skip it or inquire with the four questions and turnaround to see whether you can gain some freedom to consider something different from what your mind is sure of.

Weaning and Feeding Your Child

As mentioned in the previous chapter, I support breastfeeding as long as the child needs it. *JAMA Pediatrics* published a study in 2013 proving that the longer a child breastfeeds, the higher his intelligence.[1] Therefore, my goal here isn't to suggest shortening breastfeeding. I only wish to ensure that the child's food is rich in the required nutrients.

Some mothers complain that no matter how much they offer food to their toddler, he seems to end up mostly breastfeeding, even at age two or so. Indeed, I notice that many toddlers finish eating and run for the breast, and generally many two-year-olds spend their day on the breast despite, or perhaps because of, being fed mostly carbs and grains.

Part of this phenomenon could be an emotional need. However, in addition, I speculate—without proof yet, and this is worth doing a study on—that a toddler will breastfeed more often during the day, or even extend breastfeeding beyond natural need, if her diet is not meeting her nutritional needs. I would love to create a survey to find out whether toddlers and babies who are fed meat, eggs, cheese, animal fats, and proteins as first foods in *whole, non-processed form* breastfeed less often throughout the day and perhaps even wean more easily and naturally. In my own anecdotal experience with clients, it seems to be so, and babies seem to love these foods.

My view is only a speculation based on my experience with thousands of families around the world and my studies of the biology of body and brain development and the nutrition it requires. However, there is plenty of evidence that a child's brain development and growth require the nutrients that only animal-based foods can provide in a way that can actually be assimilated by the child's body.

Providing all the studies and proof for each nutrient would turn this book into an academic biology paper. Please do your own study to determine what to feed your baby. While doing so, it is best to stay away from ideology, commercials, your own diet (which may or may not be best for your baby/child), or cultural and social and even political pressures.

Humans have been eating high-carb diets only in very recent history. It has been 10,000 years or so since the agricultural revolution, and our greater reliance on processed and sugary carbs is much shorter than that. For most of human history, we ate very few carbs, very few plants, and nothing processed. Protein powders, baked goods, and cereal are certainly not hunted or grown on trees.

Food as the Toddler Grows

As mentioned, it is ideal, when possible, to keep children eating real, low-carbs foods. The well-known extreme harm of sugar of any kind, excess carbs, and processed modern food causes friction between parents and children. Many parents don't realize that it starts with the introduction of foods to the baby. When a toddler's taste buds grow to depend on carbs, they end up addicted to them. Supplements are not the solution as they are highly processed and don't assimilate well.

A baby comes to us with a clean slate. If you put real food in front of a baby who is ready to chew, the baby will not choose vegetables but that which ate the vegetables: meat. That's nature. Children take years to acquire a taste for vegetables for a reason. They don't have four stomachs or beaks. They are ketogenic, with an acidic digestive tract. Listen to their bodies, and they will stay trim and healthy.

Here is Linda's inquiry about feeding her three-year-old daughter, Lisa.

Linda's mother suggested that Linda feed her child, Lisa, meat and eggs. Linda had a few thoughts impacted by very common beliefs, teachings, and advice. She felt stressed and confused by her mom's advice. Her thoughts were:

1. *Vegetables and fruits are the healthiest food.*
2. *My baby should eat plant foods.*
3. *My baby should not eat meat.*

Linda: "*Vegetables and fruits are the healthiest food.*"

Naomi: Is that true?

Linda: Yes.

Naomi: Can you absolutely know that it's true?

Linda: No. It's what I heard and read that other sources say.

Naomi: How do you react when you believe this thought and your mother says to feed Lisa animal foods?

Linda: I feel confused and stressed. I trust my mom; she raised four children very well. But I am also a believer in the plant-based approach to eating. I feel torn.

Naomi: How would you be without this thought?

Linda: I would wonder what to feed my toddler. I may listen to my mom actually and explore the subject.

Naomi: So you would be interested, curious, and peaceful about hearing your mom's advice?

Linda: Yes, I would.

Naomi: So, *with* the thought, stress and rejection of your mom's guidance, and *without* it, an open mind.

Linda (smiling): Yes. Such ease. Yes, I can learn something and then decide without having to contract inside and be defensive.

Naomi: So turn the thought around.

Linda: *"Vegetables and fruits are not the healthiest foods."* I guess I should explore the facts. I never considered that.

Naomi: An open mind is a peaceful one that can learn even from Mom. A mind that doesn't know is open. You have no proof that she is right, and you don't have to do what she says, but now you are free to consider all possibilities.

Linda: Yes. And I will. It actually makes me doubt a bit how good it is for me too. I always say that I eat so healthy and feel good, but, after eight years, I actually have some issues I didn't have when I ate animal-based foods. I burn in the sun much more easily and also need sunglasses. I have joint pain when I carry the baby on walks. I have some eczema that I didn't have years ago, and my digestion is not great. Hmm. I will explore more.

Linda didn't need to inquire into the other two thoughts after doing this one. Obviously she realized that she doesn't know whether her mom isn't right after all. She ended up putting many hours into researching the subject for a couple of months, after which she decided to find a middle way and give Lisa both plenty of animal foods but also vegetables and very little fruit. She decided against all grains, beans, nuts, seeds, and products made from them—in essence, she chose a ketogenic diet. Her freedom from her own thoughts is what allowed her to study and feel both connected to her mother and clearer on how to feed her child.

The Common Narrative Versus What Nature Provides

Where do all the food slogans come from? Obviously, from the industry that wants to make a profit. Creating foods from grains, beans, and plants is cheap and can be made to be addictive. But don't believe me, either. Do some research to find out what a human adult and a human child should eat based on science and history. Chips, pasta, bread, and breakfast cereals are highly processed foods that create carb addiction and harm one's metabolism, which leads to most of our modern health issues. These foods did not exist until very recently.

Going back to ground zero about food, it seems to me that we have lost touch with what food is. We make food. But real food comes prepared. "Ingredients" is a strange idea. Children like what is healthy and simple, which is the ingredient itself, as is, like an egg, an avocado, meat, fish, milk. Perhaps anything that cannot be eaten as is and by itself isn't really human food.

We have turned food into entertainment. If this is your passion, enjoy, but for your child, think of what you wish his body and brain to be made of and what his taste buds and body would get accustomed or even addicted to.

With all the theories going around, how do you know which is true? Why not learn from your child? A baby who is introduced only to unaltered food—the actual foods, not what we make of them—will not choose wheat or soy. Bread does not grow on trees. Wheat is not edible. Leaves are bitter and rough. The baby is right.

Even modern fruit is not only loaded with plant toxins but is much sweeter than it was originally in nature, and is available in unnatural quantities, out of season, and in locations where it does not grow. I trust nature.

I recall seeing a mother telling her child not to feed chips to the deer in our yard. She was clear that chips are not species-appropriate food for deer. Why are we so clear about this with animals and not with ourselves? Why feed chips and other human-made concoctions to children? Even when homemade, it is still not real food the way nature intended it to be for our digestive tract, brain development, and growth. Nature provides the right food for optimal nutrition for our babies, children, and ourselves.

Today, many people are very passionate about one way of eating or another, often so much so that changing or learning becomes impossible. Perhaps my own example can inspire. I went through all the diets. I was vegetarian, then a devoted vegan and raw vegan versed in healthy combining and all, later macrobiotic, followed by Mediterranean, primal, ketogenic, and so on. I get that this sounds extreme to some, due to how far humans have strayed from nature's food offerings. Obviously, you will go your way with food. I hope this is an intriguing food for thought, regardless of your choices.

CONCLUSION

Your baby's first food is mother's milk—animal proteins and fats with rich nutrients, cholesterol, and no fiber. This is your *cue*. Feed your child in continuation to what nature provides in breast milk.

Animal proteins and fats from grass-fed animals are predigested (by mostly ruminant animals with four stomachs) and therefore easily assimilated by humans, especially young ones. Although plants, which are relatively new to human consumption as a main source of nutrition, when fed in correct combinations have many (not all) of the needed nutrients, humans, especially young ones, are unlikely to be able to assimilate those due to the many plant toxins—antinutrients—that disrupt their absorption.[2,3,4] In addition, recent studies[5,6,7] show that all plant oils, especially seed oils, as well as carbs and sugars, are highly inflammatory.

The baby is ketogenic from the start. Carbs will get the baby out of ketosis and create a dependency on carbs and result in poor nutritional habits. Do your research free of ideology and personal preferences so that your child can grow well, healthy, and intelligent from consuming real, whole, organic food that was intended for humans.

Chapter 4

Sleeping Like a Baby: Co-Sleeping and More

Sleep is a hot topic when parenting a baby. Like other issues, it is surrounded with myths, expectations, ideology, and for-profit products. Clearing your mind and responding only to the actual baby is therefore crucial. The many theories are all well intended, yet they often overlook the importance of listening to the baby and respecting nature's design for her safety, nurturance, growth, and emotional well-being. In this chapter, you will separate the dogma from your primal loving response to your baby.

Sleep in Contact with Your Baby

The baby's close proximity to his mother's body optimizes his safety, builds self-confidence, and grows a strong bond of trust. It prevents his need to cry to get Mom's attention. A brain that is not anxious about where its lifeline is grows peacefully and optimally. When stressed, much energy is wasted on anxiety rather than on growing up. Brain development is harmed by stress, and unfortunately, the anxiety becomes a pattern that can continue through childhood and into adulthood.

What's more, the baby's proximity to his mother's body ensures that he breastfeeds often enough at night, which is the time of growth. When not next to their mothers' bodies, babies don't breastfeed the optimal amount because they don't wake up as often. Yes, we do want them to wake up more, not less, as needed. It is best for the baby to follow nature's design rather than be shaped for what's convenient to us.

If the baby is away from your body, he is likely not to wake up as often, but this is not good for the baby. Sleeping by Mom reminds the baby to wake up often enough to breastfeed according to his body's signals.

Moreover, the amount of milk a mother produces depends on the frequency of breastfeeding day and night. When the baby is not in contact with his mother, he will wake up less often and the milk supply will decrease. Most important, the hormonal bonding of mother and baby depends on physical closeness day and night. It builds not only the mother's milk supply but also her instinctual understanding of the baby's needs.

Breastfeeding may prevent ovulation only if it is around the clock. Such consistent breastfeeding is induced by physical contact, as nature designed. Even then, it is not always reliable, but if you are not breastfeeding around the clock, do not count on breastfeeding to be your contraceptive.

Co-Sleeping Considerations

Knowing that a baby wakes up the right number of times under the optimal conditions of care tells us that it is best for her. It actually says that when away from her mother, a baby might not be waking up frequently enough to nurse. This makes bed-sharing crucial and optimal. It is actually strange that we have to "defend" the obvious in today's modern society.

A baby often sleeps without interruption the first three to four hours. Using that time to be with your partner is fine if you have other ways to get some extra sleep for yourself. I often recommend that mothers go to sleep at the same time as the baby to get those few hours of uninterrupted sleep. It is easier if you gradually shift the baby's bedtime to align with yours—or adjust your own bedtime to match your baby's. This way, you get sleep when the baby is asleep, and breastfeeding interruptions are easier on you.

"Isn't co-sleeping controversial?"

Imagine that, for a couple of hundred years, each family member went to their own room to eat. Then, at some point, someone came up with the idea of eating together around one table. People would say, "That's crazy," and label the new idea "table-sharing" or "co-eating." The subject would become controversial; families who start eating together would be criticized, and the media would point out dangers. Maybe they would say that with company, you may talk while you eat and choke to death. Or they may say that seeing people eat is unsightly, disgusting, and should only be done in private, much like going to the bathroom. If a child or adult chokes while eating at the table, the media would promptly publicize, blaming "co-eating" and warn parents to avoid it—even though more people die when choking on food with no one to assist them (same as in a crib).

"Co-sleeping" is the way of nature just like "co-eating." It shouldn't even have a name. It is separate sleeping that is actually bizarre. Why would we put a helpless being who needs constant skin-to-skin contact and care alone in their most vulnerable state of unconsciousness? There are countries such as Japan, Egypt, India, and Sweden where parents sleep with their babies regularly. Tracy Cassels, PhD, is the founder and director of Evolutionary Parenting, a website focused on disseminating the research on parenting. She shares studies on cultures who sleep with their children until almost puberty, both historically and currently. For more information on Cassels's findings, visit EvolutionaryParenting.com.

Until recent history, natural societies haven't heard of "separate sleeping," "bedtime," or "putting children to bed." Indeed, sleeping together flows naturally and is best for babies and children. If you live your life with your baby in your arms through her awake and sleep times, she will sleep and wake as needed, and naturally go to bed when you do.

My memory of sleeping with our children includes some of the most enjoyable times of my life. It was a slumber party every night, and everyone turned out excellent, independent, and healthy deep sleepers. They slept well as babies (woke up often) and as children all along. Your child knows where to sleep, and your heart knows it too. The guiding manual is in the baby's brain, and he reads it to you with clear cues. Where does the baby want to sleep? Right on or next to your body.

The baby has no concept of having to change location to sleep. For the baby it makes no sense whatsoever to be anywhere else but with his mother. He needs and wants to be in your arms at all times, asleep or awake. When awake, he can enjoy other caregivers, but when going unconscious, the baby is guided by a primal fear to seek Mother's or, later, Father's closeness.

The baby needs the security of your presence—your smell, warmth, nourishment, and comfort. He cannot make any sense at all of being separated from you. On the contrary, while his eyes are closed, physical touch or other signals of your presence are the only way he knows you are still there. His feeling of survival is at stake. Indeed, sleep can seem scary to a little one as it is the closest to the experience of death. Therefore, the baby's need to stay in physical contact with you is the greatest when asleep, and it is the demonstration of ultimate trust.

"Once my baby is asleep, can I leave the room?"

If a baby falls asleep with you but then wakes up to find himself alone, he panics—and with good reason. Without your presence, there is fear for survival. The infant has no way of assessing that he exists when his eyes are closed, nor a way to know that you and the rest of the world persist while he vanishes into sleep. *Your body contact is his life-affirming experience. He unconsciously trusts that you will always be there.*

Therefore, if he falls asleep with you but you then leave him in bed alone, he may wake up instinctively and feel alarmed, to say the least. It's not that you cannot leave the bed; just stay close enough that if he wakes, you can hear it before he becomes aware so you can go over and lie right next to him, reassuring him that you are with him.

If a baby repeatedly wakes up alone and cries, he may develop light sleep and a habit of waking up more often, and more than he would need to, in an anxious attempt to guard that you do not leave and to check that you are there.

Co-sleeping makes a huge difference in the development of a healthy human connection, body assurance, and emotional and intellectual confidence. A well-connected child has the foundation for healthy emotional development. He experiences a sense of peace, self-worth, and contentment. A baby who is peacefully born into his mother's arms will expect to not be removed from her body. If your baby has experienced painful birth, separation, or medical intervention, constant body contact both day and night will help him heal and rebuild a positive concept of himself and his relationship with you.

Many difficulties are rooted in the first imprint of birth and even pregnancy. All mammals and most of humanity sleep with their young for a very good reason.

The Impact of Isolated Sleep

Separate sleeping is a new idea of Western civilization (the result of affluence) and is the cause of many of our emotional and behavioral ills today. Feeling isolated, depressed, anxious, lonely, worthless (not deserving of care), stressed, angry, dependent on approval, addicted, and unable to maintain close connections are some of the difficulties we assume are part of life. They need not be. The causes are, for sure, more than one, but sleep security is a giant one.

Indeed, caging babies away from their mothers is a new and bizarre invention that goes against nature's intentions, and it imprints a high level of emotional hardship. The concept of needing a cage—the crib—for safety proves that point: The baby is not safe by himself. It is not the way humans have done it throughout history.

Parenting is so much more enjoyable when we don't fight the child's innate direction and when we flow with the unfolding of creation.

Trust that what the baby/toddler wants is what is good for him, and you will have peace and teach peace by your way of being. Indeed, peace on Earth starts with peace with your child. (This does not mean that we give the child whatever he wants, which differs from responding to primal needs, as I will elaborate on later.)

Modern traditions tell us to fight against the baby's nature (and actually all of nature, including our attitude toward health, comfort, food, sun, and so on). Yet, when we flow with nature, children grow up without many of the behavioral issues that result from such oppositional practices. Based on your beliefs, I suggest you trust nature—or God. Mother Nature didn't goof in creating babies and in *giving you their cues for how to care for them.*

You don't have to fix creation. Think of nature and reality as your guides. How do you know what your baby needs? By observing and listening as nature speaks to you through your baby's cues.

We don't train an infant to get out of the uterus, and we don't fight against his hunger; we don't teach a baby to breathe and, later, to play. Why wage war against anything that comes from the baby's true nature? (Note: This differs from wants that develop through habit and addiction.) Trust and follow the instructions that come naturally with your baby, and you will have peace while raising a competent and thriving child.

The best part about co-sleeping, aside from the physical, psychological, and intellectual benefits, is the joy it offers parents and the ease of bedtime. Cuddling with your little darling is so tender; you will not want to miss this short and precious ride. It is certainly much more enjoyable than uninterrupted sleep (which you don't get anyway as having to get out of bed is a much greater disruption of a mother's sleep).

"How do I keep my baby safe from SIDS?"

Safety is crucial, no matter where the baby sleeps. Statistically, most SIDS occur in a crib and not in the family bed. According to the research of Professor James McKenna, PhD, from the University of Notre Dame, the one factor that is in common with SIDS in the rare case that it occurs in a family bed is that the baby is *not breastfed.*

When being next to her breastfeeding mother, the baby's sleep cycle synchronizes with the mother's. Mom often wakes up on her own to breastfeed even before the baby makes any signal. She then responds promptly without the baby having to cry. Without the arousal caused by anxiety and by having to wait or cry, both mother and child can go back to sleep more easily because they never really fully wake up or experience any stress or arousal.

Safety issues that apply to every baby, no matter where she

sleeps, can also be related to the environment of the room such as being smoke-free, parents not being overweight or drinking, and the setup of the bed, pillows, blankets, spaces, and furniture around the sleep area as itemized further in this chapter.

SIDS is much less likely when Mom is close by. Motherly instincts tend to wake her up if anything is wrong and, even more important, a baby whose mom is right there and who breastfeeds will wake up more often for nourishment. As mentioned, babies are not meant to sleep through the night. Waking up often prevents the baby from the deep sleep that can lead to apnea (when breathing stops). Babies are designed to breastfeed often at night for optimal growth and for safety.

Mom benefits from co-sleeping as well. She is more relaxed about the well-being of her baby, which helps her sleep better while helping the baby feel secure and breathe with ease.

Please do your own research on other causes of a baby's sudden death. It has been proven to be connected to medical issues, toxic air, vaccines, or other particular situations this book cannot delve into. The Vaccine Adverse Event Reporting System (VAERS) and the National Library of Medicine both provide statistics connected to vaccinations that you may wish to investigate. The book *Vax Facts* by Dr. Paul Thomas and DeeDee Hoover offers balanced information on childhood vaccinations with real-life statistics. *Miller's Review of Critical Vaccine Studies: 400 Important Scientific Papers Summarized for Parents and Researchers* by Neil Z. Miller is also a worthwhile read. And Dr. Suzanne Humphries's and Roman Bystrianyk's book, *Dissolving Illusions,* covers the whole history and why and how we became confused about vaccines. Be diligent on studying resources that have not been paid for by the manufacturers and make your own decisions.

If you do vaccinate your baby, it is even more important to sleep with her, so you can catch any medical issue in time.

The Downside of Separate Sleeping

Getting up from your bed to nurse a baby in another room or even in a bassinet next to you fully wakes both you and your baby. To get your attention from another bed, the baby must go beyond a gentle signal. It is only when she is stressed enough to cry that you know she needs you. By the time you show up, she may have been awake for a while, sensing around her, checking for you, scared, expecting your response, and then, when realizing that you are not there, melting down into crying. Eventually she learns to go directly into crying; she learns, long-term, to ask for what she wants through stress and tears.

In having to get out of your bed, your sleep is further interrupted as well. By the time you relax and fall sleep, your baby may be calling you again. As you can see, this is not the kindest way to accommodate both your needs and your baby's.

Your baby may wake up less frequently when away from you. She may be willing to get less feeding and contact than what she really needs because the response is difficult to get. Indeed, waking up more frequently safeguards the baby's breathing and her sense of safety, and she is fed optimally through the night as nature designed.

In other words, when a baby sleeps alone, she may experience serious anxiety and stress, which are harmful. She learns that crying and tantrums are the only ways to get the care she needs.

Bed-Sharing Safety Guidelines

- The baby should sleep on the outside of mother and not between parents.

- Mother should breastfeed on baby's cue, ensuring optimal wake-ups and lighter sleep, which then prevents apnea.
- Do not smoke in the bedroom where your baby sleeps or leave matches, ashtrays, or cigarettes lying around. (Ideally, do not smoke in a home with babies and children.) Do not smoke or be around smoke while pregnant as it predisposes your baby to breathing issues.
- Do not sleep on a waterbed, couch, or beanbag, but only on a flat, sufficiently hard bed where a baby can't roll into an unsafe position between cushions or into the body of an adult.
- To sleep with your baby, you must be aware. Do not use drugs, alcohol, sleep-inducing pills, or stimulants—ever.
- If you are exhausted and may sleep too deeply to respond to your baby, do not sleep on the same bed and make sure someone else is available to be aware and responsive.
- Always place baby to sleep on his back until he can easily turn himself.
- Protect the edge of the bed so the baby cannot roll off, and prevent any space between the mattress and the barrier. A mattress should fit tightly against the rail/barrier or be flush up against a wall, ensuring crevices are filled.
- Avoid fluffy bedding, pillows, and comforters. Never cover the baby with a comforter that may cover their face.
- Never put your baby (with or without you) on a waterbed or any soft surface.
- If other children are in your bed, keep the baby on your other side, away from them.
- Attend to your baby. Don't leave her/him to sleep alone in an adult bed.

- Keep the baby on the cooler side and avoid overheating; Mother's body adds plenty of heat.
- Make sure the bed and area are free of loose, unsafe items (clock, pen, paper, pins, and so on).
- Avoid items that emit electromagnetic field (EMF) radiation such as electric clocks, radios, or placing the bed on the other side of a wall adjacent to rooms with operating electronic and electric devices or panels such as a washer, refrigerator, stereo, computer, cooking stove, breaker, and such. Those emit EMF that go right through the wall.
- Make sure there are no electric outlets within reach.
- Avoid night-lights, both for safety and to prevent habituating your baby to light while sleeping. Babies who do not experience dark tend to become afraid of it and to eventually, due to the night-light, wake up and stay up to play while you are asleep.

You can find a list of bed-sharing safety guidelines also on www.AttachmentParenting.org and in Professor James McKenna's book *Sleeping with Your Baby*, as well as in other attachment parenting guiding books by Dr. Sears and others. When you decide where your baby will sleep, make sure that the sleep area is safe. Being next to you is the main safety feature, but the technical details are crucial too.

One of the most desirable results of the quick response enabled by sharing a bed with your baby is that the baby learns that life flows easily and calmly. She has no reason to develop anxiety about getting her needs met nor any doubt about trusting herself and feeling deserving of care.

Getting her needs met with ease ensures the development of a calm child who asks for what she wants in gentle ways; she has no need to throw a fit to receive care.

CONCLUSION

Sleeping can be safe and nourishing to both parents and babies if you follow the baby's cues. Babies need constant human contact, awake and asleep. When alone, the baby is scared for its survival. Before Western culture introduced separate sleeping with cots and cribs, humans, like all mammals, simply kept babies with them. The baby is safest and most content next to his mother with free breastfeeding access throughout the night. The baby needs to wake up a few times per night to feed. Mother's sleep is enhanced too when the baby is in bed with her; she doesn't need to fully wake up and can stay in the dark and go back to sleep, often while still breastfeeding. The baby learns to ask for what he wants with gentle cues and is stress free.

When sharing your bed with a baby, follow the above safety details and enjoy your nights.

Chapter 5
Sleep Struggle Solutions

Common expectations about babies' sleep obstruct your ability to respond to your own baby on her terms. Ideas about sleeping through the night, sleep regression, dressing the baby for sleep, and other physical and emotional issues create struggles that are easy to resolve once the real need is understood. In this chapter, we will be looking at some common bedtime and sleep struggles and how to resolve them.

The Illusion of Sleep Regressions

One of the most common uses of the mistaken concept of regression is about a baby's sleep. When the baby seems to not wake up as much, we build an expectation that this should not change. Then, when the baby wakes up more often again or won't fall asleep easily again, some parents label it a "regression." In a similar way, parents talk of toddlers who used to be independent and became clingy. However, there is no regression in the baby/toddler. It's the baby's next step forward.

Babies, toddlers, and young children move *forward* in many phases. It is not helpful to expect the little one to stick to whatever you see as an achievement or progress from your adult point of view. For a baby, each step is forward and is a temporary one, which must and will change in unknown ways that don't fit our concepts of linear thinking.

There is no regression. The baby is doing what she must do to move forward. The only exception is when parents, unknowingly, create insecurity in the child by being anxious, fixing too much, rescuing the child unnecessarily, and giving the child a sense that it is unsafe to be more independent. Otherwise, all babies constantly move forward, even when it seems to the adult that they are not.

Applying adult expectations and labels to the baby's or toddler's unfolding is not helpful, as it brings you stress, which also passes on to the baby. If you become impatient, it is due not to the baby's sleep but because of your expectations. The baby may feel that she is expected to sleep and is disappointing you; she feels your frustration. Calm yourself by inquiring into the thoughts that make you impatient or anxious.

At her session, Paulina did an inquiry on her baby's sleep.

Paulina: *"The baby was sleeping through the night; she shouldn't regress to waking up a lot."*

Naomi: Is that true? What's the reality of it?

Paulina: The reality is that my baby is now waking up often. So, no, it isn't true that she should sleep through the night.

Naomi: How do you react when you believe that she should not wake up as often?

Paulina: Stressed, frustrated, trying hard to rock and sing her to sleep . . . I feel impatient and oppositional.

Naomi: How would you be without this thought?

Paulina: Fine. I would notice that the baby needs to wake up a lot during the night. I would not compare now to the last month but trust this moment.

Naomi: Turn it around.

Paulina: *"The baby should wake up a few times a night now, regardless of how she slept before."*

Naomi: Prove to yourself that this turnaround is more true: What are some possible needs the baby fulfills by waking up more often?

Paulina: (1) A growth spurt that requires her to breastfeed more often, (2) she is waking up more often and that proves she has to, (3) she is teething, and (4) she is maturing and more aware and needs to make sure I am next to her.

Naomi: Trust your child and nature's design. She is progressing, not regressing. If you see a new or returned need, meet that need.

Emotions and Other Factors That Hinder Sleep

In the past, your baby was not aware if you left him in bed after he fell asleep. At some point, the baby or toddler becomes aware and wakes up to get you back. Then, although you may be sleeping next to him, he will be anxious that you might leave again. He may wake up frequently to make sure you are there.

Another reason a toddler may be restless in his sleep is having unexpressed energy or emotions. Many young toddlers need to be physical at bedtime to let out excess energy. Parents often think that good sleep come from "calming" the child down with songs and stories. However, if energy is bottled up in the child, then this energy may show up in restless sleep. Indeed, before being able to sleep, most wee ones need to exert energy—laugh, be noisy, run (if mobile yet), tumble, and get a bit "out of control."

For mobile toddlers, power games, as described in my book *Raising Our Children, Raising Ourselves,* are a wonderful bedtime activity that let out energy and include lots of laughter and emotional healing. Even some babies may need more motion and stimulation before settling in on the breast and falling asleep. Others may need to rage, cry, laugh, and let it all out before they are ready for songs, nursing, and stories. They sleep much better once excess energy and stress is out of their system.

Physical Issues and Sleep

Another cause of restless sleep is physical discomfort, the most common of which is being too hot. A baby may move to get out of the heat of adults' bodies and find a cool place on the bed. Most parents overdress their wee ones, and the thick blankets and body closeness make it all too hot. They want the body closeness, but for many, the heat is too much.

My babies preferred to be almost naked and be covered with nothing, other than perhaps a thin cotton blanket (the climate was cold where we lived, and we slept with an open window). Just as some adults sleep best with a mountain of down blankets while others open the window, babies differ in their needs, and many become easily too warm.

Other kinds of physical discomfort might include itchy pajamas, an uncomfortable diaper, a tag on the shirt, or the chemical in the sheets. Be aware what you wash the linen with and choose organic cotton linen with no flame retardant. Lack of fresh air, dry air, an uncomfortable mattress, thirst, and other real needs can cause the baby to move around or wake up often.

Your goal is not to get away from the problem but to solve it so your child can have the closeness she needs at night.

"My toddler moves so much in her sleep that I cannot get any sleep myself."

When we sleep with the infant from day one and she is used to our physical, uninterrupted presence, she is less likely to develop a restless sleep, but it is possible that there are other causes to the baby's motion that can be addressed, as covered in the previous section.

Instead of *not* sleeping with the baby, find the cause of the restlessness so the baby can sleep next to you. It is that important. Instead of giving up, figure out the root cause and solve the issue.

Andria felt exhausted by her baby's roaming the bed at night. "She is all over, above my head, on my face, sideways in the middle, and more. I just don't get my sleep this way."

Andria: *"The baby shouldn't be so restless at night."*

Naomi: Is that true?

Andria: Yes. She moves a lot during the night. She ends up above my head.

Naomi: Can you know that it is absolutely true under *all* circumstances?

Andria: No, I cannot know that.

Naomi: How do you react when you believe this thought?

Andria: I feel angry. I remove my baby from the family bed, and she cries. I feel terrible about it.

Naomi: Who would you be without this thought?

Andria: I would be fine. I would wonder why my baby moves so much and find a solution.

Naomi: Turn the original thought around.

Andria: *"My baby should be restless at night."*

Naomi: Can you find truth in that?

Andria: I suppose if the conditions were different, she wouldn't need to move so much.

Naomi: Well, look and see. What could be causing her to move so much?

Andria: Possibly some discomfort? Or wanting direct body contact with my face?

Naomi: Yes. When we question what we think, we start looking for solutions.

As itemized in the previous section, the causes of restless sleep can be diet (of Mom, the baby, or both), being too hot, rough linen or diaper, other physical discomfort, or a desire to be in a different part of the bed.

Let's consider food, for example. Any sugar or carbs is likely to prevent calm in the child's body, even if natural and organic. Fruit, especially when consumed in the evening, can affect sleep. Likewise, if you breastfeed and you eat sweet foods or stimulating substances such as tea, cocoa, or coffee, your baby can be stimulated.

Remember, babies are ketogenic. They burn ketones. Breast milk is low carb. It teaches us how the human body is supposed to function. Our goal is to keep it this way as it is the ideal metabolic state for babies and human beings. Therefore, if your toddler already eats solids, feed her plenty of wholesome, organic, and unprocessed animal protein and fats, especially in the evening. Eggs, dairy, or ground meat at bedtime is much more calming than bread (which is not real food) or grainy snacks. Most fruit is not advisable, either, but some types of fruit that contain tryptophan such as cherries and bananas in a small quantity and perhaps mixed with protein such as yogurt can be fine for some toddlers.

However, all protein foods have this calming effect and other benefits for good sleep. The same is true for your breast milk, which even contains some serotonin and melatonin in the evening to help the baby's sleep and teach her body the circadian cycle.

Andria experimented with some changes in her baby's clothing, food, and room temperature. She actually adjusted all of these. With fewer sweet foods, a cooler room, and nothing but a diaper on the baby and a cotton sheet for cover, she slept without moving around.

"We don't have enough room in our bed for more than two."

Beds and bedrooms in Western culture are not designed for the family but for the couple. We do not have to let the industry dictate our practices through their products. For starters, be creative in making your environment fit your family preferences. Ask yourself, "Is the size of our bed really a reason to deny my baby or child her basic and crucial need?"

Listen to your baby and to your heart and nothing technical will stop you. I know families who got a larger bed, but many others simply got rid of the bed and put the mattress on the floor. Then, when a second baby joined, they added a partial or single futon or mattress until, in a small room, they had a wall-to-wall bed.

Here is a thought: "*A bed must be a manufactured, elevated piece of furniture.*" Is that true? It is not true in the majority of the world, and it is often less safe and can be inconvenient. If your priority is "My baby must sleep with me," you will find no limit to ways to meet that need.

"I cannot sleep because my baby nurses five to seven times a night or she stays on the nipple for a long time."

Your baby grows constantly and can be very hungry at night. Many babies wake up often to breastfeed; it is a real need that must be met. Co-sleeping helps them to breastfeed as often as they need, as nature designed it. When far from your body, the baby may actually learn to skip meals that she needs.

Telling yourself that you cannot stand being woken up every hour and that you will be tired is causing you more upset and exhaustion than the actual disruptions of sleep. In any event, keeping your baby in your bed, in the dark, to breastfeed does not require you to fully wake up or get out of bed. Each wake-up is a time to cherish; it will pass all too soon. Enjoy and go back to sleep or at least rest. Don't keep track of the time or how often the baby wakes up. In the morning, don't worry about how many hours you have actually slept. (If you do, this thought will make you tired.)

If you try to retract the nipple from your baby's mouth after she falls asleep and she wakes up, just give it back to her. There will come a time when her sleep will be deep enough that you can do so without waking the baby up. With experience, you will learn to recognize the signs that tell you that she is in that deep phase of sleep. Another way to undo the grip on the nipple is to slowly replace it with your little finger (clean and with a clipped nail). In addition, it is fine to fall asleep while your baby is suckling.

Although, most often, sleeping together means more interruptions, without getting out of bed or even sitting up, these are less disturbing of your sleep. However, even if you find it hard to wake up often, I suggest that you make a clear choice about your focus and commitment. When you focus on "I want uninterrupted sleep" and you don't get it, you feel stressed, resentful, and tired. Who would you be without that thought?

You will have uninterrupted sleep most of your life. Instead of devoting yourself to this Western culture's idea, you may want to focus on doing what is best for your baby and most nurturing of you as a mother. Isn't snuggling with your baby far more enjoyable than having uninterrupted sleep?

The good news is that it is possible to have a baby and get enough sleep. If you go to bed at the same time as your baby and have light-blocking curtains, you may be in bed nine hours and get six or seven hours of sleep. I know many mothers who found that co-sleeping was the best way to get sufficient sleep.

"My baby likes to sleep by herself."

Parents sometimes tell me that their baby prefers to sleep separately. My years of experience with thousands of parents tell me that sleeping alone is extremely unlikely to be the authentic wish of the baby. Instead, it may be the baby's confused response to his experience of birth and what occurred right after his arrival or other emotional confusion. Separation at birth and other birth or after-birth trauma can confuse the infant to the point of fear of closeness.

Other reasons can include that the baby mirrors your anxiety or your preference to sleep separately or that the baby is physically uncomfortable in the family bed. Perhaps the room isn't dark enough, there are sound distractions, the baby is too hot, or there are other causes that must be addressed as itemized earlier.

The confusing thought may be, *My baby wants to sleep alone.*

Is it true? Can you absolutely know that it's true? When you examine how your own thoughts impact the baby's response, as well as other possible factors, you may be surprised to discover that this is not true and that other issues lead to this choice, including the possibility that it may be your wish to sleep without the baby.

Co-sleeping is still the best solution, especially if there are emotional reasons for the baby's confusion. If your baby sleeps in your bed and has a need to create distance, he will (once he can) scoot away on his own, and you can respect him and keep that distance, even giving him his own blanket while still being right by his side. He knows you are present. Gradually, he is likely to get closer. Such a baby needs to heal his ability to feel at ease while being touched and connected. If it is truly his nature to need distance while sleeping, he still needs to know you are physically in touching proximity.

If an infant had an early experience of being held and hurt (perhaps at birth or a medical procedure), his mind may signal to him that human contact is not safe for sleep. Such babies are often less cuddly during the day as well.

You may think that nothing happened to your baby, but simple interventions—such as being turned upside down to breathe at birth, being injected with something, having blood drawn, getting drops in the eyes, undergoing circumcision, or being separated from mother by a nurse—can qualify as forms of trauma associated with human contact. In other words, I am suggesting that the baby who seems more comfortable sleeping alone is suffering an emotional discomfort that requires healing.

You can heal your baby's discomfort about night contact by giving him the safety of night closeness gradually and gently. If he can sleep gradually closer to you in a cot attached to the bed (within your touch), then move to the bed with his own blanket and experience your comforting presence, his anxiety will subside over time and his natural need to sleep close to you will recover.

The Baby May Respond to Your Hesitation

Another cause for a baby to reject sleeping with you can be confusion about your feelings. Some babies and toddlers are so in tune and sensitive that if you have any hint of hesitation about sleeping in one bed, they will sense it and prefer to sleep separately.

This is not the baby's authentic choice but a mirroring of parental doubt or anxiety.

From the moment they are born, babies try to figure out what we expect of them. They want to find out how to survive and belong. They can therefore become the projection of their parents' emotional states.

Without a painful experience at birth or sensing parental confusion, like all mammals, the human baby wants to sleep in their mother's arms or right next to Mom or Dad. A baby needs to know that Mom is always attached and never leaves while he sleeps. This will also help him develop good sleep habits, free of anxiety. Even babies who, by their nature, are less affectionate are guided by their primal survival need to be in very close proximity to their life source and protection, especially when sleeping.

Check whether it is you who hesitates to sleep with your baby. If that's truer (as you'll see in the dialogue below), there is no need to feel shame, only to heal. Vicky was convinced that her baby preferred to sleep alone. She came to this conclusion because he cried only briefly when left in his crib and slept with fewer interruptions. And sometimes, when extremely tired, he didn't even cry. When he slept in the family bed, she noticed that he woke up more and seemed restless. She did the following inquiry at her session:

Vicky: *"My baby likes to sleep by himself."*

Naomi: Is that true?

Vicky: Yes.

Naomi: Can you absolutely know that it is true?

Vicky: No. I cannot know that.

Naomi: How do you react when you believe this thought?

Vicky: Anxious and confused because I am not sure what is best for him.

Naomi: Who/how would you be without that thought?

Vicky: Relieved. Also a bit anxious about how it would work.

Naomi: That's a useful find. Let's see: Turn it around.

Vicky: *"The baby wants to sleep with me."*

Naomi: Is that as true or truer?

Vicky: Perhaps his initial crying is a truer indication of what he needs.

Naomi: Can you find proof that this could be more true?

Vicky: Yes; he is a very accommodating baby, so perhaps he cooperates with us putting him in his crib without much protest, but it isn't really what he needs. And perhaps he thrashes around in the family bed due to other reasons or discomfort.

Naomi: Can you see another turnaround?

Vicky: *"I don't want to sleep with my baby."* Vicky pondered a moment and then says with a shaky voice: I never had such closeness as a child, not even during the days.

Naomi: What an amazing discovery and an opportunity to heal. Find out the thoughts that drive this discomfort and write them down.

Vicky wrote down a few thoughts and did several inquiries with me and by herself. Within a week, she was ready and took the baby back to the family bed. She said she hardly slept but to her amazement, the baby did not display a need to be by himself and slept very well. The next night, they both slept well, and the baby was clearly happy. This was a clear case of a baby mirroring his mother's emotional state.

When you are free from any anxiety related to sleeping with your baby, you will be able to know what your baby truly needs. It is the kindest path toward your own inner peace and your baby's best.

"My toddler is used to sleeping by herself. Should I move her back to our bed?"

Most parents who ask me this question describe a scenario in which they put the child to sleep in her own bed. They lie beside the child until the little one is asleep, and then they leave. In the middle of the night, the child wakes up and cries, and the only solution is to take her to their bed. Or, if the child in question is older, she wakes up and goes to the parents' bed on her own. The parents report this as a positive situation since the child is free to join them. Sometimes the joining occurs only in the morning, simply because the toddler or child sleeps through the night.

The preference for the baby is clearly to sleep with her parents. It is never too late to do what is better. The child who prefers to join you in bed may as well feel more completely fulfilled by spending the full night close to you.

The bottom line is simply to take the route that brings the most joy and ease: If your child is happy to join you in the family bed, let the fun begin. If you doubt yourself, you are most likely listening to advice that is not your own truth. Notice whether your mind wanders with thoughts such as *What will Grandma say? or Am I harming my child by letting him sleep next to me at this age?* The mind can go to absurd places such as thinking that being loved and cuddled in bed with you can cause harm.

If you were to reword the original question, the result may be alarmingly like "If my baby is already used to being deprived of her need for closeness at night, she may as well keep being deprived." Putting it in such a strong way may startle you right into the obvious turnaround: *"The baby got used to less than what is best, so we should hurry and remedy the issue and provide optimal conditions for her sleep."*

If you still hesitate, notice how much of your worry has to do with the opinions and judgments of others or thoughts that you did not investigate. How would you feel without all these concerns? How would you be if there were no others, or if they all supported bed-sharing at any age? Who would you be then? Give yourself that freedom. When you listen to your own heart and to your child's deep yearning to be with you, you will find that it is never too late to cuddle together for the night and that it is always highly beneficial.

A couple of years back, a mother called to seek my guidance with regard to her eight-year-old son's aggressive behavior. After exploring the possible causes of his distress, I made a few suggestions, including to ask him whether he would like to move back to the family bed. The boy had slept with his parents until a year or so earlier, and his aggression had started at the time he moved to his own room for sleep. Our follow-up Zoom session was canceled. Instead, I got a thank-you email from the mother, saying that the child was eager to return to sleeping with his parents and that, as soon as he did so, all his anxiety, stress, and aggression completely vanished.

In his work in the Mother-Baby Sleep Laboratory at the University of Notre Dame, Dr. James McKenna has demonstrated the health and psychological benefits of this primal and natural way of caring for the sleeping baby. He is the author of the 2020 book *Safe Infant Sleep*. For more on Dr. McKenna's research, visit cosleeping.nd.edu. It makes sense that feeling secure at night and having body contact enhances the development of self-confidence, self-reliance, and ease of human connection. Not having such closeness is stressful for the baby, and stress always gets in the way of healthy development. These benefits, in turn, support higher intelligence and peaceful demeanor.

Babies can't fathom sleeping away from their mothers, and most children are scared when left alone to fall asleep. For most young ones, it feels very lonely to move from consciousness to unconsciousness without the physical touch of a loving human being. Unless trained out of their nature, babies cry when left to sleep by themselves and do so for a good reason. We can trust them, knowing that what they want is what they need and what is best for them. If a baby who is put to sleep alone has given up and won't cry anymore or is very accommodating by nature, it is even more important to help her return to her authentic needs and to trusting herself. Getting such a child back in your bed will reawaken in her the need for such closeness, which will be of great benefit to her.

Humans do adapt to deprivations for survival, often through addictions, denial, food disorders, and so on. Ideally, babies—and all children, for that matter—are best off not being made to adapt to deprivations of valid needs. To alleviate the pain, they numb it and create reasons for this being the way it is. A baby does so by not crying, sucking on a pacifier or a thumb, rocking their body, and so on. While numbing herself, however, the baby does more than shut herself off from the one issue; she numbs emotional openness and learns to ignore her own inner wisdom and needs. In turn, this can translate to confusion, anxiety, self-doubt, and insecurity.

Your young child will benefit from co-sleeping any time. Just because she has missed it for a few months, or even a couple of years, doesn't mean she should miss even more. Most babies and toddlers will celebrate returning to their parents' bed. It is easy for them and, as long as they sense your complete confidence and joy in wanting them in your bed, they will forget about their own bed in no time.

Your baby counts on you to make her needs a higher priority than your inclinations to fit in with norms or even your sleep convenience. Listen to her. She learns that she is worthy when she experiences your confidence in caring for her on her terms. It is rare that a baby would reject the family bed and prefer to stay in her own bed out of habit, but if she does, sleep with her in her bed for a while. She is not likely to give up snuggling with you once she has the experience again.

An older child may prefer her own bed. There is no reason to coerce her to change. However, now that you know how important your physical closeness is at night, offer it generously while letting her be in charge of her choice to cuddle with you. With all the options open and enjoyable, she will choose whatever fits her best, and you can respond to her choice.

Your attitude will impact the child's desire to co-sleep. If you love cuddling with your little wonder and you let her know how much you cherish your closeness with her (without imposing), she is likely to enjoy it. If she moves back to your bed and then wants to return to her own bed, let her, but don't give her the impression that it is better for her to sleep alone or that you expect it. Avoid implying that she is "a big girl" if she sleeps by herself or that it means anything to you. Tell her that you love snuggling for the night next to her so she doesn't try to impress you by sleeping alone. At the same time, let her know that you love her no matter where and how she prefers to sleep so she doesn't feel an obligation to sleep in the family bed but chooses freely.

The conventional thinking of separate sleeping is actually most unnatural and strange; it is historically unheard of until the last two hundred years or so and is still not practiced in most of the non-Western world. It is strange because it goes against nature's design, makes things more difficult, has absolutely no benefits, and can cause much harm. However, as I said before, don't believe me. Just find out what your child wants, and forget about what anyone says. Live your life, not anyone else's. Learn to trust your child. What a joy nature designed for us in cuddling with our babies and children.

"I am so tired. How can I get enough sleep and still meet my baby's and my toddler's needs?"

What is most kind to your baby is also the kindest to you. Sleeping with your baby gives you more and better sleep. When your baby wakes, you do not need to fully awaken; you can stay in bed and just offer the breast. It is less stressful to both of you; your baby need not cry, you don't need to worry about him, and there is no need to get out of bed or turn on the lights. Just breastfeed and doze off back to sleep.

Some parents turn on a light and get up to change a diaper. Yet I recall being in the dark while changing a wet diaper. All-in-one cotton diapers are easy to use this way. Keeping the lights off makes it easier to go back to sleep because the light stops the presence of melatonin. When you must use light, for a soiled diaper and such, you may wish to purchase a blue-light-blocking bulb for your bedside lamp.

When your baby is next to you, your sleep cycles become one with hers. This means that when she is waking up, you may be already awake or in a light sleep phase. Not being woken out of deep sleep, you will find drifting back to sleep much easier.

Based on the above, the issue of lack of sleep is actually nonexistent most nights as long as you listen to the baby and keep her next to you. Of course, the beginning may take some adjusting and learning, and if a baby is sick or teething, some nights would indeed be less restful for both Mother/Father and baby. This is true with or without a baby. None of us always sleeps well. Step one is therefore to sleep with your baby and breastfeed. Let's look at other challenges that may cause a mother to feel tired.

The argument that *"I must sleep with no interruptions"* is worth inquiring into for yourself. When a night without interruption is unavailable, as designed by nature, does this thought bring you stress or peace? During our session, Daphne did this exact inquiry.

Daphne: *"I must sleep with no interruptions through the night."*

Naomi: Is that true?

Daphne: No, I don't know if it is a must.

Naomi: How do you react when you believe this thought?

Daphne: I resent my baby for waking me up. And I feel tired during the day.

Naomi: And how would you be without this thought?

Daphne: I won't resent my baby when she wakes me up. But won't I still feel tired?

Naomi: I don't know. In my experience, I can feel tired even when I have enough sleep, and other times, I feel alert all day after a short night. Ask yourself how you may feel without the thought that you must sleep without interruption.

Daphne: That makes sense. I believe that my sleep wasn't sufficient so I feel tired. Without it, I don't know.

Naomi: Yes, give it a try and let your body, rather than your thought, give you feedback. Turn the thought around.

Daphne: "I don't have to have an uninterrupted night's sleep."

Naomi: Is that possibly as true or truer?

Daphne: Very likely.

Naomi: Try another turnaround.

Daphne: *"I must have interrupted sleep at night."* (Laughs.) That's more peaceful because it's what I have.

Naomi: Indeed. When you have a baby, you must have interrupted nights. We have babies for a chunk of our lives. Later, we have interrupted nights for other reasons. Can you think of other reasons a human's sleep at night would be naturally interrupted?

Daphne: In the old days, tending to a fire in the winter, taking turns guarding the tribe . . . and in later age, going to the bathroom? Or a partner who wakes up or snores, an elderly parent who needs care, hunger, dogs barking . . .

Daphne was on a roll. She had numerous examples that debunked the myth of the need for uninterrupted sleep. She laughed and said that she was ready now for whatever night sleep is due while being a mother to a baby.

Our culture has developed the idea of long, uninterrupted sleep at night. It is a myth hardly anyone can keep up with. In many tribal societies, people nap during the day and sleep in short segments during the night, waking up to tend to a fire, as Daphne mentioned, or care for children, and take turns protecting the family and other natural needs. Our Western idea of sleeping only at night and with no interruptions creates anxiety and lots of profit for the manufacturers of sleeping aids and pills. Obviously, there are sometimes actual sleep disturbances that require medical or psychological care, but having a baby, by itself, is not one of them.

Here are some helpful ideas to get more sleep in the family bed. You can use any number of these ideas or come up with more of your own. Choose whatever fits your needs.

- You can go to sleep at the same time your baby does so you get the longest part of the uninterrupted sleep, which is the first part (sometime three to four hours). Gently push the baby's sleep ten minutes later each evening until it is late enough for you to be able to go to sleep at the same time regularly.
- A baby who knows you are always there will sleep soundly and move gradually toward sleeping for longer stretches of time in line with her real needs and not based on anxiety. Lie next to your sleeping baby even if you are not yet tired. (I kept a book by my bedside with a small light. If I wasn't tired enough yet, I could read.)
- Hang light-blocking curtains in the bedroom. Some babies sleep later in the morning if the room is dark. You can sleep longer too and make up for lost sleep by having a longer time in bed.
- If you have a toddler or a child in addition to the baby, keep her in the family bed as well. In the safety of your presence and with dark curtains, she, too, may sleep longer. (Don't expect it, though. Some wee ones wake up no matter what.)

- If possible, take a nap with your baby. If you have only one baby or if your toddler naps, too, take a nap in the afternoon with them. If your toddler does not nap, then this is the time to give her one-on-one attention while the baby is asleep on you or right next to you.
- Start the bedtime process way ahead of time. If you have a baby and a child, starting ahead of time will allow you to be patient, and the children will have time to adjust. Use the time to let your child exert energy and do power games as explained in my book *Raising Our Children, Raising Ourselves,* so that he goes to bed relaxed, free of the day's stress or excess energy. Let the toddler run and jump as long as he needs to. If you are the one to stop him, his pent-up energy can hamper his sleep and yours. Let him finish his "job." Story time and a lullaby work best after all the excess energy (or what you may call being "overtired") has been spent.
- Physiologically, your blood sugar has a lot to do with feeling exhausted even when you get enough sleep. Do yourself and your baby a favor and eat only wholesome, real foods that are nutritionally dense and easily assimilated by the human body. Eat food that keeps your blood sugar even without glucose spikes and that gives you long-term energy rather than ups and downs. Real food is eating without turning "ingredients" into something else. Real food looks like what it actually is and requires no "making" it into food. Real food provides all the nutrients we need without needing processed powders or supplements. When eating healthy, organic, nutritionally dense, and unaltered foods, many find

they need a lot less sleep and feel alert more of the time.

- Make up sleep if and when you have support—for example, when a partner, grandparent, or a friend can take your baby for a stroll and let you stay in bed or take an afternoon nap. Use this on the rare occasion of special hardship with sleep due to sickness or other causes.
- Get some exercise daily or, with your baby in a wrap or other in-arms baby carrier, go for a walk in the fresh air. It is good for both of you.
- Let your partner, friend, neighbor, or a relative hold a happy or sleeping baby and take a ten-minute nap; it can make all the difference.
- Let go of your idea of how much your baby should sleep and how much sleep you need. Your thought that *"the baby will be cranky"* or that *"he is not getting enough sleep"* or that *"I didn't get enough sleep"* adds further stress to your day. These, too, are not your thoughts. Respond to your baby on his terms, and sleep will more easily flow.
- Happy babies may not need as much sleep. Often, when you think your baby is tired and cranky, if you stop trying to put him to sleep and instead play with him, you will discover that he is not tired at all. Or you may find that he needs to do some "cranking" and crying and when done, he is either wide-awake or ready for bed with no resistance. This will help the baby sleep better and develop a healthy attitude toward sleep, and you will get better sleep at the same time.
- Examine your limiting concepts about sleep: Notice thoughts such as *"If I am interrupted a lot, I will be tired,"* or *"If I get*

only four hours of sleep, I will be exhausted and cranky." Obviously, take care of yourself in ways that are possible. But free yourself from anxiety about sleep that is rooted in ideas of the mind and not in motherly or fatherly reality.

With my first baby, I was counting the hours of sleep and the number of times I was woken up to breastfeed or change a diaper. As a result, I believed I was tired during the day, and so I was. One day, I explored this belief and realized it was not true. I stopped counting the hours and the number of wake-ups and found out that without the thought about my broken night, I was awake and peaceful no matter how little I slept. I didn't remember to be tired; it was simply not a problem anymore. Yes, sometimes, while breastfeeding or reading to a toddler, I would notice a sluggishness (this would happen even when I had plenty of sleep), but without giving attention or meaning to it, I noticed that it vanished as soon as I was in action again, drank a glass of water, or went outside with my little one. That, too, was a fine experience.

The most difficult thing to say to you about sleep is that much of it is an attitude. Although you do need to take care of yourself and find ways to get sleep as suggested above, what constitutes "enough sleep" is strongly affected by your preconceptions. In addition, more exhausting than the lack of sleep is the struggle against reality. When you say yes to whatever occurs and whatever the baby wants, life is peaceful, and your energy isn't spent on this inner struggle. Of course, take care of getting sleep some other time by planning, as explained earlier.

Yes, sometimes you don't want to be strong and you just want to cry and feel your feelings. Be kind to yourself, and do that with all your being. Let go, and feel it fully. When done, you will feel temporarily better. But it won't solve the problem long-term because it actually reinforces the suffering. Questioning the thought that causes you to cry and to feel overwhelmed is a long-term help because it frees you from the painful thoughts that produce the intense emotions in the first place.

When your baby sleeps with you, you will generally get plenty of sleep except for the rare occasion of a teething or sick baby. If you get only four hours of sleep on a given night and you tell yourself, "I hardly slept—I am so tired," chances are you are going to feel exhausted. Without a devotion to this thought, you may forget how little you slept and feel fine most of the day. Your beliefs reinforce tiredness. Some typical beliefs that cause us to feel more tired are:

Breastfeeding is tiring.

One must have eight hours of sleep each night.

One must have uninterrupted sleep for a few hours.

When I lie in bed awake, I don't get any rest.

If I am short on sleep, I am grumpy.

I am so tired.

I hardly get any sleep.

I am exhausted/overwhelmed.

I can't do it.

It is too much for me.

I need more sleep.

Question these and similar thoughts, and you will find your own resilience and real solutions. Of course, having a resilient attitude does not replace implementing suitable sleep conditions as discussed. These include sleeping with your baby, keeping the room dark, napping with the baby when possible, and making smart food choices. Take care of yourself, but when life hands you a challenge, take it on—not as a victim but as a grateful and skillful warrior.

The Sun and Your Sleep

Spend time in the sun with your child during the day. Your sleep and their sleep will be sounder if they get sun during the day, starting when they get up. The sun not only gives you both much-needed vitamin D but also ensures the correct timing of melatonin production, which helps with sleep. For the sun to be effective, avoid burning by keeping the skin's natural oils working for you and your wee ones according to this guidance:

- Avoid direct sun in the hottest hours of the summer, depending on where you live and on the season. Use wide-brimmed hats and keep the children in the shade in hot hours, taking your child's skin color into account. Daylight still affects your child in the shade as it is reflected from trees, homes, grass, the sky, and clouds.
- Sun is life-giving. In safe hours, let the bare skin absorb it for nourishment.
- To allow the skin to absorb nutrients and not burn, avoid drying it with soaps and lotions. These not only take the natural oil of the skin away but change the composition of these natural oils and thwart their ability to absorb nutrients rather than burn.
- Minimize or avoid using sunscreen. Instead, in the hot hours, use natural animal fats such as butter, lard, or tallow, and keep the child in the shade and with a wide-brimmed hat when the UV is too high for too long.

- Eat and feed your child a diet high in healthy animal fats to maintain the skin's ability to absorb nutrients from the sun and avoid burning.
- Avoid consumption of all seed oils; their excess linoleic acid and other toxins cause mitochondrial damage in human cells, greatly increasing the skin's susceptibility to burning.
- If you must put sunscreen on your child, use an organic animal fat–based one, or use hats, shaded play areas, or long pants and sleeves when needed. In extreme snow/sun exposure, combine zinc oxide with butter or coconut oil for sunblock.
- The sun is especially nurturing through the eyes. Obviously, we don't look at the sun directly. However, it is healthy when the sun is red, at sunrise and sunset. When the sun is above, we get nutrients through the eyes by being in the shade (such as under a tree or hat) and looking at clouds or the sky. Your baby needs the sun. Follow these guidelines to provide the benefits without doing harm.
- There is a debate among scientists and physicians about the sun being the cause of skin cancer or whether lack of it is the real cause. My thinking is that it is humans who created the problem by altering the way their skin acts in the sun through diet, soaps, and other modern interventions. Regardless, burning is clearly unsafe, just like standing in the rain and cold for too long isn't safe, even though water is healthy and life-giving. Being in the cold is healthy; freezing is not. Likewise, the sun is healthy; burning is not. Nothing is healthy when overdone.

You can explore this subject for yourself and see why, for millions of years, humans lived mostly outdoors in the sun with bare skin and had no skin cancer and why, in modern society, soaping the skin, being indoors, eating food that dries the skin from inside, and many other factors literally created an easy-to-burn and disease-prone skin.

Once you understand how to take advantage of the sun, your child can benefit from its amazing gifts and sleep better at night.

"I am tired physically, even if I don't think I am."

One mother who called for my assistance used my guidance and managed to have sufficient sleep. However, she found that she was tired no matter how much more sleep she got. In her session, she found a treasure in the form of a limiting thought: *"I want my husband to see how difficult it is for me to be a mother."* She did an inquiry with me, going through the four questions and turnaround:

Pamela: *"I need my husband to know how difficult it is for me to be a mother."*

Naomi: Is it true that you need him to know how difficult it is?

Pamela: Yes.

Naomi: Can you absolutely know that it's true?

Pamela: Yes, I really can.

Naomi: How do you react when you believe this thought?

Pamela: I see my days as difficult, and I get impatient with my baby and yell at my husband.

Naomi: How do you feel when you believe this thought?

Pamela: Tired. Cranky. Overwhelmed.

Naomi: How do you treat your husband when you believe that he must see you as suffering and working so hard?

Pamela: I am a drama queen: I act, I sigh, I tell him how hard it is and try to elicit his pity and care. I believe that he would not value me otherwise or would expect too much of me if he didn't realize how hard it already is . . . oh, I see. This is such nonsense. (Laughing.)

Naomi: Who would you be without your story?

Pamela: I would enjoy my baby and feel alert and needing nothing.

Naomi: What a discovery. How does your husband like you better, complaining or happy?

Pamela: Happy, of course.

Naomi: Turn the thought around.

Pamela: *"I don't need my husband to see me as working so hard at being a mother."*

Naomi: Is this as true or truer than the original thought?

Pamela: It is truer. I see that I get stuck because I tell myself that he won't appreciate me if mothering is easy. . . . I can see that this is not true at all. He hates when I complain. He tells me so.

Naomi: Try another way to turn the thought around.

Pamela: *"I want my husband to see how easy it is for me to be a mother."* Oh, yes. He would love it so much better. He adores when I am happy. He says, "She is a natural mother. . . ."

Naomi: Can you see another turnaround?

Pamela: *"I want me to see how easy it is for me to be a mother."*

As an aside: We are not talking about denial and pretending but about actually noticing moment by moment without the story about "hard and difficult." It is not a denial of challenges but a celebration of each moment's victory of an honest and grateful spirit. The inquiry continued:

Pamela: Something inside me rebels. It is not easy to let go.

Naomi: Yes, the mind rebels. That is its job—to protect the beliefs that are in the "software." It wants to keep you a believer in its "program." So, look again and see yourself caring for your baby without this story.

Pamela: It is easy—just one thing after the other. Nothing difficult about changing a diaper, holding, breastfeeding, kissing . . . I love my baby and enjoy doing these things.

Naomi: Doing one thing after the other is never difficult. So, without trying to show up as a victim in your husband's eyes . . . ?

Pamela: I would be fine. Since we go to sleep at the same time and we have the dark curtains, I actually get plenty of sleep most nights and am really fine.

Our level of energy is affected by our thoughts. I am not suggesting that we don't sleep at all or shrink our night on a regular basis. Get the sleep you can get, exercise, be in the sun, and eat nutritionally dense foods. But when life dictates less sleep, you would be better off believing your body can handle such a naturally occurring setup without being cranky and exhausted. You will enjoy life more. You get whatever sleep you get, and being upset does not improve the outcome nor guarantee a change. It only tires you.

Instead of saying, "I am short on sleep, and I feel exhausted and irritable," you can try, "I have been nursing a lot of the nights and I get up early, yet it is amazing how my body can handle it, and how when I am engaged with my child(ren), I forget about how little I slept." Decide to feel refreshed and at the same time be creative in using the above and your own ideas to allow yourself times of rest.

And, yes, take care of yourself in the many ways suggested earlier. And choose your priorities such that your self-care comes ahead of a clean house, an email, or even cooking dinner. Real food comes prepared. Cooking and "making" non-food into foods is only one option. The dishes can wait too. Many things we spend time on are not a must, and letting go of some of those allows us more breaks and rest. You can do them in a better time, with baby in arms, or if you have someone who can help, count on them to hold the baby or to do the chores.

Too many parents say years later, "I wish I had been more present. I wish I had ignored my tiredness and just enjoyed the moment." This period will all pass so fast that, looking back, you would be sorry for any minute spent complaining rather than enjoying, or cleaning rather than being with your children. So, wake up; this scene will never repeat itself. It is now.

"What about our sex life?"

Regardless of where your baby sleeps, your sex life will never be the same as it was before the birth of your first child. Your sex life is not about your baby's sleep location. Your baby's existence changes everything. We don't deny the baby's needs to retain our conveniences or habits. We learn to live with the baby and alter things as needed.

How wonderful to move on to a new phase of romantic and sexual relationship! In our youth, while we didn't have children to consider, we also might have had more limitations, depending on our age and living situation. We had to be flexible in finding the time and place to romantically connect with a partner. We had to improvise but the limitations offered an element of excitement.

At this stage in our life, keep that same element of excitement going by being flexible and keeping your mind open. How romantic to embrace a baby with your partner and kiss! Sleeping with your baby can actually make sex more possible, more peaceful, and yes, even more frequent than when a baby is tucked away elsewhere. Interruptions are for sure less dramatic when the baby is right there, so you don't need to go to another room where a baby is already too awake from crying and completely interrupt your intimate connection.

Here are three thoughts that limit our joy in this new phase of sexuality:

1. Sex must occur at night.
2. Sex must take place in the bedroom.
3. Sex must be uninterrupted until both reach orgasm.

Please be kind to yourself and let go of these and other imprisoning ideas. My husband and I used to count the number of times we were interrupted; this brought only laughter into our intimate connections. Our record was making love in five "episodes."

Being in the same bed with the baby makes things a lot easier because you can respond before the baby is fully awake and, often, lull her right back to sleep. A cuddle or a touch is often enough to prevent a full wake-up, and often breastfeeding will put the baby back to sleep.

Therefore, the bedroom may be ideal in the first year or two depending on the nature of your baby's sleep. Later, it may be simpler to be in a different room while the toddler is asleep in your bed or during the weekend if you are lucky enough to have grandparents, a friend, or a babysitter to take him to the playground in the middle of the day. You may need more planning on the one hand, and flexible spontaneity on the other. Flow freely and creatively with an open and curious mind. At the same time, if you can't get help and the conditions limit your sex life, embrace it—let it nurture your yearning and affection. It is only temporary.

Nothing is ever the way it was.
It is always the way it is.

CONCLUSION

In the early years, parenting and especially mothering, can be a shocking shift in reality. Nothing is what it was. We can yearn for the way it was and suffer, or we can walk the new path with curiosity and open arms. As nature intended, regular sleep deprivation is unnecessary. And uninterrupted sleep is probably not going to be part of life for a while. Inquiry into the stressful thought brings gratitude. Sleeping with the baby during the hours the baby sleeps maximizes the mother's sleep.

Chapter 6

Your Toddler/Young Child's Sleep

Toddlers can walk, but they are essentially still babies, and they need what babies need. Most often, they can still be breastfeeding. With or without breastfeeding, they need constant contact just like they did before when we called them babies. Their emotional need for constant human physical contact has not changed. Being more aware, their need can feel even stronger. They want to be with you, to sleep next to you, to be included, and not to be left alone. This chapter covers toddlers' sleep and how to recognize the cues when your child may be ready to move to her own bed. Allowing the child to decide where she should sleep is crucial for her development of self-reliance and independence. When it is her independent choice, she learns to trust herself and to trust you to respond to her valid needs.

Your Child Wants to Be Included

One reason a child doesn't want to go to bed is that they hate to be removed from the excitement of life. They don't want to miss anything. As long as you are awake, they expect to be included. They will struggle to keep their eyes open when tired in order not to miss anything. They are also likely to be fearful of being alone in bed if they know that you won't stay in bed with them. As I hear from children—and from parents sharing their childhood memories—lying alone in bed and hearing adults' voices from the living room can be a nightmarish experience. Others feel isolated and excluded, uncomfortable, or anxious. Yes, some fall asleep peacefully and feel calm when waking up to find themselves alone, but if your child isn't one of them, respond to her specific need.

The toddler's innate instructions are to be with you at all times. She can fall asleep on you or next to you, feeling your presence even while you stay up. Likewise, the toddler can sit in your lap or run around until ready to sleep. Simplicity and peace come from surrender to the call of nature's design. The instructions are given to you by your child.

Any time you struggle, you can bring peace back by surrendering instead. I use this word in its deeper spiritual meaning of flowing with the gifts coming your way until you realize that nothing happens to you but for you. Questioning your thoughts is the most direct way to quickly find this liberating experience.

As Byron Katie, the creator of the self-inquiry method known as The Work, says,

"Life is simple. Everything happens for you, not to you. Everything happens at exactly the right moment, neither too soon nor too late. You don't have to like it. . . . It's just easier if you do."

Let's look at how such surrender and flowing brings joy to bed-time with a toddler.

The Overtired Toddler

When, at the end of the day or at nap time, a toddler seems indecisive and out of control, many mothers are convinced that the child is overtired. They struggle to put the child to sleep against the child's will, being sure it is best for him.

In her session with me, Tania asked what to do when it is clear that her toddler is ready to go to bed, but he refuses to go to sleep.

Tania: *"My toddler is tired and should sleep now."*

Naomi: Is that true?

Tania: Yes. He is overtired.

Naomi: Can you absolutely know that it is true?

Tania: No. I cannot.

Naomi: How do you react when you believe this thought that he is overtired and should sleep now and he wants to run around?

Tania: I am stressed and struggle with my little one. I am impatient and irritable.

Naomi: Where do you feel it in your body?

Tania: My throat is tight and I sometimes get a headache.

Naomi: How would you be without this thought?

Tania: At peace. Enjoying my toddler.

Naomi: Turn it around to the opposite.

Tania: "*My toddler is not overtired and should not go to sleep now.*"

Naomi: Yes. He knows his own body. Turn it around to yourself.

Tania: *"I am overtired and want to sleep. That is true. I am trying to get him to sleep to get a break and to get to bed soon too."*

To clarify again: "Overtired" is an adult concept and does not resonate with the toddler's experience of himself—no matter how logical our explanation. Babies are born knowing to sleep, to cry, to breastfeed, and so on. By responding to the baby's cues, parents are confirming that the baby's own sense of himself is right and worth trusting, and he grows up to respond well to his own body.

When we oppose the toddler's experience, we wage war on forces beyond our power. Inadvertently, we then teach the toddler not to trust us—and, more importantly, not to trust himself and to fight against his own inclinations. He may even feel wronged and like he is failing to live up to your expectations. The confusion between the toddler's experience and your fight against it can create insecurity, emotional dependency, and confusion.

I shared this with Tania, but she wasn't sure:

Tania: But what about the fact that he is cranky and crying for little things . . . he is not having a good time.

Naomi: When cranky let him crank. When crying let him cry. These behaviors are not the same as needing to sleep. An upset and out-of-sort toddler doesn't need to have his expression suppressed or stopped by sleep. He will sleep more calmly and more deeply if his emotions are expressed first.

In reality, a child who is allowed to go through emotional meltdown with a loving and validating parental presence is done with it, and then he either goes to sleep calmly, or, more often, he plays because he isn't tired yet. To support your toddler's need to unleash emotions, stay close, listen, hold affectionately but with respect, and let her know that it's fine to cry. If verbal, ask questions that can help the child to tell you more, but be careful not to go beyond her wish to talk.

However, most often the meltdown is a response to being made to go to bed when the child is clear that he is not yet ready to sleep. Therefore, if you listen to the child's inner guide, there may be no cranking or meltdown at all, but simply more play. As you may recall from Chapter 1, your idea of tiredness is very different from a toddler's. When you listen to your toddler's choice to sleep or not to sleep, he learns to recognize his own body signals and becomes a healthy sleeper.

"Until what age can our child sleep with us?"

Check to see whether you have a belief that says that at some point your child cannot sleep with you. There are stories floating around about sexual harm and lack of independence. Check those for real and hard truth. Blindly believing whatever society tells us is not helpful. Here are some thoughts to inquire into:

My child should move to her own bed by a specific age.

Humans should sleep separately.

Sleeping alone teaches independence.

My child will be sexually confused by sleeping with us.

Sleeping with parents prevents becoming independent.

What my relatives/doctor say is true.

What my child feels is not valid.

Add any of your own thoughts to the list. Check inside which thoughts are stressing and limiting you so you can freely respond to your child. Here is one example of the first thought: "*My child should move to her own bed by a specific age.*"

Dave was pushing to get his older daughter, age six, out of the family bed. A three-year-old also shared the bed. He and his wife consulted with me and did an inquiry on Dave's thought.

Dave: "*My child should move to her own room and bed now that she is six years old.*"

Naomi: Is that true?

Dave: I don't know. So it's not true or I would have known for sure.

Naomi: How do you react when you believe this thought?

Dave: I feel stressed about my children still sleeping in our family bed.

Naomi: How do you react when you believe this thought when your girls are in your bed?

Dave: I try to stay calm and happy, but I am a bit tense inside, worried that I am harming at least my older daughter.

Naomi: How do you treat your children in the family bed when you believe this thought?

Dave: I try to be kind and playful, but since I am ambivalent,

I am sure they sense it. Sometimes I ask my older child if she would like to try to sleep in her own bed in her own room. She always says no.

Naomi: Who would you be without this thought?

Dave: I would enjoy sleeping with my children and have a ball every night. It is so fun, after all.

Naomi: Turn it around.

Dave: My child does not have to sleep in her own bed in her own room.

Naomi: Is that as true or truer?

Dave: It sure feels good. A great relief. Must be truer.

Naomi: Indeed. Truth is peaceful. Can you see another turnaround?

Dave: *"My child should sleep in her own bed when she feels ready and wants to do so."* This feels joyful. But then I was just looking for reassurance—why didn't you just tell me that it's fine?

Naomi: You should be reassured by someone else . . . is that true? And isn't it best if you find reassurance within? When reassurance is external, doubt is likely to reemerge. You are your own best teacher for lasting clarity.

Pediatricians and other parenting professionals keep changing their theories about caring for babies and young children because they don't really know what's best. They are confused by making up theories or repeating others' instead of observing real life and responding naturally to babies and young children, believing the mind is often the source of harmful choices because the mind is fed by these unreliable sources. Even when based in so-called "research," the mistakes continue because they miss the obvious: *trusting the child's innate blueprint.*

Children have slept with their parents for the whole of human history—and still do, at all ages, in most cultures. They don't develop strange sexual interests from co-sleeping. On the contrary, they feel at ease with their own bodies and comfortable when connecting with others, without misinterpreting closeness as being sexual in nature.

Children's independence is enhanced by co-sleeping because:

1. It's their independent choice to sleep with their parents. Their need for dependence is fully satisfied so that they move on with ease when ready, precisely because they are complete.
2. The child's choice to sleep with you is a lesson in self-trust and self-reliance. If you go against it, you teach her to be dependent on the choices others make for her and ignore her own sense of herself. That's the opposite of developing self-reliance. If you honor her choice, she learns to listen to herself, which is true independence.

As for healthy sexuality, sexual issues are more likely to occur in families where sex is taboo and where the child can be found alone in her room vulnerable to the whims of predatory relatives, visitors, or others who may be present in the home. Privacy in a child's own room protects the intruder, not the child. The child who is alone in his bed feels insecure in the face of mistreatment and is therefore willing to hide his abuser's secret. The family bed is a much safer place because the baby or young child is not alone, and because the adults can develop a positive and responsible connection with the child.

Obviously, nothing guarantees the child's safety if parents themselves are not emotionally well, but in that case, the family bed doesn't make them more vulnerable but rather less so because the other adult is there as well.

Please don't believe what I say. Check inside yourself: If you never heard any negative opinions about co-sleeping, would you hesitate to cuddle with your baby or young child throughout the night?

We live in a puritanical society; we forget that, in some societies, children witness sex naturally and don't think much of it. I am not suggesting we become such a culture, but rather we should realize that babies don't see sex as a problem or a prohibition. Believe no one but yourself and your little one, and your nights will be some of the sweetest times of your life.

"How do I get my child out of my bed for my sake?"

Some parents think that they will sleep better without the toddler in their bed. As you have now learned, it is actually the other way around. Once we take care of the cause of thrashing, we find that when they are in our bed we sleep much better and sounder because we don't have to get up to breastfeed or care for the child.

However, this question is sometimes motivated by wanting privacy for intimacy, often by the father, which is understandable. But even when that is the motivator, when such fathers consult with me, they always seem to admit that they enjoy cuddling with their toddler or young child, but, like Dave, they worry that it isn't good for them. So it becomes a mix of wanting privacy and having doubts about what's best for the child. When doing the inquiry on the privacy aspect, most men realize that they do have other times to be intimate with their wives without the children around.

It often comes back to thoughts. The voices of media, other parents, and the majority in this culture (the minority worldwide) do not have your child's best development in mind. They, too, are caught up in believing what others are parroting. They are saying what is recorded on their minds. Choose which guidance you want to follow and, ultimately, listen to your child and to your heart. Then you can adjust your privacy needs rather than ask your child to give up on her valid needs.

Always come back to questioning the thought that says, *"I need my family's and/or friends' approval."* Freeing yourself from that shackle will allow you to respond to your child with confidence and love. Check and see for yourself. Listen to your child. What is the problem? I promise he won't want to sleep with you when he has a girlfriend—and obviously much sooner.

Human development does not need our help, only our love. It occurs on its own, and your child follows it to the letter. When fully nurtured rather than shaped, the child unfolds as he should and on time.

Parenting is simple when you follow nature's instructions without trying to change reality or wishing it was other than what it is.

Fear, which is based on untrue thoughts, is the only obstacle to flowing peacefully with this wondrous ride. Without fear about the future, you can follow the path as paved by nature/God and be at peace. If you believe it is your own original opinion, put it on paper, then question it and turn it around. No one is born with thoughts.

Flowing with your child propels you to grapple with your own fears and limitations. Instead of pushing the "lesson" away by coercing your baby to fit your limitations, follow her direction, and you will grow in emotional wisdom and clarity.

"I need my child to adjust his behavior so that I am comfortable"—can that be a true priority? Does this thought bring you peace or stress? A connection to your child or disconnection and a need to control? After you ask the four questions, turn it around, and you will find that, in fact, adjusting the child so you are comfortable or so you can please others is like throwing away the lesson of love and maturation.

Your child does not need to adjust to your fixed mindset; it is you who has the *opportunity* to free yourself from all limiting mind talk. You have no control over what your mind is saying, but you can choose whether to obey it or not. Remind yourself that your mind is not you. If you had grown up in a different family or culture, your mind would say something else. It doesn't know the truth—you do. Who would you be if your parenting thoughts were erased or exchanged?

Your child needs a parent who can lead by responding with love and clarity to reality, not to a conjured fantasy. We can't always do that. Our triggers may get us, and we lose our clarity and love. But with inquiry, you have recourse—a way to question the cause of the distress in a given situation and to walk out of it with understanding, forgiveness, and making changes when needed.

"So, when will my child move out of the family bed?"

When asked in a workshop, "But when will my son move out of my bed?" someone from the audience shouted spontaneously, "When he has a girlfriend!" This elicited both laughter and a sense of relief. It didn't mean that the child would necessarily sleep with his parents until puberty (not likely), but it reminded us all that no grown child wants to sleep with his parents, and so there is no need for worry.

The thought *"If I don't get him out of my bed, he will sleep with me forever"* is clearly not true. They don't stay in your arms forever, they don't breastfeed forever, they don't pee in diapers forever, and likewise, they don't stay in your bed—or even in your home—beyond their need. They all grow up and move on from each of these stages.

"My toddler gets up at 5:00 AM and is still tired. I get up with him, but I wish he would sleep longer."

If you have dark curtains and no night-light and your toddler still wakes up and gets up, then make peace with it and with afternoon naps. He is obviously wired from inside to rise with the sun.

If, however, you have been using a night-light and the light is not blocked, the early sun may be waking him up. It is completely possible to adjust things so your toddler may be able to sleep later in the morning. In addition to making the room dark, changing what your toddler eats, activity, time in the sun, and some other details mentioned earlier can help to shift his schedule gradually.

Often, parents think the child needs more sleep than he actually does. Thinking he is not sleeping enough causes parents much stress. Therefore, another possible answer to this question could be simply starting bedtime later. You can move his bedtime gently just ten minutes a day.

There are a couple of inquiries you can do to clarify which direction would be most peaceful and healthy for your child. One is inquiring into your thinking about the timing of going to bed, and the other is to investigate your idea of how many hours your toddler needs to sleep. It seems a combination of both will help bring you peace and creative solutions.

You say he is still tired when he gets up, but can you really know that this is true? On his terms? Obviously, he is waking up and getting up. So either accept his inner rhythm or apply some changes to enable him to stay in bed later in the morning.

"My four-year-old sleeps in her bed but wakes up and comes to our bed. What should I do?"

What is her choice based on her actions? What is she telling you? Most likely, she doesn't want to sleep separately for any part of the night. Simplicity is peace. Follow the instruction manual based on her cues.

Stephanie and Rob attended my workshop and shared a similar issue. I asked the audience how many parents experienced this scenario: Most hands went up. Stephanie volunteered to come onstage to do an inquiry:

Stephanie: *"My child should sleep in her own bed and stay there."*

Naomi: Is that true?

Stephanie: No. The fact is, she is not staying there.

Naomi: How do you react when she comes to your bed and you believe the thought that she shouldn't?

Stephanie: I resent her for waking me up and not staying in her bed. I feel stressed. I accept her, of course . . . but with a sigh inside me. I resist and am impatient.

Naomi: Does believing your idea create connection or disconnection with your child?

Stephanie: Disconnection and stress.

Naomi: So, how can coming to your bed be the problem? You are saying that your thought is what's causing stress and disconnection.

Stephanie: Yes. I see it now.

Naomi: When she comes to your bed, with your thought, you feel stressed and resentful; how would you be without your thought?

Stephanie (laughing): Delighted to snuggle with her. Grateful. Gosh, this is embarrassing.

Naomi: Well, being a human can feel this way. Turn the thought around.

Stephanie: *"My child should not sleep in her own bed and should not stay there."*

Naomi: Is that as true or truer?

Stephanie: Oh yes. Because that's what she does. So this way I am at peace with my child.

Naomi: Yes. So simple. Can you find another turnaround?

Stephanie: *"I should sleep in her bed and stay there."* I do lie with her till she falls asleep, but I don't stay. . . . Oh I see, she needs me to stay. Oh wow, so, she may as well sleep in our bed with us from the beginning of the night.

Our bladder sends us to the bathroom, and we don't look for a remedy against it. Our hunger sends us to the kitchen and our thirst to a source of water. When we are cold, we respond with heat or warm clothes, and when we are tired, we give ourselves a place to sleep that is comfortable and emotionally supportive. When we need to relax, we arrange the time for it; when we need a hug, we seek it; when we feel loving, we offer affection. We don't fight against all these natural "instructions" that arise in our own bodies and souls as nature designed. Likewise, there is no need to go against a child's healthy and timely inner guidance.

Western culture has been indoctrinating us with thoughts of not trusting babies and children and of literally fighting against their healthy natural inclinations. *Why take the ideas of other people (which are not their own thoughts either) more seriously than the clear choice of your precious and authentic child?*

In addition, notice that you may be focusing not on the correct need of your little one but on your or your partner's convenience.

Again, this is nothing to feel guilty about; it is considered culturally correct. And yet, is it what you want to focus on? Inquire into all your assumptions about your little one's sleep location, and find the answer that is in peaceful harmony with reality.

If your priority is sleeping without your child, tell her the truth: "I want you to sleep in your bed because I want my bed to myself with Daddy." Sounds awful, right? This is because it is most likely not true for you. Spelling it out in this jarring, honest way can wake you up to reality and to happily cuddling with your child the whole night.

Affection and closeness while we sleep is the nature of love.

What About Bedtime?

Although parents often like to believe that the baby is tired or even overtired, the real "baby manual" is the child himself. If the baby doesn't sleep even though he breastfed and is in a quiet place, he is not tired enough by his own self-assessment.

Again, the voices of magazines, doctors, in-laws, and friends recite, "He is overtired! Look at him, he is rubbing his eyes, and he is out of control. . . ." But is he falling asleep? It is much simpler to use reality as evidence. He is not asleep. So however tired we think he is, he is not ready to sleep from his point of view. We say, "He is fighting it," which he does, and that is his way to get to his idea of being tired.

It is true that if you felt the way your baby does, you might have called it "tired." But babies evaluate their body sensations differently; they are much more excited about life than most of us are and often prefer to stay awake until their eyes shut on their own. If we don't respect their perception of themselves, babies have no opportunity to learn to recognize their own tiredness and become healthy and sound sleepers.

If we always decide for our children when to sleep, they are coerced to sleep before they have a chance to recognize their own tiredness; they miss the learning-to-fall-asleep part. The result is years of bedtime difficulties and possibly sleep issues later in life.

No matter how tired the baby or toddler is by our perception, when we try to get him to sleep before he feels ready, he is likely to stay awake longer, resisting our attempt to take his autonomy away. In contrast, when we let go of our own idea that he is overtired and take the fact that he has not fallen asleep as the simple proof of his sense of himself, we can spend the time playing rather than struggling. Or if the little one must cry, just be with him peacefully.

If the baby's timing is respected, he will not associate falling asleep with stress. When tired on his terms, he will sleep—and not a minute before. You can spend the time struggling, or you can play. Letting your baby learn his own body signals means allowing his trials and errors in order to support his self-awareness.

I recall a three-year-old who was at my house with her family for a family intensive retreat. The first two nights, the mother did her usual routine. She struggled to "put the toddler to sleep" as the child kept getting out of bed. It took two hours of breastfeeding, singing, hugging, and the toddler getting up again and again before she finally stayed in bed and fell asleep. On the third day, I suggested to simply not put the child to sleep and let her be in charge of herself. She played happily for those same two hours, running around while her mother was having a session with me and playing with her child as needed. After two hours, the girl climbed onto her mother's lap, nursed, and fell asleep within minutes.

Same two hours. One way was a struggle in which the child did not learn to recognize needing to sleep and instead learned that going to bed is difficult while the other way meant two hours of joy and the child feeling in charge of her body and learning to recognize the need for sleep.

Time to Go to Bed?

We have created artificial reasons to "put" children and babies in bed earlier than we go to bed. We created adults-centered reasons such as sexual needs or work schedules and adult time without children. But does it fit the child's real and valid need? It is easy to be fooled by the fact that it is possible to manipulate a baby to our needs, but over time, children become aware and have their own direction from within, which we want to encourage and nurture.

The child's need to connect with us as long as we are awake has rarely been considered in our modern hectic scheduling and plans. We may want to consider being more child friendly and less adult centered. In this way, instead of "soothing" the hurting child after separating her from us, we keep her with us, and she need not be "soothed" for anything.

No, this does not imply child-centered parenting, where children become self-absorbed and rule the house. It is about their own autonomy, not about doing anything to others. In fact, as children mature, it is when their primal needs are met without struggles against them that they become more aware of others and accommodating of everyone's needs. They simply don't develop anxiety around getting their needs met. It is all a matter of responding to the little one's needs and abilities in harmony with each stage of development.

Many young babies fall asleep early and give us a break in the evening. We should not grow to expect this trend to continue; sometimes it does, but it often doesn't. Giving the toddler a pacifier or trying other ways to get her to sleep and give ourselves a break is more likely to create stress; it is a way to teach her to shove her emotions down and be quiet for our sake rather than respond to her real needs.

I have observed many couples who find a peaceful and enjoyable way to nurture the baby's sleep without causing struggle for anyone involved. If you are able to respond to your baby's cues for sleep and then sing, nurse, or rock her with an easy flow, by all means do that, and enjoy your "baby-free" time.

I do recommend that you stay very close by, so if your baby awakes, you are right there and she need not cry to feel your presence. Babies who wake up to find themselves alone tend to feel scared. With such repeat experience, a child can develop anxiety associated with sleep and difficulties falling asleep or staying asleep. As they grow older and understand that it takes a few seconds for you to show up, staying so close becomes less important but is still very kind.

For those whose baby won't sleep as long as you are awake, consider letting her stay with you. Keep her with you to sleep on your body or play for a while longer. When she is feeling secure in staying with you, not fearful that you would leave her to sleep alone, she will most likely fall asleep in your arms or on the couch next to you.

When another family was studying with me, our youngest demonstrated this idea. He was three and clearly tired by adult assessment, but we and the other family were still in the kitchen, engaged in a counseling session. My husband offered to go to bed with him, but he refused, which we respected. In no time, he was sound asleep on the kitchen floor. My client sat on the floor and took him in her arms. She said, "Oh my gosh, he is sound asleep," to which my husband commented, "Our children eat when they are hungry and sleep when they are tired. It is simple Zen."

The above way of responding to a child's tiredness is not only more peaceful, but the child gets more sleep and has a healthy attitude about going to bed and about trusting his own body.

Your job is to question everything your mind says and to respond to your unique baby through the changes she presents. The instructions are in your baby and nowhere else. And they change all the time, so don't get used to a specific pattern. Just listen and find what is most peaceful, connecting, and nurturing of the baby's trust in herself that is also what would ensure the optimal amount and quality of sleep for her and for you.

Only thinking gets in the way of noticing and responding.

Your goal is to set things up such that there is no pain that has to be "soothed," but a flow that lets your baby feel secure and trusting of herself and of you.

CONCLUSION

Sleep comes to the baby and child from within. It cannot be orchestrated externally without a cost to the child's self-reliance and quality of sleep. If you struggle with your baby or young child at bedtime, the struggle is not in the child but in you. The child is "declaring" the instruction she senses from inside. Bedtime can be joyful, active, and peaceful when we tune in to the child's needs. When we trust creation and listen to the child, life can flow in terms of sleep location, timing, bedtime, and specific age and emotional needs. It's the end of war and the celebration of peaceful connection.

Chapter 7

When the Baby Cries

No baby ever cries for no reason. In this chapter, you will learn how to understand why you should take your baby's crying seriously, how to understand the valid need, and what to do when you cannot figure out the cause or need. Your baby and young child counts on your response, nurturance, and protection. A baby never cries with an intent to trigger you, nor does she ever cry for nothing. Yet sometimes she needs to unleash emotional stress through crying, and that too is a need that requires your care.

Crying is the baby's last-resort communication. She does what she can to communicate with you without crying. If you wear your baby (that is, your baby is mostly in arms or close to you), she develops non-crying strategies first. The result is that she manages to cue you without crying. But her system isn't perfect because some needs aren't obvious and because your reading of her cues isn't perfect. When the message does not elicit your correct response, the baby will cry both in an attempt to get your correct care and in despair when failing.

When the cause of crying is not a basic need, such as physical pain, gas, teething, fear, and other unknown issues, the baby will cry as long as she has hope that you will respond. She will stop crying when her need is met, or when her need is not met, she might stop crying in resignation if she concludes that you are not responding, which is obviously traumatizing. The baby will notice your attempts and intent and you will, with the help of this chapter, be able to provide compassionate and reassuring care.

Crying for a Need or a Need for Crying?

Always hold your crying baby. Obviously, first address real needs. Your baby may need to sleep on your body and not alone; she may need movement or to be on the floor; she may have gas or discomfort with her clothing; the environment may be too warm, too cold, or too noisy; or perhaps you are trying to put her to sleep rather than letting her fall asleep according to her autonomous sense of herself. Yes, babies scream, "Don't put me to sleep!" and parents often call it being "too tired." (Check page 125 for dealing with a baby you assume is "overtired.")

Giving the baby a pacifier in these situations is, with loving intentions—and please excuse my bluntness—like rejecting his need and saying, "Don't do what you are doing." There is no need to feel guilty. We honestly feel like we are helping the baby when we try to stop his crying. But the crying is the valid and needed expression, not the issue that needs care.

A crying baby needs either to be taken care of, in terms of needs, or held and validated so he can know that it is fine to cry and that we love him and approve of his need to cry. As soon as you realize that the baby needs to cry, it will be easier for you to connect while providing physical closeness and compassion—and not distraction. To get your own triggers out of the way and focus on the child, write down what your mind is dictating to you, and question it.

In her session, Athena shared with me how frustrated she feels when her baby cries and she doesn't know why.

Athena: *"My baby shouldn't cry, so I should give her a pacifier when she does."*

Naomi: Is that true?

Athena: No, she is crying, so that is what she needs. (Assuming all other needs are met and sucking isn't one of them.)

Naomi: How do you react when you believe the thought that she shouldn't cry?

Athena: I am stressed out, anxious, and I think I am a bad mother. I want to stop her crying.

Naomi: How do you then treat your baby?

Athena: I try to stop her crying, even give her a pacifier. OMG, I see that's like I am shutting her mouth. (Athena closes her eyes, feeling pain.)

Naomi: Who would you be without the story that the baby should not cry and that you should stop her by putting a pacifier in her mouth?

Athena: I would notice the baby. I would connect with her and hold, validate, be present, and be with her, not against her.

Naomi: That's who you are—compassion and love. Turn the thought around.

Athena: *"My baby should cry and does not need a pacifier."* Yes, this is more true because she *is* crying and spits out the pacifier. All her needs are met, as far we can tell, so she needs to cry (after a pondering silence). But what if she needs something, and I don't understand it?

Naomi: If it is the case, you still want to be with the baby who needs to cry for not being understood, feeling helpless because she cannot get through to you and has a real need plus a need to be understood and cared for. All that can be validated—"Oh dear, you need something, and Mommy and Daddy don't understand"—while holding and loving your baby. Turn the thought around to yourself.

Athena: "I should not cry . . . about her crying." Which makes me shove a pacifier in her mouth. Yes, I see.

Another thought Athena brought up that stopped her from focusing on the baby was: *"If my baby cries and I don't know why, it means I am a bad parent."* Feeling like a bad parent is a common fear that arises around other issues as well. It is a thought that is self-focused rather than focused on the child. Athena explored this painful thought:

Athena: *"If my baby cries and I don't know why, I must be a bad mother."*

Naomi: Is that true?

Athena: No, babies cry. I do everything I can to meet her needs and keep her content. And yet, she cries.

Naomi: How do you react when you believe that when your baby cries, it means you are a bad parent?

Athena: I feel down, like a failing parent. I am focused on myself, needy of approval, and not focused on my baby.

Naomi: Who would you be without this thought?

Athena: I would be focused on the baby and on being there for her.

Naomi: Turn your thought around.

Athena: *"If my baby cries, it means I am a good mother; I am able to hold her and be present and loving."* And another turnaround, *"If my baby cries, it doesn't mean anything about me."*

You keep learning the same principle that without the anxiety-provoking thought, you don't make up a meaning about yourself or about the baby. Instead, without it, you stay focused on the baby so she can feel heard and connected, and she then senses your care.

Humans cry, and tears are healing. No matter how attentive we are, babies need to cry sometimes, and we often have no idea why. We want to stop them because we think they don't want to cry and that their suffering will vanish if they don't cry. But, in reality, if they cry and all other needs are fulfilled, then they do need to cry, and they need us to flow with their need and to be a loving listener.

To Pacify or Not to Pacify?

Most often, the pacifier is used for a purpose that is not for the baby's benefit and not his real need. When we give a pacifier to have quiet or to stop the baby's crying, we do so because we think the baby should be happy. We think it calms the baby. But the baby may need to cry and not shove his emotions down by putting something in his mouth—a habit that he may end up falling back into later using food, nail-biting, and/or smoking as a pacifier.

A mother wrote: "My baby uses the pacifier, but at night, he keeps spitting it out, and he cries, and I have to put it back in his mouth over and over again. What can I do?" (This baby was sleeping in a cot.)

You can use this question to explore and find that you already know the answer and know what to do (if you have read this book so far). The many thoughts you have inherited block your instinctual ability to read your baby's cues. Your doctor, your mom, your siblings, and your friends don't know what your baby actually needs. Your baby knows, and when you listen, you know too. So notice him and look inside yourself. Ask yourself the following questions:

- Why is the baby crying?
- Does my baby really want or need the pacifier?
- What is the hurt for which I want to soothe him with a pacifier?
- Does he need soothing, or does he need something else?
- Does he need the breast?
- Does he need to be held?
- Does he need to cry in arms with full attention?
- Is he not tired enough (in his own experience, not mine)?
- Does he want to be included and not be put away?
- Why do I give him a pacifier? For my sake or his?
- What does he really need?
- Where do my opinions about giving a pacifier come from?
- How would I respond to him if there was no pacifier?
- How would I care for my baby without the story that he needs a pacifier?

When you answer these questions honestly, you may find, again, that your concerns are not really yours. You were told this and that, but is it true? What are the facts? What is true for the baby? Let's look at some honest answers from different mothers:

"Does my baby really want the pacifier?"

"He seems to," says one mother, "but only if he cannot get to be held or breastfed." Indeed, the baby does not want a pacifier. She wants the real thing, which is you.

In the situation above, the baby is crying because his need for human touch and closeness is not met. The mother said, "My baby wants to sleep with me. He is upset about being left in a separate bed. I put him in his cot with a soother because I fear that otherwise he won't develop the ability to self-soothe and to be independent."

The mother who expressed this concern realized that she has no proof that crying himself to sleep or sleeping by himself with a pacifier in his mouth would help the baby become more independent.

The reality could be exactly the opposite: Learning to ignore his own inner voice, the baby or young child becomes dependent on others to tell him what to need and even what to feel. The baby learns to ignore his own inner guidance and to look to others for direction, discounting his own feelings and following external ideas.

To build independence, let your baby be independent from day one. It is his independent choice to stay close to you or sleep with you. He will become independent through the experience of his own inner guidance being taken seriously and affirmed in action.

Pushing babies and children ahead of themselves creates emotional dependency. The result is often teenagers who follow peers and the media and adults who cannot think for themselves and who look to satisfy what they have missed by consuming goods, drugs, food, and other emotional and physical addictions offered to them by others. They value external guidance more than their own.

"Why do I want my baby to have a pacifier?"

Here, I receive one typical answer: "So he will stop crying and soothe himself." One very candid father added, "So we can have a break."

Soothing seems to be a goal for a baby who is in pain. What is the real need for which the baby is crying; why "soothe" her? Why not simply meet the need? She may have given up hope that her discomfort can actually be taken care of. And she may have learned that we don't want her to cry and that she should suppress her emotional expression and put something in her mouth instead. In her books and articles, developmental psychologist Dr. Aletha Solter elaborates on the harm of suppressing the baby's crying with any kind of distraction. For more information on Solter's work, visit the Aware Parenting Institute at Awareparenting.com.

The baby doesn't need us to give her a way to numb her pain or feelings about her needs not being met. She counts on us to meet her real and valid needs. Most likely, the baby is scared and lonely because she needs to be next to your body. Meet her need, and no soothing is required. Instead of depriving her and then providing tools for numbing herself, take the cause of pain away and have a content baby.

If she cries even when she is with you, then there may be another need, not instead of but in addition to needing to be with you. If you stop the crying with a pacifier, you will not know what that need is, and you are teaching the baby to put something in the mouth to avoid painful feelings (as we do when we use alcohol, drugs, sugar, and other destructive habits).

The pacifier suppresses the expression—it does not solve the cause of the need to cry. It tells the child, "Don't cry; don't feel; don't express yourself"; it shuts the baby up without addressing her real cause.

What your baby needs is exactly the opposite: She needs to learn that her cues produce a fitting response: She is heard and taken care of. If she needs to cry, it is best to hold her and allow the crying to be a healing emotional time. She then learns that it is fine to have and express intense emotions and that the need to cry is embraced too.

Needing to Suckle and Thumb Solutions

Sometimes suckling is the actual need. A baby may need to suckle without the milk coming at him. If your baby feeds on one side for long enough to empty the breast, that can provide the suckling. Otherwise, you can offer a clean finger with a smoothly cut nail, and eventually the baby will find his own finger.

The drive to suckle can become strong, and a pacifier can sometimes be the kind solution. Just be sure it's not a cover for other needs and try other direct human solutions as noted above. Generally, a pacifier's a last resort that I don't really recommend as it can lead to early weaning.

Many babies do find their own fingers by a few months of age. If fully breastfed, thumb-sucking does not usually become a habit and passes on its own. Keep her close to your body and not by herself, and let her find her own natural solution. It is best not to teach her to be dependent on gadgets.

If thumb-sucking leads to braces, my view is that it's worth it in self-trust and peace. But, of course, some parents like to avert such a possibility, and that's fine as long as we don't teach to suppress crying or to please us by being quiet and by giving up on one's real needs. You can read the blog of holistic dentist and facial structure expert Dr. Kevin Stock (www.KevinStock.io) to explore whether thumb-sucking does any damage when breastfeeding is continued.

When it comes to why so many of us end up needing braces, it's not just about habits like thumb-sucking. A big part of the story has to do with diet and how our jaws develop. Anthropologists have found that our hunter-gatherer ancestors, who ate tougher, less-processed foods, usually had wide jaws with plenty of room for their teeth—and rarely any cavities. According to one theory, things started to change when softer plants and grain-based and cooked foods became the norm, which meant less chewing and, over time, narrower jaws and crowded teeth. If you're curious and want to dig deeper, check out Dr. Weston A. Price's classic *Nutrition and Physical Degeneration*, and find Dr. Kevin Stock's website and the other sources listed in the Resources section under health and food.

Even if you choose a pacifier, keep your baby in your arms so that it is only about needing to suckle and not about being alone and suppressing emotions. If the baby is in your arms and she spits out the nipple and the pacifier or finger and she is dry and healthy and has no other needs, she may actually need to cry and unleash her feelings in the safety of your embrace.

Crying is therapeutic and healing. Life can be overwhelming

at all ages and more so for babies and toddlers. However, for a wee one, crying by oneself is frightening and painful; it does not bring on healing without being in the arms of a loving parent. Feeling lonely and scared only adds despair and fear to the cause for crying. Hold your baby and validate the possible stresses she may have experienced that day in a factual way without drama.

Distracting the baby or child from crying teaches her to internalize the message, "I shouldn't cry." The child learns to suppress emotions. This harms her development and her ability to feel, to listen to herself, and to connect with you and with other people.

Suppressing a need to cry leads to many behavioral, health, and learning difficulties. I have seen aggression, ticks, and compulsions vanish when a child is free to cry and express her emotions. And I have also seen shifts in learning abilities and focus. Once emotions are fully expressed with a compassionate and affirming listener, the baby or child is relieved and can be fully present, focused, and calm.

The "Colic" Crying Baby

The assumption that the baby who cries a lot has digestive issues may or may not be correct for your baby. But it is a possibility to consider, as a first step, to eliminate any cause of digestive discomfort. If the baby cries and arches his back, it is possible that the new digestive system is having a hard time and you will need to restrict your diet (see next section). But even before your diet change, breastfeed with the baby in a more upright position. Make sure to burp the baby. Other helpful treatments include the following: Raise the baby's knees to her chest and move in circles to let gas out. Massage the lower back, massage the bottom of the feet lengthwise, provide warmth as in a bath or a warm (not hot) rubber bottle in a towel.

Sometimes a chiropractic doctor or an osteopath can be very helpful. But, ultimately, if digestion is the culprit, you will have to change your own diet for your breastfeeding baby.

Diet for a Breastfeeding Mother of a Colicky Baby

The surest way to avoid all gas is a complete elimination diet. Zero carbs means zero gas for you and for your baby. Mothers who try elimination of all plants and carbs for a while see excellent improvement. It is worth trying. Give it enough time for both your body and your baby's body to adjust (at least a couple of months, in my experience). Start with eating nothing but fatty red meat and organ meats with added animal fats. You'll get all the nutrition you both need and zero gas. No supplements needed with this protocol. Fish may be added next. Then eggs or chicken. Take a whole week for each added food. To help with your own digestive adjustment, make sure to add plenty of animal fats such as butter and tallow. This elimination diet requires your digestion to adjust, which can constipate you if there isn't enough fat—or the opposite if there's too much.

Once you have added back all animal foods, but not dairy, if the issue has improved, stick to the diet for a couple of months. By then, the baby's digestion will be more mature. Then, you don't have to change, but if you want to, you can add back to your diet one easy-to-digest item per week and none of the usual offenders—no onions, radish, beans, grains, sugar, nuts and seeds, baked goods, anything in the cabbage family, tomatoes, raw vegetables, fruit, sugar, and anything made with the above. If you like dairy, stick to grass-fed and raw. Start with easy-to-digest foods, and take it slow based on the baby's response.

Regardless of colic, always avoid coffee, black tea, chocolate, seed oils, and sugar. Your baby will be healthier and calmer without such stimulants and addiction-forming substances.

I am sorry to say I do not have as good a solution for you if you avoid animal foods. Unfortunately, plant foods are likely to be the culprits for gas and indigestion in your baby.

As mentioned, I was vegan for many years. I can say with confidence that, if my baby were suffering, I would let go of being vegan until the baby stopped suffering. That would be my priority. Maybe you can find vegan foods that won't irritate your unique baby's young digestive tract by trial and error, but it's a long process, and meanwhile your baby will be in pain. If you find a way, please share with other vegan or vegetarian mothers. Keep in mind that your milk supply and quality are best on our natural human diet of animal foods.

Evidence suggests that animal foods played a central role in our diets long before agriculture. Our forward-facing eyes, strong stomach acid, and reliance on key nutrients found in meat point to this heritage. While people today eat a wide range of foods, many find that reducing processed carbs and even whole carbs, and increasing nutrient-dense animal foods supports health, energy, and even fertility. Personally, minimizing or avoiding carbs and plant foods has saved my life (and the lives of many others) and supported my children's well-being. It is worth considering.

If you cannot breastfeed and your baby is suffering from indigestion, avoid formula and other so-called milk from grains, beans, nuts, or seeds, and with added sweeteners and flavors. These will irritate the immature digestive tract, and the nutrients are not bioavailable to a baby. In fact, formula is the worst substitute due to such ingredients. It is highly processed, made of sugar in the form of corn syrup, soy, artificial vitamins/minerals, is difficult to digest, and is unhealthy. The artificial nutrients added are hardly bioavailable.

Mother's milk is, of course, raw; when unavailable, another mammal's raw milk is the closest. Raw milk does not usually cause allergies. Pasteurization alters the milk to make it less bioavailable, often causing gas, and leaching minerals, including calcium, out of the body. Raw milk from organic, grass-fed, and free-grazing animals from a known and clean source is safe and best for most healthy babies. I share from my experience and knowledge from working with thousands of families worldwide and my own studies. This isn't a diet book, so I encourage you to explore the research and make the decision that feels right for you.

Other Causes of Excessive Crying

The transition from the womb to this reality can be overwhelming. In addition, if shortly after birth, your baby had any medical intervention, such as being turned upside down for resuscitation (a near-death experience), undergoing circumcision, being separated from Mother, getting drops in the eyes, being poked, or another scary, unplanned experience, he needs to cry about it in order to recover. Some babies who experience traumatic pain in the early days cry a lot for a few weeks or even months. It's their self-therapy.

Of course you do your best to avoid such experiences, but

sometimes things don't go smoothly, or you may not have a say. I do highly recommend avoiding circumcision, which is elective and neither necessary nor natural. I grew up in a culture that circumcised. I succumbed to the pressure with two of my sons and finally retained my conviction with the third. These religious rituals are excruciatingly painful and traumatizing for the infant and, as it turned out, harmful long-term. This is my knowledge and experience. If you are part of a culture that still does this (they are stopping it even in Israel), I suggest that you consider learning more about it before subjecting your baby to such pain and altering of his body. Check out Gloria Lemay's website (WiseWomanWayofBirth.com) for reasons to avoid this old, harmful practice, and also visit the website of the National Organization of Circumcision Information Resource Center (nocirc.org).

Therefore, if food elimination does not resolve the crying and your baby is healthy, with no medical issues, diaper rash, discomfort with clothing, or being left off your body, then, keep in mind that he may need to cry for emotional reasons as itemized above. If your baby is not suffering from indigestion but still cries a lot, especially in the evening, your job is to propel the healing therapy. Hold your baby lovingly, validate possible feelings, and be affectionate and present. It is best not to soothe, not to say "shush" or keep offering the breast or a pacifier. Those just say, "Shut up and don't feel your feelings." Luckily, a baby won't listen to these initially, but as she grasps the tone and more of what is being said, it can teach her to avoid emotions.

Stopping the expression does not resolve the feelings; it becomes a habit of not expressing emotions. Many babies cry for an hour or two in the evenings. Being loved in arms, the baby learns, "It's fine to feel and to cry (do my therapy). No one is falling apart. No one is trying to stop me. It seems I am fine to be crying."

CONCLUSION

We will never actually know why babies cry. It's all based on speculation. But we do know that if a baby cries, he has a valid reason for it and needs us to either attend to the need or, if all needs are met, provide a loving listener while he is in our arms. Distracting with toys, sounds, songs, or other entertainment is the same as shutting down the emotional expression with breastfeeding, swaddling, or a pacifier. Let your baby know that you've checked and met all his needs, and that it's okay for him to cry. Hold a crying baby in your loving arms, with a fully attentive heart.

Chapter 8

Emotional Needs and Growth

A human being is born with a character of her own. As she moves from babyhood into becoming a toddler and a child, you will learn gradually who your "guest" is, and she is rarely who you expect her to be. Let go of all expectations and be purely curious and supportive, and your ride will be full of joy. It isn't always easy; there is no other human being like this child. Flowing with your child is not the same as relinquishing leadership. Yet, being a leader is not being a boss.

In this chapter we will examine the many difficulties and issues that arise with toddlers and young children, and how to respond as leaders who nurture who the child is, without giving her power over others—from car rides, toilet training and routine, to behavior, name-calling, sensitive child, and much more. These examples will provide you with the principle of questioning your own thinking and responding to the child rather than reacting with your own emotions.

Babies and Children Are Innately Self-Motivated

The toddler is unstoppable as he learns to stand, walk, talk, and master many skills. The child often refuses to stop his project or go to bed while trying to run, climbing, working on a puzzle, figuring out a new song on the piano, creating something, or learning to do cartwheels. It is the adult who loses patience and wishes that the child would stop. Motivation for success is the best trait of children as long as we do not hinder it by pushing or engaging with our own ego.

From day one, babies push themselves all the time, challenging themselves endlessly. Their brain and emotions are noticeably engaged and unstoppable, pointing at things, asking for things, and crying when frustrated in the face of challenge, yet not giving up.

Often, we thwart our babies' and children's efforts exactly when they persist with a challenge. We pick a baby up from a safe and challenging situation, and we literally tell children to stop, to change activity, to go to bed, and to do something else when we sense their frustration. As they grow and go to school, we ring bells to disrupt their focus and persistence, and we tell them to give up when they are frustrated yet wanting to persist.

In her session, Robin said that her toddler was building a tower that kept falling. He repeatedly built it again, hoping to build it taller without it falling. Robin noticed that he was frustrated, yet persistent and focused. She decided that it was bedtime and that he was getting agitated anyway and would be happier if he was distracted from the task. She suggested to him to stop building and get into his pajamas for story and bedtime. Aaron said, "No," and continued building his tower. She came over and lifted him up in her arms saying, "It's story time and then sleep," and she carried him to the bathroom.

Needless to say, the child melted down with a terrible tantrum, which delayed bedtime far longer than if he had just finished his task. Most important, it was completely unnecessary. Robin wanted to know how to do better next time. She wrote down and questioned her thought:

Robin: *"When frustrated and it's bedtime, Aaron should interrupt his play and go to sleep."*

Naomi: Is that true?

Robin: No, he wanted to continue working on his tower.

Naomi: How do you react when you believe this thought?

Robin: Well, I react with impatience and anger. I feel frustrated and tight.

Naomi: How would you be without this thought in the same scenario?

Robin: Not sure. I still want him to go to bed at that time.

Naomi: That's *with* the thought. How would you react without the thought that he should stop and go to bed?

Robin: Oh, right. I would be fine.

Naomi: And how would you act without this thought?

Robin: I would just wait till he is done or stops on his own.

Naomi: Turn the thought around.

Robin: "*When frustrated, at bedtime, Aaron should not stop his activity and go to bed.*"

Naomi: Does this feel more peaceful and true?

Robin: Yes, certainly much more peaceful. But he may get more frustrated if the tower falls, and have a meltdown anyway.

Naomi: Can you find three reasons he should not stop building the tower, even if he ends up crying?

Robin: Well, it's his business what he does. It's good for him to challenge himself. He learns a lot from struggling or failing. He was focused and I disturbed him.

Naomi: And another turnaround?

Robin: "*Aaron should continue with his focused play until he is done or decides to give up.*" Yes, that sounds much more respectful and peaceful.

Naomi: Indeed. Who likes to be interrupted when fully engaged? Can you find reasons why it is good for him to continue his focused play until he's done or gives up?

Robin: He is learning to make his own decisions. He is learning perseverance. And if he fails, he learns to accept failing, and if he needs to, he can cry until he feels better and learns that crying is good too."

Naomi: Can you turn it around to yourself?

Robin: "*I should stop my mind from telling me to interrupt my toddler when he is challenging himself.*"

In an email a day later, Robin added another turnaround: "*When*

I am frustrated with my toddler's frustration, I should interrupt myself and calm down."

No Need to Push for Mature Behavior

Many parents push toddlers in terms of behavior. The thought "I can't get him to be quiet, listen, sleep, and so on," becomes the cause of your hardship as a parent. Eventually the child internalizes a self-perception of "I am not good enough; my parents are displeased," resulting in low self-image and dependency on external guidance and evaluation. They may feel something like "They want me to act in ways I cannot. I cannot know for myself what is good for me. I should rely on others. I am not good enough."

If you are worried about what others would say and it gets in the way of knowing how to be a parent, then you yourself are suffering from this same yearning to live up to expectations. Do an inquiry about yourself on a thought such as "I need to impress, or to please, or to live up to expectations." When you find your own freedom from such constraints, you will see your baby's and child's abilities more clearly.

Give your child a better foundation than you had so he doesn't learn to live for the sake of impressing others but to fulfill his authentic, powerful, and loving self.

The Sensitive Child

Tender souls are a gift and not to be hardened or suppressed. But today children are taught to be easily offended. Being offended is not the same as being sensitive. Only the ego is easily offended, and today the trend is to teach little ones that they are special and unique and that no one should ever criticize or point out their faults.

Although the child may also be, by nature, aware and tender, being easily insulted is not the same as sensitivity and tenderness, nor a natural or a positive trait. Instead, it is self-centered worry about one's own image. A tender soul cares about the feelings of another and notices nuance of behaviors and emotions of people. Not that I expect a three-year-old to focus on the other who calls them names, but if we did not teach them to take it personally and to be defensive, they would not feel hurt.

When a child's friend or sibling says, "You are stupid," most parents rush to erase what they think would cause pain, thereby teaching that it is supposed to hurt. Parents tell the "offender" not to speak this way, or they say to their own child, "You know you are smart," and ask the other child to apologize. This teaches the child that being called something like "stupid" must be painful and has to be fought against.

Indeed, on his own, the young child would not usually respond in this way, and if he did, our job would be to help him with inner peace, no matter what anyone says. If your mind tells you that not defending oneself when criticized is being submissive, know that this is exactly the opposite. Not having a need to be defensive is powerful. Such a child grows up to be able to connect with anyone and stay rooted in himself. He will not feel threatened by other people's opinions of him and instead will be open to consider the feedback and stay peaceful.

"A friend's child called my toddler stupid."

Most often, the toddler/child doesn't even care or grasp the meaning of such words, and so there is nothing you need to do. But if the child has already learned to take such words badly, your job is to help her take it in with honesty and gratitude. Aren't we all stupid sometimes? Recognizing it and getting feedback doesn't hurt unless we let it and then become defensive.

In a family intensive retreat, I was in the car with the mother and her two children, who started fighting in the back seat. When the older child called the younger one "stupid," I chimed, "I am stupid too." I promptly gave an example of my stupidity: "Yesterday I stood right by the stove, cooking and talking to my husband, and my food burned while I was right there."

The children cracked up. All defenses went out the window. Instead, each child came up with examples of their own stupidity, embellishing their stories and cracking up. The mother got the idea and added her own stories. We all laughed and felt real joy and connection.

The children learned "non-defense," the willingness to find truth, connection, honesty, and emotional resilience without feeling threatened or diminished. After all, none of us have yet met anyone who has never done or said something "stupid." The burden of having to be always smart, good, or successful can be overwhelming.

Therefore, instead of teaching a child, "Oh, no, that hurts," teach the child, "Oh, yes, I can find that quality in me." This way, not only does it not hurt, but the burden of having no flaws is lifted, allowing emotional strength and freedom.

If your child is easily offended, check yourself to figure how you have taught such a need to be perfect and a knee-jerk reaction to defend oneself. Turn it around to compassion or to acceptance and humor—depending on the situation. The idea that your child is "sensitive" and needs "protection" is turned around to realizing that your child is aware, caring, and emotionally resilient. He needs no protection because he is not attacked but given words that can be taken with gratitude and humor depending on what is being said.

A situation that calls for compassion and not humor is still best without defense. Obviously, a child who already learned to take things personally should not be belittled with humor when upset. We can be compassionate without teaching defense. It's not about negating with "No, you are not mean" (for example) but about connecting with the child.

You can offer a hug and, if the child is verbal and conversational, you can do a mini-inquiry, saying, "Are you upset because you told yourself that you must never be mean?" (because that is not possible). Or you can do what I have done in the story above and say, while hugging the child, "I am mean sometimes. Remember yesterday when I . . ." and you tell or make up an example. Your compassionate hug combined with your peaceful mention of your own fallibilities, when repeated, will gradually release the child's anxious need to avoid imperfection.

"Should I challenge my toddler to overcome difficulties to achieve a goal?"

No matter the age, young children often challenge themselves to the point that we may worry about their safety. That is their program—to try to achieve and overcome and master their bodies. We must hold back our enthusiasm and allow the toddler space to generate their own motivation without being confused by our input or emotional reaction to her progress. We can do so by following their cues—not by pushing, but by allowing them to explore opportunities while discreetly ensuring their safety.

Our culture sometimes glorifies pushing the very young against limitations or against their fears or disinterest. Such parental reactions can get in the way of the toddler's innate direction. Our job is not to push but to remove obstacles if needed and guard the child's safety. It is not up to us to decide what the toddler is achieving. We want to provide opportunities without imposing an agenda.

In his session, Antonio told me that, at the playground, his daughter, Lucie, seemed unwilling to try new things. She also didn't respond to other toddlers or children at the playground and was mostly by herself doing one easy thing and watching other children.

Antonio asked me how to "help" his toddler be more daring and to relate to other children. He was worried that she was too shy, insecure, and fearful. He wrote down his thought: *"I know what Lucie should be able to achieve. Lucie should go down the slide on her own."* Here is his inquiry:

Antonio: *"I know what Lucie should be able to achieve."*

Naomi: Is that true?

Antonio: No, I cannot know that.

Naomi: How do you react when you believe this thought?

Antonio: I push my little one against her will and encourage with "You can do it."

Naomi: And when you oppose Lucie's choice with these words, are you stressed or at peace, disconnected or connected with her?

Antonio: Oh. I am anxious and pushy and impatient . . . clearly not connected to her.

Naomi: Who would you be without this thought?

Antonio: A happy father who celebrates my child's ability to assess her own skills and interests.

Naomi: And isn't that a much more important achievement?

Antonio: I didn't think of that. Yes. Much more important.

Naomi: Turn the thought around to the opposite.

Antonio: *"I do not know what my child should be able to achieve."* That is more true. I cannot know.

Naomi: Indeed. Her decision is her business, and she is the one who knows. Turn it around to yourself.

Antonio: "*I know what I can achieve.*" Oh yes. Easy. And Lucie knows what she wants and can achieve. I get it. She is achieving things that are not on *my* mind.

Naomi; Indeed, like what?

Antonio: Making her own choice without any worry about what she looks like to the other children.

Naomi: Wow, that's huge. Can you see the turnaround about yourself hiding in this revelation?

Antonio: I guess. *"I should know myself and what I can achieve."* Oh, yes. *"And not try to achieve things through my toddler."* It's true. I worry about what she does in terms of looking good as a father. She is much more free than I am. And I don't want to ruin that.

Naomi: Incredible find. How do you feel?

Antonio: Much lighter and excited to take Lucie to the playground tomorrow and watch with delight.

Achievement can only apply to oneself and not to another. A person who grew up rooted in herself will freely choose the purpose of her life and will follow her own passions in her own time and ways.

Being pushed against one's will and against one's choice does not foster a future ability or desire to challenge oneself and may even thwart it. A child senses the parent's desire. She feels it's not hers and is likely to go against it, even if it may be fitting her. Or she may get attached to doing things that would please the parent and others and go through with the achievement, becoming dependent on approval. There are many such success stories—great success of unhappy people. See the discussion on praise on page 228 for more on this issue. The human ability to push to the top of the mountain can only work when it is the person's free will and wish to get there.

The "Clingy" Toddler

Parents get used to their toddler's progress and expect it to continue. Yet the toddler is following an internal program that has lots of moving factors we may be unaware of. In this section, you will follow inquiry into what really drives a toddler to need to be closer to you even after she seemed capable of being without you for periods of time. The only difficulty is not the child but the parent's mind that expects an uninterrupted linear progression.

"My once-independent three-year-old has become extremely clingy. How can I get him to go back to being independent?"

Barb and Lou were confused by their three-year-old. In their session, Lou explained, "He was staying with the babysitter he totally loves without a problem. He did a lot of things by himself that now he asks us to do for him and to be with him all the time.

Is there something wrong? How can we get him back on track to where he was?"

Lou: "*Our toddler should move forward in progressive order.*"

Naomi: Is that true?

Lou: No. Obviously not true as he is not.

Naomi: How do you react when you believe this thought?

Lou: We both get anxious, comparing to others and feeling like we are failing as parents. And I become pushy trying to coerce him into doing what he used to do last month.

Naomi: Who would you be without this thought?

Lou: I would be patient and enjoy my child immensely, just the way he is.

Naomi: Turn it around a few ways.

Lou: I have three turnarounds: (1) "My toddler should not develop in any particular order." (2) "My toddler should develop the way he does." (3)"I should develop my parenting skills in an order that fits my child."

Naomi: That number three is such a helpful revelation. As one wise client, a mother, said with a smile in a Zoom session, "It always comes back to me working on myself, doesn't it?" Indeed. Now, can you find three reasons and/or benefits for your toddler to return to dependency?

Lou: (1) He is more aware of dangers. (2) His brain is planning a big leap and he misses the "good old times" with "Mommy and Daddy holding me." (3) Similarly, fear of change: "Let me experience this amazing closeness for a bit longer before I take off."

It is not possible to control the child's development, but it is possible to control oneself. You cannot turn the clock backward or forward. Your young developing toddler has to go through the many stages of getting close to you and away from you. Don't get used to any of them; they don't last. Going back and forth between experimenting with independence and staying glued to you is nature's way.

Child development is always forward, including when the wee ones return to an older or previous habit; it's their process. It is only us, the adults, who are limited by linear thinking. The child is simply doing something now, and then something else, which is all part of her progress and is essential for her unfolding and for trusting herself. In a way, the human being is born like a fixed time machine, unraveling according to its program precisely and in time, including back-and-forth periods.

Enjoy when your little one clings for a while—lucky you, get an additional treat! It won't last either. These incredible experiences with our wee ones are such a tiny part of our lives. Enjoy and cherish every extra treat.

No Need to Fight Clinginess

If you give your toddler the message that she is not supposed to be so close and dependent on you, she will be afraid to take the next step toward self-reliance. She is "clinging" again because she needs to be sure that, in her attempts to become independent, she won't lose you. "Is my safety net still available to me? Can I go back to being a baby if I need to?"

If such a "return" is available, she can feel safe to take the next step away from you again, knowing she is the author of herself and will do so at her own perfect timing. Have no expectations, and each moment will be precious. Whatever your child needs is what is best and right for her. When she wants to be dependent and close to you, follow the instructions with confidence in the design of nature. There are no mistakes; you may as well celebrate every passing moment.

The choice to cling or not to cling is your toddler's independent choice. This builds his self-reliance and propels him toward independence on his own self-directed terms!

"My child only wants Mommy."

Babies and toddlers go through times of needing only Mommy or Mommy and Daddy but no one else. When a baby is born, it seems anyone can hold and care for her, other than for breastfeeding. As time goes by, at three months and beyond, the baby starts noticing who her lifeline is and goes though periods of being calm only in her mother's arms. This is natural. If you wish grandparents and other helping adults to be able to help with your wee one, let them be present without the baby losing you. If the baby doesn't associate them with losing Mommy, over time, he will be at ease being with these people and later with others—initially in your presence and eventually without you for limited durations.

The wish that your wee one would be less needy of you is not only far less important than her trust in herself, but it actually gets in the way of it. When you respond to her sense of what she needs, she learns to trust herself and you. That is the nature of being self-confident.

There is no such a thing as a "wrong need." The only exception is when we, unintentionally, cause the child to need something that isn't really his authentic need. For example, we may get upset and yell, or take sides with the child's teacher against him. The child may respond with needing to hit us or scream. Even then, the child's response to the situation is the right response that requires our attention, not our opposition. In the vast majority of cases, you can simply trust the child and adjust your ways with him. Often, we get upset with a child for behaviors he cannot control or because our expectations don't match his ability.

Every stage in a child's life is there for a purpose. When the need is fully satisfied, the child moves on, on his own.

Trying to propel a young one to move on ahead of his own choice to do so both slows down such development and hinders his confidence in himself because the message he gets is, *"Do not trust how you feel inside; instead, follow the direction of someone bigger than you and take cues from their anxiety, fear, or concepts."*

"Can small children be too isolated with just their parents for company?"

There are situations in which a child who spends her day only with Mom, or with Mom and Dad, may have difficulties and social anxieties. These generally fix themselves over time because the need for connection has been met with no stress or separation anxiety. But if the connection is more of an enmeshment, by overprotective parents and parents whose ego is mixed with the child's direction, it may cause a long-term difficulty.

My approach is one of trust. Therefore, no matter what happens, a child's path will propel her unfolding uniquely to who she is and to her specific childhood relationships and circumstances. Experiencing difficulties because of parental choices is unavoidable; no parent is perfect, and no one ever turns out without emotional challenges to work on. Therefore, nothing I say implies a need for worry or panic—only a call to keep learning and do our best to allow the child to unfold authentically.

What we call being "clingy" or needy of Mommy only is not a description of the toddler but of our own wish to have time without the little one and our mistaken thought that she should be able to be without us. A healthfully bonded toddler experiences something like a combination of being in love and feeling scared yet excited. The being-in-love part is easy to understand. The fear grows with age for a while. The newborn doesn't know enough to feel fear of other people; her fear is focused on survival, needing to always be carried on a human body and being fed. As mentioned before, most newborns can be passed from person to person and seem oblivious. Outside a primal sense of needing body touch, care, and nourishment, the infant is unaware of other dangers.

As the baby becomes more aware, she starts to fear strangers and to feel the safest with Mom, or Mom and Dad and siblings, or other consistent caregivers in her life. As her view of reality expands between ages one and three or four (sometimes even later), fears may grow. Parents often say, "We were already able to leave our toddler with Grandma or go for a date and leave him with a babysitter. All of a sudden, he cries and won't let us leave." *Yes, this is normal.* There is no regression in a child's development, only in our view of it as we compare it to some mythical ideal of how she should be.

Therefore, if you find yourself isolated as a family or a single parent, it is helpful to expand your community so your child has more relationships and a wider view of a community. But if you find yourself unable to provide more company in your child's life, it is also important to not despair. Instead, recognize that while the child may face more social challenges, she will find her way as long as she experiences herself as an autonomous, emotionally self-reliant person.

Separation Anxiety

When my third child was still a toddler, I started taking public speaking engagements far from home. If it was in my state, we would go together as a family. At some point, my older two were excited about staying at home with extended family. At that time, whenever I had a speaking engagement, I started taking only my youngest with me, with my husband in tow to care for him.

I recall preparing for one such trip. My youngest was about two years old, a breastfeeding and co-sleeping toddler. As I was making my plans, a therapist friend of mine visited me and inquired:

The friend: Why do you take the toddler with you?

Me: He is not ready to be without me.

Friend: How do you know?

Me: His need for me is obvious.

Friend: So, what will happen if you left without him?

Me: He would cry a lot, daily, and suffer in a harmful way.

Friend: But then his crying will be a good therapy to release and heal from previous separation experiences.

Me: He doesn't have any separation anxiety because I never left him, and I am not about to give him a traumatic experience now.

No trauma means no therapy needed. By not leaving your child before she is ready, you prevent separation anxiety. If it had already occurred, then crying in arms and with a validating and loving listener, in a safe setting, is the healing. "Providing" another trauma is not the way (unless in play therapy with dolls, when it is not really happening).

The point of this story is that, as much as possible, we can avoid creating trauma that requires therapy or generates separation anxiety. Therapy, including crying, is very important when a trauma or ongoing distress was not avoided and has already occurred, or a situation is unavoidable, such as sickness or death of a dear one. Indeed, we cannot prevent all painful experiences. As parents, we know that things happen, and indeed, crying is healing when it is supported and listened to without dramatizing. But we need not, knowingly, create trauma or any kind of anxiety.

When a rare situation occurs (for example, injury of mother or other unique unplanned situation), the person staying with the crying child should provide a therapy session to the child by listening, allowing her to cry, validating without drama, and doing so as often as the child shows the need, until Mom's hopeful return.

In ordinary situations, if you try to leave and your child shows you that he is not ready (even if he was able to stay without you before), that is a natural and healthy response, letting you know what he can and cannot handle at that time. Respect and trust your child's communications. He is not "wrong" to feel what he feels and does not need to be pushed ahead of his inner schedule. Do your best to plan life in a way that you need not traumatize your toddler.

Theo, a single father, came to his session hoping that I would help him empower his child, Leah, to manage being apart from him during a two-day trip. He planned to have his sister, Leah's aunt, take her to her house. Being a single father, he was working from home and had never left Leah before. She was almost three and a half.

Theo: *"Leah should be able to let me go for the day or a couple of days."*

Naomi: Is that true? Is she?

Theo: No.

Naomi: When your child says no and you believe your thought, how do you react?

Theo: Honestly, I feel frustrated and even resentful toward her. I am stressed and irritated.

Naomi: In your mind's eye, look at Leah not wanting you to leave. Who and how would you be in that moment without the thought that you should be able to leave?

Theo (sighs and takes a minute to ponder): I would just hug her and know that I am not leaving. I wouldn't want to leave then.

Naomi: So, *with* the thought, you feel resentful toward your child, and *without*, you are happy to stay with her and not go on your trip. So this has nothing to do with her, only with your thinking.

Theo: I see that. I just really wanted to go on the trip. But I guess I can't.

Naomi: So, if the first thought isn't true, what is true? What is the turnaround to the opposite?

Theo: *"My child should not let me leave her when she is not ready."*

Naomi: Isn't that what you really want for your little one? To be in touch with herself, assertive and clear? And you want to know what is best, and since your child has the instruction inside her, you can follow peacefully, knowing how reliable she is within. Can you find another turnaround?

Theo: *"I should leave my idea behind and respond to my child's clear request that I don't go."*

Naomi: Can you find three reasons why Leah should not let you go on this trip?

Theo: Yes, she is obviously not ready to be without me. It would hurt her emotionally. And it may harm the trust between us.

Naomi: What a relief to know that you don't need professional guidance or books to figure it out, because your child is the book and the guidance about her own being.

Separation anxiety can only occur if the toddler had a painful separation experience. We will be able to go on trips, movies, and restaurants for the rest of our lives. Most parents realize that they would rather wait than create any kind of anxiety in their child. The trips can wait; the toddler's need for you cannot.

"Is a routine as important as people say it is?"

The answer to this question lies within your innate parental wisdom in response to your baby's cues. You will probably say, "I don't know." Not knowing is an excellent place to start as it generates freedom from all the "knowing noise." Not knowing means listening to the baby, questioning, and paying close attention to find out. Then, trust your baby, and trust yourself to respond with kindness.

Many ideas that float around from generation to generation are the result of overthinking and of needing to control or to fit in with the narrative of the time. Simplify. The question may be either irrelevant and not coming from you, or it may have a simple answer in the reality of who your baby or toddler is. Each baby is different. Live your life, and your baby will flow with you while you respond to her.

Life is rhythmical by nature.
There is no need to manage it; it is already the manager.
Who needs the burden of micromanaging God?
Surrendering is flowing with the
river and its rhythm.

Natural rhythms create routine without our management. Respond to the baby, to the seasons, to day and night, cold and hot, tired and awake, hungry and satisfied, outdoor time and indoor time, with Daddy and without, and so on. The rhythms and routines are already here and unfolding with this baby and creating predictability and a sense of safety and belonging. You don't have to manufacture the seasons, dark and light, weather, or human needs; these all just happen rhythmically.

Your baby may develop a natural rhythm that is noticeable and organized for a while, or his rhythm may seem uneven in relation to you and your habits. Ride the wave and notice the beat, which you don't cause but you respond to. Your baby's routines come from within and in response to nature; it will change as she grows. Notice and make space for her ever-evolving direction.

Some babies seem to thrive on strong routine, usually for a limited duration. Notice that, too, and if that is your baby's source of security at the time, then, by all means, provide it. However, rigidity is not healthy. So even if your baby needs routine, make sure to have days that do not follow it, and let it slide over time as the baby changes and the child grows. Children who depend on routine to feel secure often become unable to be flexible and flow with life. Keep in mind that life creates its own rhythms, and seasons change all the time. Life is not rigid and has constant variations that are a good model for how to be human. Unexpected things happen, and to be resilient, the child benefits from having to deal with changes and deviations from what she is used to.

If a child grows with no changes to routines, her ability to deal with change may be hindered, and she may become anxious when a change is needed or develop compulsive tendencies and an avoidance of change. Life is full of both natural cycles and deviation from those. We want to allow the child to build a muscle in adopting to both routine when needed and the flexibility and ability to flow with change when these are required.

All in all, my personal recommendation is to flow and not impose a human-made routine. Even if your baby seems to be calmer with routine, provide it for a short while, and then let go and see how she is doing when she follows her own natural rhythms. In other words, as your baby grows into a toddler and beyond, an imposed routine can become a crutch. Let go and allow days and evenings that are not identical, including plenty of special occasions of later bedtime, skipping dinner (for a light snack later), and other variations. Most of all, let the baby and, later, the child create her own life rhythms and flexibility, autonomously.

When Car Rides Aren't Joy Rides

In the early days, you may find it doable to take your infant in a car. She may fall asleep, and you get to where you need to go. Over time, most babies develop an aversion to car rides as they discover that they are tied down and physically restricted, separated from contact with you, and unable to move. This experience can be scary or at least extremely unfitting with a baby's and toddler's need for movement, freedom, exploration, and physical connection. The misleading "original" thoughts to question are:

The toddler should cooperate with buckling up and riding in a car.

These errands must be done now.

There are no other ways or times to get these things done.

No one can help.

A baby crying in a car seat is harmless.

These and other similar thoughts hinder your ability to be clear on reality. Once you face reality rather than your thoughts, everything has a peaceful solution. You realize that there are plenty of valid reasons for your child to dislike car rides and plenty of ways to honor his needs.

The best general solution is to minimize car rides, and when you must, avoid being the driver with no other adult in the vehicle. If possible, and if you have the support, have your spouse or someone else do the shopping and errands. If no one else is available, start by doing the inquiry so you can understand your baby and find the best solutions, such as walking, biking, ordering food, or at least minimizing the length and times of taking your baby in a car.

It is too painful for a baby or toddler to be dragged along on an adult's boring shopping and errands. The only time I put a baby or toddler in the car is when I am not the driver. I will sit then next to the baby, who is facing the back and therefore could have eye contact with me. In fact, in this way, my husband and I have done long rides and even weeks of travel with a baby.

While riding, when the baby is awake and needing attention, I would provide it as needed. I always had books, toys, and dolls. We sang, danced the dolls, talked, and laughed as if we were at home. When the baby needed to breastfeed or a change of diaper, we stopped the car and took a break, often adding some outdoor time. Once our firstborn became a toddler, we made sure to take playground and running-around breaks as needed, always preventing suffering by anticipating it and stopping for movement *before* the toddler could associate the car with discomfort and frustration.

Prevent the child from associating the car with suffering. If you have errands and you must do it yourself and have no one who can be with your child, here are a few ways to make the best of it:

1. Make sure to add going to the beach, lake, or playground (a place your toddler will enjoy) to your errand list for the day.
2. Play music your child likes and take along toys, books, and food.
3. Install a rear-facing car seat mirror so your baby can see you while you are driving.

4. Between errands, take breaks to breastfeed, go for a walk, play, or just sit together.
5. While driving, if needed, relate to your baby by singing and talking.
6. When possible, walk or take public transportation to run errands.
7. If you must take your child grocery shopping, get enough food to last a week or longer so you don't have to shop as often.

Replacing human contact with screens is obviously not a healthy solution. When my children were young, we didn't have those, luckily, and so we had to create opportunities for human contact and incorporate word games, pointing to views, counting cars by colors, singing, and so on. It was fun in the car, and so the children loved it. But babies are too young to engage with in such ways until they understand more. Therefore, do your best to avoid car rides so your baby doesn't develop a dislike of being in the car in the first place. Some single mothers or fathers say that there is no way to avoid errands with the baby along, but once they brainstorm with my facilitation during a session, they always find ways to get some help.

"What if my baby or toddler already cries in car rides?"

Parents often realize that they have already created a negative association with the child being buckled in the car and wonder how to undo the difficulty. In that case, your first goal is healing the emotional reaction associated with car rides.

For two weeks, sometimes more, take your baby nowhere. Your partner can do the shopping or, if you are alone, get enough nonperishable food in advance, order in, or ask others to do the shopping for you. During this time, you want your child to forget about car rides and not be negatively triggered by entering the car. After two to three weeks, bring the car seat into the house and place it in the play area. Observe your child's reaction to know whether he is healed. If the car seat elicits a negative reaction, take the seat away and give it more time.

With a toddler, you can play positive pretend games about car rides, read books, or tell stories. You can use toy cars to pretend you are going in the car to the zoo and having such a good time, then riding back and getting home and eating tasty food. Make up whatever story your toddler may be excited about. After a while, test the car seat in the play area again. Put a doll in it and talk about a wonderful ride to Grandma's or the zoo. If the child seems more ready, he can pretend to buckle up the doll.

At this point, if the association is healed, most toddlers will want to sit in the car seat themselves while in the house. Let her do that, and watch as she imagines a wonderful trip. Be humorous with ideas such as "Now I will be the driver." This can lead to playing a ride with you as the driver, literally practicing future rides. Do not push it or hurry. One step too soon, and past memories can resurface, forcing you to start the whole healing process over.

If all goes well, keep the car seat in the play area for a while so the toddler can keep playing and pretending while enjoying himself. If your baby is very young, you can skip bringing the car seat into the house. When he starts crawling, bring it into the house and place a doll in it, and let the baby crawl into it or try to. If he does or wants you to put him in, do so and give him something he enjoys a lot, such as yummy food or a favorite toy. Let him choose to get out of it at will. Once your toddler is enjoying the car seat, you can say, "We can put it in the real car and go to the playground. Would you like that?" Some toddlers need to play pretend in the parked car first, without going anywhere. That's excellent too.

Understanding this principle of allowing the child to forget the painful association and find joy in car rides is the key but not the end. After your little one is excited about going into the seat in the car, you must keep the rides short, enjoyable, and leading to something he loves to do. Yes, that means that you still make every effort not to take your baby or toddler in a car for errands, and you continue to find creative solutions to needs that depend on driving.

Keeping car rides enjoyable is a childhood-long project, so keep at it, and your children will run to the car enthusiastically. Obviously, if you have to drive by yourself with a baby, your challenge is even greater. But then it is even more important to minimize car rides, find other methods of transportation, and plan activities and fun while in transit.

"My toddler holds his poop in. We tried everything from poop softeners to suppositories."

The cause of a toddler's constipation can be related to food or emotions. When a toddler feels that she cannot hold on to something she needs, she may sometimes tighten herself in other areas of the body, and tensing the bowel is one typical way to "hold on." The little one is anxious about losing control in some way, so she holds on to her poop as if to say, "You cannot take this away from me." Other children are emotionally attached to their "creation," and they hold on to "it" with no emotional issue. And, often, constipation is a combination of emotions and/or food.

To address the emotional cause, ask yourself what your toddler may perceive as being taken away from her, or what may be thwarting her sense of autonomy, whether on a daily basis or in a single instance of loss. It can be a forced bedtime routine or food control issues (regardless of what she eats), premature separation from Mom (such as day care or staying with a babysitter), issues with siblings, jealousy of a new baby, or some restrictions that hinder her sense of self-governing.

More often than not, it is less obvious and more general. It can be the yearning of the child to be herself when she perceives that we expect her to act differently than the way she is. With the best of intentions, parents often take away a child's sense of self by dictating how she spends her time, taking her to day care or to be with someone she doesn't like, or having to behave in more mature ways than she can.

Another major emotional need to hold on to something is hindered self-expression, such as the need to cry, rage, or stay close to Mommy. If the child doesn't feel safe to rage or cry, is shamed when having intense emotions, or is asked to be quiet when she needs to be loud, the child may apply the same skill of suppressing her emotions to suppressing her bowel movements.

As a side note, such a reaction is only one way of responding. Some little ones do exactly the opposite; when their emotional expression is hindered, they may let it out (unconsciously) by wetting the bed or having a meltdown, becoming out of control. Each child is unique and develops her own strategies for coping with emotional issues.

Once you have an idea of what the issues may be, make the changes that would relieve the toddler from the need to hold on. Enable her nature; allow her to pursue herself, when safe and possible, on her terms; meet her needs for closeness or for independence; and let tears flow if needed while addressing the underlying cause.

How to Detect and Alleviate Emotional Causes of Constipation

To alleviate your toddler's need to hold it in, catch yourself acting or making comments that imply disapproval and restriction of the toddler. Notice any disapproval of exploration, or of self-expression such as crying, expressing fear, or being shy or insecure. Here are examples of phrases that easily suppress a young child's expression:

- When the toddler is afraid: "There is nothing to be scared of."
- When the toddler doesn't respond to an adult who is talking to him: "Tell so-and-so what you did today."
- When the toddler is crying: "Nothing happened, you are all right. . . ."
- When the toddler is exploring something unsafe, saying a harsh "No!" instead of gently removing him.

These are just a few examples of how, unaware and with the best of intentions, you may deny the child's experience and teach him to ignore, deny, or suppress his emotions and feel shame. I have included a more in-depth discussion in my book *Raising Our Children, Raising Ourselves,* about making it safe for the child to express feelings around you.

Once your toddler's life flows in harmony with her inner guidance such that her natural direction is not thwarted or judged, most often, the problem will resolve itself. In the meantime, if you are concerned, it's fine to try a suppository to help it out. Just don't focus on that as the solution. If the constipation is emotional, the suppository is a bandage, not a cure, as it does not address the cause. The cause is not the constipation; that's just the manifestation of something else. Once the toddler's life flows in such a way that she has a sense of power over herself, the constipation often subsides on its own.

Food Corrections to Relieve and Avoid Constipation in Your Child

Babies who are fully breastfed rely heavily on fat for energy since breast milk is naturally rich in healthy fats. As children grow, their digestion often works best when their diet continues to include enough nourishing fats, along with other whole foods. If constipation becomes an issue, first consider whether certain foods in your toddler's diet (or in your own diet if you're breastfeeding) might be the cause. Adding healthy fats like butter, cream, avocado (not seed oils and not fried), are helpful and healthy. Also pay attention to hydration, and reduce known constipating foods.

The use of "fiber" to relieve constipation has recently been found to be often ineffective and sometimes even constipating as it burdens the intestines with undigestible matter. You can try it, of course, but feeding the child fat is not only healthier but also oils the inside of the intestines, thereby making the process painless for the child.

If constipation persists, a step-by-step elimination and reintroduction approach can help identify triggers—or reconsider emotional issues as the cause.

Primal Needs Versus Wants and Preferences

Coming from the old culture of child abuse and of expecting obedience, we have now bent the stick the other way, which has created imbalance and confusion. To get back to balance, we must realize that a child, regardless of age, does not have to always get what she wants. And when she cannot get something, there is no need to distract the child from her emotions of disappointment or sadness.

By confusing wanting with primal, basic needs, we create self-centered people—or even narcissists—and people who get depressed when life does not dance to their tune. In reality, getting whatever one wants is not about respect, freedom, or primal needs. And getting what one wants is not happiness, either, but the opposite, since true joy comes when one needs nothing, is not focused on self, and when joy is not dependent on external fulfillment.

The confusion of wants with primal needs starts with babies and toddlers. From day one, we can either cultivate emotional resilience or cultivate children who are never satisfied and always want more. We have a choice. At the same time, keep in mind that a highly alive, happy, and engaged child is not a problem but a good sign of a secure and thriving human being. The distinction here is to know when your child is unable to handle things that don't go her way or when she cannot have what she wants.

Your goal is to raise a child who is vital and assertive, not dependent and needy.

Obviously, I am not talking here of depriving a baby or child of actual emotional or physical needs. Primal needs are love; food/breastfeeding; clean, dry clothing; affection; being in loving arms; sleep; connection; intellectual stimulation; air; gravity; safety; cleanliness; and so on. These differ from wanting a toy, a candy, to be first, to win every game, or to have things go one's way.

Again, to be super clear, we do our best to provide a life that flows and that says yes to the child's intent and explorations. We babyproof the house to make it safe to explore; we remove dangers and obstacles; we stay with the little one and protect him from unsafe situations and people; and we say yes to choices about physical and emotional needs as much as possible while staying healthy and safe and being considerate of the needs of others.

The problem starts when we treat wanting a toy or a candy as though these were actual needs. They are not. When we keep offering distractions from crying and constant entertainment with things, actions, tastes, and visions, we literally train the child to be dependent—addicted—to wanting and getting what she wants. Many children today have very low emotional capacity to handle real life, which doesn't cater to their wants.

As the baby becomes a toddler, if we make the mistake of overstimulating her, taking her with us shopping in toy stores, giving screen time, and offering constant things and experiences, we risk creating a dependency on always wanting more. The child equates life and joy with constant stimulation and a focus on getting what she wants. Such a child grows up entitled and unable to handle not getting her way. She tends to have more tantrums and be easily upset and demanding. We taught her that she cannot handle reality, by the fact that we always offered something external to entertain her eyes, hands, taste buds, and all senses.

When we distract an upset toddler or child, she gets no practice in handling things when life does not go her way, and she internalizes what she experiences as "My parents rush to get me out of feeling sad, so it must be bad to feel sad," and "I cannot handle strong feelings, and Mommy is teaching me how to run away from such emotions."

Screens Add to the Overwhelm and the Addiction to Constant Gratification

Toddlers are attracted to our phones and larger screens. These become yet another instant gratification habit in which the child is a receiver or a responder while motionless. This deserves a whole chapter, but it is not my expertise. In short, my recommendation is zero screen at these ages, and after the preteen years, minimal device use until the late teenage years. Even then, we must provide enough human contact and activities such as physical, artistic, music, dance, sports, and outdoors, among others, to minimize the use of screens.

For toddlers and young children, every minute on the screen is a loss of true learning time and development. The young brain is designed to learn through full body engagement with humans, nature, and motion.

The screen reduces the child into a passive receiver or responder to this external two-dimensional input, which takes time away from real engagements with people and life. It also harms the eyes and the brain, and is a major cause of a short span of attention and a constant wanting for instant gratification.

To learn about how incredibly harmful screens are to children's mental health and development, I highly recommend Jonathan Haidt's bestselling book, *The Anxious Generation: How the Great Rewiring of Childhood Is Causing an Epidemic of Mental Illness.*

"My toddler learned to depend on wants and stimulation. What can I do to change that now?"

The cure is simply to stop feeding the dependency on constant entertainment of any kind. It does not mean saying no to everything; we are still providing a flowing and kind life for the little newcomer, with respect and in a way that allows her autonomy to flourish. Autonomy is not about getting everything she wants but about being rooted in herself. When something isn't possible, available, or healthy/safe, autonomy includes the experience of disappointment, sadness, or anger and knowing it is *fine* to feel this way. The child learns that she can handle it, and that she is heard and understood.

In a life that generally flows her way—where her primal needs are met and exploration and play are rarely obstructed—a child can be at peace during times when she cannot get what she wants. Her autonomy is then her inner experience, which you can affirm: "I see you wanted to play with that doll and your sister got it first." Pick her up in your arms if the child is receptive to touch or otherwise respond to her need on her terms. (She may need nothing, so be careful not to offer more than is clearly cued or asked for.)

If the upset is great, it tells you that the addiction to wanting is strong. You can further validate as needed: "You love playing with that doll." And if she cries, you may say, "It is fine to cry. I will be with you, and you can cry with me holding you as long as you need." This lets the toddler know that:

1. Crying is safe and fine.
2. The crying or tantrum isn't going to change reality.
3. She can handle not getting what she wants.
4. She is emotionally capable of handling intense feelings.
5. She is loved unconditionally.

When she is done, she will realize that she survived and that life is good. She will move on, having learned to respond powerfully to real life rather than to illusions parents create for temporary gratification.

Powerful and emotionally resilient people are not those who always get what they want or who fall apart when they don't, but those who can do without and accept reality peacefully. Eventually, a child who gets balanced practice in a life that does not always go her way will become one who can handle life's offerings with emotional resilience. Such a person is not only powerful but happier and flexible.

CONCLUSION

The daily behavior and emotional challenges you encounter with toddlers are more about your resistance than about your toddler. Toddlers follow their inner guide with gusto. They need your leadership and guidance for safety, for nurturance, and for knowing that their intense emotions are part of life. Be sure not to be the one causing unnecessary stress, but when life doesn't cater to every whim, always allow the expression of emotions without adding drama or distraction.

The solutions to challenging moments are loving who they are no matter what occurs and how they feel about it. They don't always get what they want, but they are given space to experience themselves without getting the message that you fall apart or panic to get them away from their own inner turmoil. Don't say, "You are all right," because that negates the toddler's experience. And be genuinely okay with the child's state of mind yourself.

When you find yourself baffled by your child's emotional storm, remember to allow it. Be the calm holder of space for your child's strong emotions. To calm yourself, inquire into your stressful thoughts about it. Then, your calm embrace lets your little one know that she can survive her feelings because she sees that you have room for her emotions and you stay calm and present.

Chapter 9

Communication That Connects and Inspires Responsiveness

From day one your baby is learning communication and social skills from you—from the way you treat him and speak to him and to others. In this chapter, you will find guidance on how to communicate in a way that creates goodwill and loving connection. You will learn what inspires a toddler to respond and participate with you and, in contrast, how common ways of speaking ignite defiance and resistance.

Amazingly, toddlers respond just like adults. They need kindness and respect the same way you do. A toddler must sense that you care and that you are on his side even when he cannot get what he wants. We are often sure that we are respectful, when in reality, we are not. You can know by taking the child's response as the valuable feedback that it is. This chapter provides understanding on what toddlers respond to, how they perceive our words, and how to connect with a toddler in a way that respects his autonomy, without handing him power over you. Strive to speak in a way so that the child always feels unconditionally loved.

How and When to Interrupt Your Child's Play or Activity

A child cannot be motivated to do what contradicts every cell in his body. For example, if he is intensely playing with a toy, he cannot be motivated to stop because we tell him to unless the reason means something to him. That said, sometimes we must interrupt a toddler's joyful engagement, but if those interruptions are few and far between and done compassionately, the child will more readily cooperate when it is actually needed because he is not distressed by repeated thwarting of his self-direction. If you respect your toddler as you would an adult guest, you will find ways not to interrupt him and be able to handle rare situations when you must interrupt your little one. Here are a few ideas:

Choose a bath time, a playground time, or any other activity when time is not limited. The adult world of scheduling means nothing to your child. Mealtime, bedtime, and other family routines don't have to be dictatorial or rigid. You can plan around them. Having to be somewhere at a specific time may mean it is not a good day for a bath unless the bath occurs plenty of hours ahead, or later. So, if you want dinner at 7:00 PM, start the bath at 3:00 PM. If you want to be home from the playground because your older child returns from school at 3:00 PM, go in the morning and take along towels, extra clothes, and food.

If there's a scheduling conflict such as with the older child who has to be taken somewhere, you can give your toddler a sense of autonomy by the way you preset the situation. Your toddler may not speak yet, but he understands the difference between dictatorship and consideration of his needs. Instead of saying, "Time to get out of the bath now. Jamie has to go to her dance class," talk to him in advance of having to go: "You are enjoying yourself in the bath so much. Hmm. Mama has to go soon to drive Jamie. How much longer do you need in the water?" Maybe help him to decide by providing a water activity ("How many water wheel turns before you can get out?") or put on music and ask, "How many songs should we play before you're done?"

Again and again, when parents communicate like this, they report that the child chooses a reasonable amount of time and gets out of the water happily. This is because the child feels in charge of himself. Sometimes, if your toddler has experienced restrictions too often, he may say, "Lots of times" or "A hundred more times." That tells you that you have been too controlling.

Children learn respect
by being respected.

You most likely know whether your child has been experiencing too many restrictions. In that case, assume he will refuse to get out or will say, "A hundred times" and linger. Start by changing your ways in other situations so that your toddler's anxiety about loss of his autonomy and about being interrupted is not triggered.

Even if your toddler is very young, perhaps nonverbal, and you have an unexpected situation such that you must pluck him out of the bath or other activities, you can do so with validation and care: "You are having so much fun. I don't like to interrupt you, sweetie, but I have to go now." Still try to get cooperation, but if you must act, then take him out lovingly, and if he cries, validate with facts, "I know. I know. You wanted to stay in the water longer. It's fine to cry while I dry you and dress you. . . ."

Unexpected disruptions are part of life but not on a daily basis. A toddler who generally has autonomy will benefit from occasional experiences of life taking an unwanted turn. As long as we are on his side, going through it not with control and anger but with love and connection, he will accommodate with ease.

"How do I get my toddler out of the bath when I must and he refuses?"

Change the question a bit to magnify the truth: "How do you get any human being, at any age, to do what they don't want to do? And why would you?"

As adults, we all do things we don't like. But we choose to do so for another purpose that is our choice. We may not like to wash the dishes, but we want them clean for the next meal. We may not like to follow our boss's instructions, but we choose to follow them because we want to keep our job and have an income to live on and care for our family (and hopefully we care about the job too). We may hate packing, but we wish to travel, or we have to travel to make a living. We dislike exams, but we want to have a degree so we can work in a field we care about. We may prefer to sit around all day, but we go and exercise and do all kinds of things for goals that are our choice.

Dori brought up this example in her session and did an inquiry:

Dori: *"My toddler should get out of the bathtub when it's time for bed."*

Naomi: Is that true? Is he getting out? Truth is reality.

Dori: No. It is not true.

Naomi: Whose choice is it that your toddler or child should get out of the bath?

Dori: My choice.

Naomi: How do you react when you believe this thought, and your toddler is not ready to get out of the tub?

Dori: I feel angry. Tense. Stressed. Disconnected. Sometimes exasperated because I am tired and want to get him to bed and go to sleep myself, or have time with my spouse, etc.

Naomi: How would you be without this thought and expectation?

Dori: I would be calmer. I may let my toddler have his bath playtime and relax about it.

Naomi: Isn't that good to know? Turn the thought around to the opposite.

Dori: *"My toddler should not get out of the water."* My proof: He isn't. He is having a blast of joy. So, I see that without the thought, all is well. He wouldn't be that long anyway.

Naomi: Turn the thought around to yourself.

Dori: *"I should get out of my disconnecting thoughts."* Oh, I see. I would start it earlier to allow enough time for his play without needing to interrupt him. He is obviously not done with his bath. It is about my convenience, wanting to go to sleep and thinking that my toddler should go to sleep. But obviously he is wide-awake and so happy.

Naomi: And it doesn't mean that you couldn't ask him to finish sooner for your sake. Do you see another turnaround?

Dori: I see. With the thought, I am irritable, so I don't speak to him kindly or honestly. So another turnaround could be: *"I should get out of my irritability and communicate kindly."*

Naomi: And with that, what would you say?

Dori: Easy. I could simply say what you teach so often, which gives the child a sense of autonomy: "Mommy is tired and wants to go to bed now. How much longer do you want to stay in the water?" Gee, I bet he would come out very soon this way.

Indeed, there is no need to believe the chatter in the mind that hijacks you away from love and kindness. Be the master of your own thinking, not its slave. Reality is much kinder and truer. As a parent, you are the leader. A leader parent is one who plans well for a most peaceful flow. Not that it always works perfectly, but most of the time it does, and when it doesn't, a respectful communication stirs things peacefully.

Children who are treated this way act naturally in caring and peaceful ways. They want to belong and feel trusted and included. The result is that parents don't have to struggle because the child wants to be part of the team.

Cooperation or Control?

Cooperation is often used as a cover-up for control. There is no bad intention—this is a culturally endorsed self-deception. Therefore, naturally, most people are not even aware of it. We consider ourselves kind and respectful parents when we ask with words for cooperation, give logical instructions, and create so-called agreements we expect children to keep. Let's look at how all these strategies are perceived by the toddler or young child:

The following is an inquiry on this basic expectation for cooperation:

Gavin: *"My toddler should cooperate."*

Naomi: Is that true? Is that what she does? (Truth is what actually occurs.)

Gavin: No. Because she doesn't.

Naomi: That is good to know. When you believe that she should cooperate and she doesn't, how do you react?

Gavin: I get angry and annoyed, and I try to control her.

Naomi: Are you connected or disconnected from her?

Gavin: I feel disconnected and not on her side.

Naomi: How would you be without the thought that she should cooperate when she doesn't?

Gavin: Oh, I see something. For me, cooperation is obedience. I don't really want that. So, yes, without this thought, I would be peaceful. In that peace, I would be curious to find out what she truly needs.

Naomi: What is the turnaround of *"She should cooperate"*?

Gavin: *"She shouldn't cooperate or obey."*

Naomi: With that truth, you can investigate what her valid need is, and why, by turning your thought around.

Gavin: *"My child shouldn't cooperate. I should cooperate with her needs."* YES! I like that.

> **Naomi:** This does not mean that you always do what the child wants. But understanding her autonomous take on herself, you can find ways to present limitations in kind ways that validate the child's intent. In this spirit, you are staying connected rather than controlling or oppositional. In such a state, you are also more likely to find a way to resolve a situation that seems impossible and discover a nuanced solution that is kind. Your child learns from you and will likely act like you.

Interestingly, the examples parents usually give are often trivial daily issues such as going to sleep, being quiet, putting a coat on, not hitting, or not tearing or throwing things. In all these situations, it is about parental cooperation with the toddler or baby's needs and abilities. Check the previous chapters about bedtime and other "must be done" issues. Many are not a must and can be done in cooperation with the toddler's ability, based not on control but on connection.

Important: Safety Is *Not* About Cooperation

- When discussing the topic of cooperation and communication (versus control), parents often ask something like, "What if she runs into the busy street?" **When it is about safety, it is not about cooperation. If your child is going to endanger herself or others, act quickly.** You can still communicate while taking action; validate your toddler's dismay, and let her know why you picked her up and took her out of a situation. Or you can validate her feelings once she is safe.

Danger is no time for a communication workshop or a lesson in cooperation.

It is the parents' job to prevent danger. In my world, no toddler walks along a busy street without holding my hand at all times (unless he is on my back or in my arms). You already prevent danger when you buckle the child in the car, put on a life jacket when near or in water, put glassware and matches on higher shelves in your kitchen, lock cabinets containing cleaning fluids, and avoid unsafe toys and gadgets. This keeps your child safe without having to "get their cooperation." Some unsafe situations may arise unexpectedly—when this happens, take action fast; do not wait for your child's cooperation.

Cooperation is more the parents' job than it is the toddler's. She will learn to cooperate from her experience of how you cooperate with her. How she is treated and communicated with is the greatest instruction. She will do to others as you do to her. Your child always has a valid need and reason for her choices. Be curious and responsive to understand her needs and reasons.

Such a habit of empowering your child's sense of self-reliance is also helpful for the child's safety as she grows older. She will be much less likely to "cooperate" with an abuser when her experience of cooperation is associated with feeling good about herself, respected, connected, and cared for. She will trust herself to cooperate with those who, like you, show up connected and truly on her side.

Who Made the Agreement?

A parent may say, "We had an agreement, and the child isn't cooperating. She isn't keeping her agreement." This one is a double bend: The cooperation we want is our wish to control and for the child to do what we want (even when it is for her sake). And our method is to create a so-called agreement. But when the child initially agreed, she had no choice but to say yes and usually no idea how she would feel in reality when she would be required to keep that so-called agreement. Or she knows she won't keep it but feels coerced to accept the "agreement."

To prevent struggles with children, it helps to become aware of these culturally endorsed deceptions. In their family intensive retreat, Sonya and Bret were exasperated by their young child's breaking of agreement. Here is Bret's inquiry:

Bret: *"We had an agreement."*

Naomi: Is that true, especially the word "we"?

Bret: No. It is a lie. (Lili, who was almost four, had not really agreed but had no choice in the matter.)

Naomi: How do you react when you believe this thought and the child is not keeping the so-called agreement?

Bret: When believing this thought and Lili isn't cooperating, I feel angry. I scold her for not keeping her (supposed) agreement. I am disconnected and annoyed, and I blame my child.

Naomi: How could you be without this thought in the same situation?

Bret: Without this thought, I would notice that this "agreement" isn't working for my child. I would feel peaceful and curious to understand.

Naomi: Turn it around.

Bret: Oh, I am clear. I have a few: (1) *"She should not keep 'our' agreement, because it isn't really her agreement. She didn't want to agree to this, because she was honest and knew that she won't cooperate with this situation in the future."* (2) *"She should keep 'her' agreement with herself, which she does by refusing to be controlled."* That's being rooted in herself and confident. (3) *"I should keep my agreement, which is to respect my child and to find ways to solve problems with honesty and connection."*

Naomi: Beautiful. How do you feel now?

Bret: I can't wait for another broken agreement. I feel sorry that I intimidate Lili so that she has no choice but to pretend to agree. But I feel happy that she doesn't keep that dishonest agreement. I will not make such agreements again.

In modern parenting, we often use altered language to pretend that what we do isn't what we do. For example, we have a special designated word for hitting children: "spanking." It gives the parents the illusion that they are not hitting their child when they are. Different words make no difference in the infliction of pain and harm.

Then we deceive ourselves with words such as "It's time to go" (to leave the playground or friend, to sit down to eat, to go to bed, and so on), when in truth, it is what we want. Even if we think we must go for the child's sake, it is still our point of view and plans, and when in opposition to the child's, we are teaching control and harming the child's self-reliance.

Be clear that I am not saying that you cannot lead the way to leave the playground or help your child go to bed. I am only saying that, with more honest wording, you are more likely to be respectful and not have unrealistic expectations. You will then have a more peaceful and harmonious flow with your child and even a more "cooperative" child, one who cooperates of her own free will. This is the topic of the next section. We can be an authority without being a controller by having a relationship of trust and respect.

Respectful Communication Allows Autonomy and Doesn't Generate Defiance

As parents, we often confuse taking care of the child with being a boss. But your child is not confused. She is clear in the moment you control her; she experiences you as going against her and is therefore likely to bolt and run away, or refuse to cooperate. If we resort to force, the picked-up toddler is going to scream and kick while being carried away or stopped from what she is doing. There are better ways to relate to a human being such that her dignity is protected and her autonomy honored. And, no, it doesn't mean that she can always do whatever she wants. It does mean that we learn to respect another human being regardless of her age and communicate in a way that elicits trust and goodwill.

For example, when at the playground, instead of the dictatorial, "Okay, it's time to go now," you can say, "Your daddy is coming home, and I want to go home to be there when he returns. How many more times do you need to go around on the carousel?"

Instead of using the "God of IT'S," as in "It's time to go to bed," speak honestly: "Mommy and Daddy need quiet time without you. We would like you to go to bed and sleep." Such honesty may cancel your request and connect you to reality, such that you find an honest solution: You can find a different way to have a couple time (a babysitter, a relative, or a different time) and realize that, in the moment, your child may need your full engagement for a while longer.

Cooperating with your child does not mean that the toddler runs your life. Instead, you choose to run your life in response to your child. Cooperation means that you are a wise and aware leader who plans life to work for everyone with respect. This way the child feels autonomous and wants to do the best she can of her own free will. If your toddler protests, consider the possibility that she may be seeking autonomy and that, to her, you appear as an obstacle. Often, we stop wee ones without even knowing why. If the situation is unavoidable, use kind communication and connection to affirm your toddler's experience, even when she cannot get her way.

When There's Absolutely No Choice

Many kind and loving parents make the mistake of doing what I humorously call a "communication workshop" with the little one when the child needs the parent's clear leadership. Sometimes there is no choice (but be honest about whether that is actually so), and if that's the case, the child needs clarity, not pretend conversation about it. The nice, long conversations do have their place when there is no time-sensitive situation or an urgent need.

For example, if you must take your three-year-old with you on an outing but he wishes to stay home and there's no one who can stay with him, validate his feelings with a benign attitude, and avoid a long conversation about majority rule or all the other times everyone does what he wants, and so on. Just say something such as "I know you prefer to stay home. We must be going. I will help you put your shoes on. . . ." Or if he won't put his shoes on, take his coat and shoes and pick him up, validating, "I know you wanted to stay home." A kiss, if the child allows, can help.

This is not the ideal way, of course; it should be used only for an unplanned, urgent situation. Ideally, prepare the child, plan for options, and do your best not to drag her around on other people's outings, or add something fun for her.

Spare the little one the "debate" that creates the illusion that if he is good with words or other toddler strategies, he may get his way when in truth there is no choice. Acknowledge the fact that there is no choice. If life, in general, flows and your child feels autonomous, my experience shows that such a child will not have an issue in times when he is required to bypass his own wishes. In addition, from day one of a child's life, let him be aware of the fact that there are other people and factors that dictate the next action. (See page 216 for nurturing awareness of the needs of others.)

"Don't we sometimes have to tell a child to stop doing something or to wait?"

Yes, there are situations when a toddler has to wait, but if most of life flows peacefully, they can usually respond with ease in such rare situations, especially when validated and treated honestly. If there's a real reason to momentarily interrupt a toddler from doing what they are enjoying, you can take action while offering validation—for example, "Whoops, I love snuggling with you now, but I must attend to Grandpa right away. When I am done, we can snuggle again."

"Why won't my toddler listen to me?"

Let's follow Monica's inquiry about her toddler, Gina. Monica told me that she often instructs Gina to no avail. Gina doesn't listen to her and ignores her requests or suggestions:

Monica: *"My three-year-old should listen to me."*

Naomi: Is that true?

Monica: Well, yes.

Naomi: Can you absolutely know that it's true? What is your proof?

Monica: She is not responding and not doing as I ask her to.

Naomi: How do you react when you believe this thought?

Monica: I get upset and feel like this little brat is passive-aggressive.

Naomi: And how do you treat Gina when you believe your thought and see her as passive-aggressive?

Monica: I first repeat my request calmly, but she still doesn't listen, and then I raise my voice or scare her with my tone.

Naomi: Close your eyes and imagine the same scene. Watch Gina in your mind's eye. Who would you be with her in that moment, without believing that she should listen?

Monica (recalling the scene with closed eyes): I see a peaceful child focused on her play. I feel curious and peaceful.

Naomi: Feel it. Take your time.

Monica: Oh, I see. She is listening to me. She hears me. She is clear that she doesn't want to do what I say.

Naomi: Interesting. So perhaps the real inquiry is on "*She should obey me.*"

Monica: Yes, exactly. I expect her to obey. Oh no. But I don't really want that for her.

Naomi: Good news. So turn the thought around. What is the opposite?

Monica: *"She should not listen to me"* . . . or, more honestly, *"She should not obey me."* That is much more true. I am so happy that she refuses and that she is not afraid of me and asserts her will by tuning me out. Wow, this is amazing.

Naomi: Now turn it around to yourself.

Monica: "*I should listen to her?*"

Naomi: Well, look and see. How could that be more true?

Monica: I will notice that she doesn't want to, that I show up as an abstraction to her direction. Yes, I see that. I am indeed not listening to her clear cues. So I need to listen and connect with her. How do I do that?"

Naomi: Connect first. For a child focused on something, how can you connect? Think of the way you would do it with an adult.

Monica: Oh. First, I would wait and not interrupt. Then, if needed, I would say, "Excuse me for interrupting. Dinner is almost ready. Do you need more time to finish your reading? How soon can you be ready to come to the table?"

Naomi: Excellent. Now translate it to what you would say to three-year-old Gina.

Monica: "Are you enjoying the new blocks? What have you built?"

Naomi: Yes, yes. Now you made a connection.

Monica: After she talks about her creation, I can say, "We are getting ready to go to Grandma's. Are you ready to go?"

(Monica imagined the scene.) I think she would get up and ask me to help her get ready. Or she would need a few minutes to finish her tower. But what if she said, "I don't want to go to Grandma's now."

Naomi: That depends. Must you go? If not, what is the harm in not going or not going yet? But imagine you must go for taking care of your mom's health needs or something else that is time sensitive.

Monica: I could say, "I know you want to stay at home and finish building with your blocks. I don't have anyone who could stay with you. And I must go now because Nanna needs help."

You can see that with an intention to connect and respect the child, there is no end to kind words. Even in an emergency, if you must pluck the child out of her activity or buckle her in the car seat against her will in a rush, you can still use validating and caring words and even affection. Your child's behavior is feedback to the way she perceives how you treat her.

Even if you must guide her away from her wish (for safety or other unalterable considerations), when you are peaceful and understand the child, you can do so kindly and clearly.

Often, our mistake is in limiting the toddler's autonomy by imposing our (often unimportant) concepts on the little fellow. We wouldn't ask a busy adult to stop what they are doing and obey our plans for them. We would ask if they could, or we would wait till they are available. We can be as respectful of a child. Imposing our will on a child (or on anyone) harms our relationship with them and produces disconnection and resistance.

Of course sometimes the kindest thing is a setup with no choice. Too many choices can confuse and burden a young child. When we are attentive, it is not hard to know when to say something kind first and allow autonomy (when there is time and possible choices), and when to just say, "I know you aren't ready, but we must go. Let me put your coat on. Grandpa said it is urgent." This is still validating and respectful.

Sheila mentioned to me how her toddler was digging dirt with a toy shovel. With excitement and joy, her toddler piled the dirt on the grass. The mother asked him to make the pile of dirt away from the grass. The toddler refused. She got angry and took him into the house, and there he had a tantrum.

Sheila's thought was: *"He should listen to me and put the dirt on the non-grassy area."*

Naomi: Is that true? What was the reality?

Sheila: Not true. He was putting it on the grass.

Naomi: And whose choice is it how he plays?

Sheila: His.

Naomi: Yes, and what is the harm in dirt on the grass?

Sheila: Nothing much really.

Naomi: How did you react when you believed your thought?

Sheila: I was enraged. I grabbed him aggressively and took him inside while he was screaming.

Naomi: How would you be without the thought that he should pile the dirt off the grass?

Sheila: I would enjoy watching my child play happily. I see. I ruined his play, and he felt helpless and hurt. Gee, I could easily clear the grass later.

Naomi: And so, what is the opposite of your thought?

Sheila: *"My toddler should put the dirt on the grass . . . because that's what he autonomously chose to do."*

Naomi: Do you see another turnaround? Turn it to yourself.

Sheila: *"I should not put the dirt on the grass?"*

Naomi: Well, sure, that is more true. It is your idea to keep the grass green.

Sheila: *"I should clear the dirt off the grass."*

Naomi: Are you sure that would be peaceful?

Sheila: Well, I am not sure now. At least not right away. My child may be enthusiastic about the beautiful pile of brown dirt on the green grass. I guess I should find out by asking him, or just let it be. It is harmless and can wait.

Sheila (after thinking for a moment): "But what about situations when what a child does is a real problem?"

Naomi: A child whose life easily flows most of the time is generally very responsive to the random occasions of limiting circumstances, especially when it is communicated with respect and understanding.

Listen Versus Obey

We fool ourselves when we say "listen" when we actually mean "obey." Obedience means fear and a relationship of control. If we train children in habitual obedience, they may grow up to obey other authorities unquestioningly—making them more vulnerable to a molester, peer pressure, media manipulation, sales tactics, and more.

Obedience is not a healthy quality to develop. It creates fear, oppression, closing up of emotions, and disconnection from self-trust and self-direction. It creates followers—people who are insecure and imitative—rather than independent thinkers who are emotionally grounded in themselves. We have repeatedly seen the destructive results of obedience both in close relationships and in social settings and politics.

True listening is an act of love, connection, and interest. We all want to be heard. You want your child to feel safe to respond authentically to your communication. Giving instructions must be done with respect, not as a commander, but actually as a listener. Watch your toddler and choose your words with kindness. You are the one giving instruction. Therefore, it is your job to listen by tuning in to the child's reaction to assess the kindest next step. The bottom line is the turnaround: *"I should listen to my child."*

"How do I get my toddler to respond when really needed?"

Ask yourself whether the situation is truly dangerous—such as when a child runs into the street or approaches the edge of a cliff. In those cases, you simply act to protect him; no listening is needed, just clear and quick action. Yes, there are less urgent situations too, involving the needs of others, but even then, it is either possible to allow flexibility or it requires taking action accompanied by kind words.

Most of the time, parents talk about "need" when referring to going to sleep, eating when everyone eats, sharing toys, leaving the playground, and so on. None of these are really needed. As previously discussed, a toddler will fall sleep and learn to be able to do so when we flow with his sense of his own tiredness. Appetite cannot be coerced, nor can sharing or interrupting fun time. The way to respond, then, as mentioned before, is to give honest information, as in: "I want you to sleep so we can have time without you" (this sounds rough so, facing this truth, you will probably want to find a different solution; see page 208), or "I want to go home now to make dinner. How many more times do you need to slide?"

Children are very accommodating when allowed to feel in charge of themselves. In contrast, feeling helpless generates resistance and tantrums. Be honest, and when honesty is rough words, rethink your plan.

When a Toddler Causes Damage

Even damage done by a toddler can be handled with kindness and leadership rather than authoritarian control. One family came to my home for a family intensive retreat, and they had a one-year-old who loved my garden flowers. Very quickly he embarked on plucking them with joy. It was obvious they would all be gone if the toddler wasn't stopped.

The father picked up his toddler and explained that the flowers have to stay on the stems. Together they put each flower back on, even though they would die anyway. Then the father put the child down and showed him how to look and smell but not pluck the flowers. This child was generally autonomous and had no issue responding to the request. He seemed enthusiastic about knowing how to be part of the "team" and never plucked another flower in all the five days that they were in our home.

In another situation, in a store, a toddler was very taken with a toy the parents did not intend to buy. Even validating and gentle ways didn't help, and he had a meltdown on the floor of the store. The parents picked him up and took him out of the store, and he cried for a while until he felt at peace again. The parents were gentle but clear and supportive of his emotional expression without making drama. Dramas and compensations only make the next upset bigger and more painful. Toddlers can handle not getting what they want when it doesn't happen frequently and when we embrace their emotional expression with calm, attentive listening.

However, such episodes can often be prevented. Being kind includes not exposing little ones to what they cannot get before they are ready to accept such limitations. Some places are not for toddlers. Stores are too stimulating. For some, restaurants require too much motionless time. Other times, it is about consideration for others who may be children themselves or who may be unable to accommodate a toddler.

At all times, stopping the toddler's intent can be done with validation of her expressed intent and without distracting her. It is fine for a wee one to experience not getting what she wants as long as it is not too often, and as long as you do so only when it is really necessary. If life generally flows with ease, the toddler can handle it peacefully. If she needs to cry, that is fine, too, when responded to with loving listening and holding.

How to Say No Kindly

A kind way to say "no" is to say "yes" to the intent first. You pick her up and say, "I see, you want to play with this child's doll." Wait for a cue that the toddler is hearing you, and then say, "The child is playing with it. We can sit here and watch if you want." Or if the toddler has already grabbed the toy, say, "We must return it to her," and go over so your toddler can give it back.

Of course, sometimes you just have to say no. It is not a taboo, but save it for danger or real and urgent necessity so that the little one learns to take you seriously. Even harmful things can be validated first. "Whoops," you may say as you pick the toddler up kindly, "it is fun to jump on Grandpa's couch, but Grandpa said it is only for sitting and lying down." If, at home, you let her jump on your couch, you can add, "When we go back home, you can jump on the couch."

Most "noes" can be presented as a "yes" to the intent first, but we need not fear being clear when necessary. Many parents who want to be gentle and kind don't dare to impose some basic ways of being. If your toddler is pulling another child's hair, it is not a time for a communication workshop. Act clearly by saying something such as "Whoops, that hurts" as you undo the grip of the little hand off the hair and make sure the other child is fine. Toddlers try things on, expecting to be guided by us. They do so innocently, so there is no need to be upset with them, only to provide a neutral and clear guidance.

Multiple Options to Choose from Is Confusing

A common misconception is that giving a child two or three options to choose from allows the child to feel free. It doesn't unless it is the condition in reality; let me explain: If you go to a restaurant, it's your choice to go there, and then you face the menu with multiple choices of foods to choose from. A child can handle such a situation. You take your toddler to the playground that she likes, and there are two swings, a slide, and some ladders to choose from. She can do that. She is looking at the choices and goes for what she wants happily.

In contrast, when you give your child two or three options, she is fine only if she actually wants one, but often she wants none and feels cornered. That is not autonomy at all. Or you may even use such options to manipulate the child to cooperate when she doesn't want to (and it is not a crucial issue). For example, when you child is not ready for bed, and you say, "Do you want the green or the red pajamas to go to bed?" Or your child doesn't want any of the foods you offer and you say, "Broccoli, egg, or tomato?" These are not real choices—they feel like a dictatorship, leaving the child cornered and helpless.

How to know when to offer choices? My answer is: never. Like with routine and bedtime, let reality do the job, and your child will feel in charge of herself and not manipulated. For the most part, toddlers feel free when there are no choices to make: There is one raincoat, one Mommy and one Daddy, boobs are only on Mommy, one place to sleep, and so on. They don't have a tantrum because they want another home, bedroom, or Mommy.

Therefore, in the early years, parental leadership is also minimizing confusion and the burden of making choices. Keep it simple. Put the plate on the table. Give a cup of water. And when the toddler starts to be interested in choosing the cup's color, let her choose from all that is safe and available—freely.

Other Manipulations Through Words

In the next chapter, you will learn how and why to avoid manipulative communication such as praise, rewards, consequences, or punishment. It suffices to mention here that praise, threats, and other techniques designed to compel the child to obey are not tools of love or connection. Instead, they create fear and do not result in the child's authentic desire to cooperate or behave well. Your child's responses guide you. To avoid manipulative parenting, carefully read your child's cues and her responses to your words so you can adjust your guidance and return to love.

CONCLUSION

Talk to your child with a purpose to connect, not to control, coerce, or manipulate. This ensures that even when she can't get her way, she knows she is unconditionally loved. The toddler's response (or lack of it) is always feedback you can use to understand her and adjust your words accordingly so she can be inspired to flow with your guidance. When your child is defiant, inquire into your thinking so you can understand how you have ignited her need to resist you or what you are missing in terms of her valid needs. Take the child's reaction seriously, and take responsibility for what you inspire in her.

When your child is interrupting, refusing to stop her fun time or noise, or causing damage, show up not as a controller but as a loving listener. Is your restriction really needed, or can you prioritize love and allow your child's autonomy? Even attempts to secure a child to do as you wish through praise, rewards, or threats are not going to generate goodwill and loving connection. (There's more on that in the next chapter.) When being kind and respectful, there is no need to turn each issue into a communication workshop. A young child relies on your leadership and counts on your kindness and clarity. There are safety issues that require brisk action and firmness, but you can follow up with honest, loving connection. For example: "I was so scared when you ran into the water. Sorry for scaring you. I am so happy you are here in my arms."

Chapter 10

Social Manners and Rethinking Behavioral Challenges

How we speak shows the root cause of misunderstanding children's behavior. A parent asked me how to *make* the child behave, try harder, or share. But we cannot *make* anyone be or do anything. We can model, expose, inspire, or guide respectfully *when asked.* For the most part, the child will acquire knowledge and skill best when it is her own interest and becomes her passion for a duration.

It is easy to notice that you cannot compel a toddler to walk or talk. His brain is programmed like a time machine, and he will unfold in his own time and way. Naturally, you don't convince or manipulate a child to talk or teach her to walk or run. Earlier, you read why not to push a child ahead of their natural evolution. In the same way, they learn social skills and behavior through immersion that feels good, exciting, and inspiring. They want to belong successfully and need no compelling.

In this chapter, you will learn how to respond kindly to the many behaviors of young children that may seem challenging. From sharing and caring about other people to aggression, biting, and many more, you will read parents' stories and resolutions that allow compassion, responsibility, and peace to flourish without manipulation.

Manners in Public

Children who are treated with respect and are immersed in social settings that fit their abilities behave well with other people, in restaurants, in stores, at family gatherings, and in the theater, of their own free will. They have the self-discipline to behave well because they want to belong and fit in.

I have seen this repeatedly with client families and my own children. They could be sitting quietly in a full-length classical music concert, behave well in restaurants, or wait as toddlers patiently by my side as I counsel, without threats and punitive approaches—ever. They wanted to be part of the experience and fit in, and they did. They were aware and enthusiastic about "playing the game" society plays. They learned to be aware of others through immersion in a family that was constantly modeling such awareness.

For example, take your baby or toddler to a restaurant only after their needs for motion and being noisy are met—meaning not after they have been sitting buckled in a car seat for a while or after they have had to be quiet and with limited motion. If traveling, go to the park first, allowing movement and noise until the child is done and eager to go eat.

When ready, choose a place that has an outdoor play area to wait while the food is being made and has food the toddler could enjoy. Be flexible but also provide clear guidance about how to behave in such a setting ahead of entering the restaurant, and if needed, again once seated at the table. Wee ones love to know the rules and to fit in. Most often, however, if your toddler has already experienced social settings successfully and enjoyably, you will not need to say anything. The child looks around, quickly figures out the code of behavior, and enjoys being part of it successfully.

In his Zoom session, Ross shared that his family cannot go to restaurants without constant struggle with their three-and-a-half-year-old toddler, Giovani. He told me, "Gio can't sit and wait for food. The baby is easy, but caring for her makes it hard to also control Gio. He goes under the table and runs around between the tables." The following is Ross's inquiry:

Ross: "*Gio shouldn't go under the table and run around in restaurants.*"

Naomi: Is that true?

Ross: Well, yes. It just doesn't work.

Naomi: Can you absolutely know that it's true that Gio shouldn't go under the table and run around in restaurants?

Ross: Absolutely? No. I don't know what is going on for him.

Naomi: How do you react when you believe this thought?

Ross: I am exploding with rage and impatience. I try to settle him and remind him of our agreement.

(See the section on delusional agreements with children on page 205.)

Naomi: Does this thought bring you stress or peace?

Ross: Clearly, stress. I don't know why I keep hoping each time that finally Gio will get it.

Naomi: How do you treat Gio when you believe this thought?

Ross: I pull him back to his chair and whisper angrily to sit down or else. . . . I come up with some threat.

Naomi: So *with* the thought, you are angry, stressed, and rough on your child. How would you be without this thought?

Ross: Ha, I wouldn't go to restaurants.

Naomi: Not a bad idea for starters. Respect Gio by not putting him in a place that he cannot yet handle. Let's see if there is also a possibility of going to a restaurant such that Gio enjoys being successful at belonging and being part of the experience. Turn the thought around.

Ross: *"Gio should go under the table and run around in restaurants."*

Naomi: Is that as true or truer than your original statement?

Ross: It's more true because this is what he does.

Naomi: Reality is truth. Making it clear to your mind is the first step toward peace. If you don't even know what is real, how can you act effectively? When you know the facts, you either don't fool yourself by going to restaurants, or you do something about it that isn't a repeat of what you have done and failed at repeatedly. Find three reasons for the turnaround; three reasons Gio *should* go under the table and run around in restaurants.

Ross: He has a lot of pent-up energy. He doesn't trust my guidance. He is bored. He needs attention. He needs movement.

Naomi: That's five and you can easily find more. So now you are starting to understand your child. With that understanding, you could perhaps come up with ways to help him enjoy sitting at a table in a restaurant. You can make sure he has lots of opportunity for activity before going to eat and go to a place he likes that has a waiting play area.

Ross decided to stop going to restaurants for a few months, simply to have a fresh start without the current habits. He worked on kinder communication and on trusting Gio with his real needs. A month or so later, Ross reported that Gio has been much more responsive at home.

I made a suggestion to play a power game of Gio going under the table at home. They did. Daddy said, "Oh no, where is Gio?" And Gio went under the table and pulled on Dad's pants. Then Gio got out from under the table and ran around as he used to do in restaurants, and his father chased him playfully. They played the game many times until Gio had enough of it.

Then I recommended playing "restaurant" with Gio being the waiter and Daddy going under the table and then running around—then switching roles. After playing it daily for a couple of weeks, Ross reported a conversation Gio started with him:

Gio: Daddy, why don't we go to restaurants anymore?

Ross: I thought you didn't really like to sit quietly in one place. It's not important. We can go again when it is fun for you.

Gio: I am ready.

Ross: We can try. And if you change your mind and want to go under the table or run around, we can leave so you can do that at home. In the real restaurant, we do have to sit on the chairs at the table.

Gio (jumping up and down, excited): Yay, let's do it.

The family went to the park to play and then to a restaurant that Gio liked, where he could play outside while waiting. Not only did he sit at the table, but he was so excited about being, as he called it, "a real restaurant man" that he didn't want to go outside to wait for the food.

Self-Discipline Is the Only Discipline Possible

The only discipline that works is one that a person applies to himself. We cannot discipline another human being at any age or compel a child to want what they don't want. We can hurt them, we can scare them, and we can coerce or bribe them to do what we want or manipulate with praise and rewards. These approaches do not create a truly disciplined child or adult but rather a scared, anxious, and insecure one who obeys for approval or for the praise or prize. The same applies to discipline in accomplishment: Genuine practice, behavior, and learning cannot be coerced or compelled.

Babies are born self-disciplined and self-motivated in a way that they can apply to their growing accomplishments, such as exploring toys, gazing at things, and practicing sitting, turning, and crawling. Similarly, toddlers are amazingly focused and self-disciplined when they practice walking, talking, climbing, and learning to make an impact through communication. Therefore, there is nothing to teach, and everything to protect and preserve. Your goal is to nurture, respect, model, and support the toddler on his many learning projects while not getting in the way.

Here are some guiding points to help your child's innate self-discipline flourish:

- Don't interrupt a focused toddler or child (this requires respect and self-discipline on your end).
- Be self-disciplined, especially in how you respond to your toddler and others when things go wrong. Do the inquiry on your angry thoughts rather than letting anger take control of you.
- Practice self-discipline in terms of learning, like your toddler. Whether practicing a musical instrument, folding the laundry, learning a dance move, doing what you said you would, practicing yoga, making disciplined food choices, and so on, your toddler is watching and internalizing.
- Do not help your child or do things for her when it comes to playing and creating. Provide toys, art, and activities she can do on her own.
- Provide your toddler with activities that challenge her to a degree she can handle—not too easy, but also not so difficult that she keeps giving up.
- Avoid manipulations through coercion, praise, rewards, or negativity. Causing a child to do things does not lead to "self"-discipline. It creates only fear-based obedience and causes similar damage, including hating to do that exact thing you are trying to make her practice.

A baby learns from day one by observing, based on the way she is treated and her innate nature. The toddler is busy learning self-discipline every minute of every day. She is driven to master life, belonging, contributing, participating, helping, figuring things out, and having an impact. Don't shape her or steer; just enable her path as a nonintrusive leader.

How Children Learn to Care for Others

A baby is born self-absorbed, naturally. She has a colossal job ahead of her—to figure out life and become herself as a contributing member of society. Therefore, being focused on herself is natural and healthy. She starts by figuring out how to get you to meet her needs and expands from there to physical skills, language, play, and unfolding her whole being.

We cannot know the baby/child experience. She may still feel as one with all beings or even things. Some people think a toddler cries when they watch another toddler cry because they feel one with them or have empathy. Others assume that, upon noticing another toddler cry, the child is scared that whatever caused the other child to cry will happen to her too, so she bursts out crying. We cannot fully know, as most of us do not recall being these ages. We need language to be able to store memory.

Regardless of these interpretations, humans are social animals and care for others naturally. At some point, a child notices the needs and emotions of others. Many children seem very caring from an early age. Others appear more focused on themselves. The development of care and compassion for others unfolds naturally and without lessons and drills. But we must be aware that such qualities unfold as a result of and in harmony with experience and observation. The toddler becomes a child who treats others based on the way she has been treated. Her experience of how she is cared for is the main teaching. Next in importance is what she observes around her—that is, how her parents treat each other and how other people in her life behave and care for one another. In short, how we behave makes *all* the difference.

"My child ruined another's child sandcastle."

Eduardo took his three-year-old to the beach, where the toddler played on the edge of the water in the sand. At some point, the little one came toward his dad, passing by the sand tower another child had built. To Eduardo's surprise, his toddler kicked and ruined part of the tower.

Eduardo asked for my guidance as he was not happy with what his son did and didn't think the child had learned anything. He told me that he promptly said to his toddler, "No, no, we don't do that, someone built this tower and wanted it to stay." He took the child over to apologize.

Although Eduardo did better than yelling or punishing, the child most likely felt confused and shamed, a state that makes learning or becoming aware of the needs of others practically impossible. It is best to move away from moralizing and shaming, and instead take actions of compassion, connection, and care.

The past is over.
Teach kindness by responding to the present
rather than reacting to the past.

The child kicks the tower while coming toward his father. I suggested to Eduardo: You could say, "Oh, ah," and walk over and rebuild the tower. If the other child is close by, you apologize (modeling behavior) while you fix the tower. Actions speak for themselves.

That's it. The child is not scolded, shamed, or put to the embarrassing task of apology without actually feeling sorry. Without these confusing emotional experiences, he is free to watch and learn. He is not blamed or judged, and he observes kindness and the correction of misdeeds with an open heart. Keep doing this. The child will adopt your ways.

The following is an example in which a child taught her father compassionate action in the present:

In a restaurant, a two-year-old toddler spilled juice on the table. The dad was angry and scolded his toddler, telling him that juice is for drinking and not spilling and making a mess. The older sister took napkins and cleaned the spilled juice.

Dad was angry because he had the thought, *"My toddler shouldn't spill the juice."* And another thought perhaps, *"If I clean it, he wouldn't learn that he did something wrong and not to do it again."* Many of us grew up with the notion that without suffering, shaming, or spelling out the right and wrong, no one learns anything. Yet, it is the opposite.

When his daughter wiped the table clean, the father felt embarrassed. The toddler looked at his father with fearful eyes. The father had the humility and strength to realize his error. He thanked his daughter and then said to his toddler, "I am sorry I got angry." And he thanked his daughter for her caring action.

How to Shine the Light on Compassion

We can enhance and support the child's natural affinity to care for people by verbalizing and engaging in the well-being of others out loud. For example, if you are at a playground and a child is upset, you may help or say (provided your child is listening), "I wonder what happened to this child and if I can help." Or if Grandma is coming for a visit, before she arrives, you can say to your child, "I wonder if Grandma will need to rest when she arrives, or if she will need to eat first, or hugs first. . . ." You can play a guessing game about it. This can apply to Daddy coming home or anyone else. The idea is to act with kindness and speak caring thoughts aloud.

If you simply treat people with generosity and kindness, your child will learn naturally because love is her innate program. Adding language to it creates a verbal connection and adds clarity about how to relate to others.

About Sharing

At a public playground, a toddler goes over to another child and innocently assumes she can take a toy of his and play. The other child is upset and not willing to share, which is fine; he has a right not to. The parents of both children are upset and trying to control and teach. The parent of the child who owns the toy had the thought: He should share. The parent of the toddler who takes the toy has a thought: She shouldn't take another child's toy.

Neither can be true when we observe reality. The little girl has no concept of ownership; she is innocent and would, herself, share generously at that age. The other child to whom the toy belongs is as innocent and had a valid reason to be upset. Therefore, neither thought is true. *The boy should not share. And the toddler should take the toy and assume it's available.* They have no reason to do anything else. Facts are the proof.

This is easy, so here is a shortcut of the inquiry:

- *When believing these thoughts,* parents are upset and go against the child, shame her, and confuse her with instructions and telling her what to do.
- *Without these thoughts,* parents observe children who do exactly what they are supposed to do based on what they know.
- *Turning* these thoughts around yields the thoughts: *He should not share* and *She should take the toy.*

With this clarity, you can easily stay peaceful and be kindly helpful.

You can pick the toddler up and validate: "I see you love that toy tractor. I think this boy wants to play with it, so let's give it back to him." Some toddlers will just hand it back, for the same reason of not having an issue about it in the first place and enjoying doing the "right" thing, playing the game the way Daddy says it goes.

If your toddler says no and holds on tight, give her a moment, and show that you are waiting, not judging.

If the boy is upset because he isn't getting the toy back fast enough, apologize to him and assure him that he will get his toy back shortly. "I know it's yours, and the little girl is learning and will give it back to you. It may take her a minute to understand and make peace with it."

The boy or his parent may come and ask her to give it back faster, and other things may occur that we cannot foresee, but the principle is to flow with reality. You can say to the child (depending on age) or the parent, "She will respond faster if you are the one who asks her to give it back." Usually this resolves it.

Toddlers are generous, both in giving and taking, because they don't yet perceive ownership. As they grow older, immersing in a very possessive society, they learn the materialistic lesson that possessions define ownership and identity.

The models are obvious every day: Adults have cars that make a huge noise if someone else dares to try to use them. Most homes are locked. We keep telling our children, "This is not yours but hers." We do that with items, with food, clothes, and money. When visiting a friend's home, a toddler naturally feels free to take food and toys. We go out of our way to destroy this natural communal inclination, and we succeed over time.

I have no value judgment on this way of living. There are pros and cons to different social arrangements. I only suggest that we realize that we are the models and make peace with the fact that children tend to practice what they see.

Not wanting to share is a clear imitation and practice of being in this society and of a sense of self in such a culture. At some point, the child learns to identify with "his" stuff and will sometimes share and other times not.

Respect Your Child's Choice About Sharing

In our family, when guests with children were expected for a visit, I always asked my three children to decide in advance what they do not wish to share. We put those things behind locked doors so they could enjoy sharing everything else. Their reason for not sharing was usually the concern that the guest child(ren) would break or damage their toys or ruin their creations.

Allowing your toddler and young child to feel autonomous about making such a choice makes their time with friends easy, and they can be generous with what they feel comfortable sharing. And

> yes, they can change their mind in the middle of the visit and put away something else or vice versa.
>
> Remind yourself that you, too, are not willing to share everything. In fact, most adults share very little and show an exaggerated focus on ownership of possessions. Children absorb this attitude and, over time, take it on with passion.

Rethinking Behavioral Challenges

Toddlers' behavior may seem challenging to us sometimes, but the toddler is just exploring innocently and is excited about life. Contrary to our perception, the child is not out to get us. When we treat the child as though he is somehow wrong, we wage war, we oppose, scare, or shame. We create a child who either behaves increasingly worse or shuts down and becomes scared and obedient. The reason such control breeds negative outcomes is that the toddler learns that life is about opposing, blocking, and struggling and that he isn't good at it and has to be constantly managed. In essence, he joins our "game" of opposition.

Obviously, we want to avoid this undesirable outcome. To do so, we must shift paradigm: from courthouse to love house and from judging to connecting and finding loving solutions. Toddlers and young children do the best they can. They have no frame of reference to what we take for granted as a way to behave. They need guidance, not control. The next sections provide examples of challenging behaviors and their peaceful solutions that help children to feel content and able to act with care and joy.

"My toddler bites me. What should I do?"

Biting is a common way toddlers assert their impact and power. The common conception that they bite out of frustration or a need to express feelings is not the case in my observation. They don't bite in the frustrating moment of failing to build a tower, and they express their feelings clearly, loudly, and openly. A toddler may try biting, and if the impact leaves an impression, she will do it again. The key is your response to the first time it occurs; be authentic rather than enabling. Many mothers say that the first bite didn't really hurt, so they thought it was cute and did not provide a clear and authentic message.

Irene was very frustrated with her toddler's biting. "No matter how much I tell her to stop, she seems to think I am playing a game," she said. "She didn't mean to hurt me. I shouldn't scare her with my reaction. It could harm her. But now she just keeps biting and doesn't respond to my attempts to stop her."

Irene: *"I cannot express that it hurts, because it would scare her and do harm."*

Naomi: Is that true? Is it true that encountering a real human reaction to pain would harm your baby or toddler?

Irene: No.

Naomi: She may cry. You can also do an inquiry on "*My toddler shouldn't cry.*" Or "*Crying is harmful.*" For now, let's continue with this inquiry: How do you react when you believe this thought?

Irene: I feel annoyed, but I pretend it's cute and no big deal. I tell her gently not to bite.

Naomi: Who would you be without this thought?

Irene: I would utter a sound of being hurt.

Naomi: Turn it around.

Irene: *"I can express that it hurts, and it won't scare or harm her."*

Naomi: Is that as true or truer?

Irene: Honestly, I have used harsh tone before, and sometimes she cries, but she is fine. So, it is more true that I should be honest with her.

Naomi: And you need not be harsh to be honest. And, yes, she may cry initially, and you can hug her and tell her you love her and that biting hurts.

Irene: I lie and my toddler has no idea . . . so she will do it again, thinking that it's an approved game.

Naomi: Indeed, she could be thinking that it's a game of "I bite and Mommy says no, and then I bite again and so on." And, yes, when you are real, she may appropriately and naturally cry. Crying is a healthy and useful response to being the cause of someone's pain. It does no harm to experience real life and not a pretense. You can validate and hold your child without canceling the impact of reality. Can you find another turnaround?

Irene: *"My toddler's response would hurt me."*

Naomi: Yes. The proofs are in real life. Ask yourself how you would respond if your toddler ran into the street. Would you worry about hurting her feelings or disturbing her intent? No. You would grab your child within seconds, possibly screaming as you do that, and she would cry, and you would hug her with relief. Of course this is not identical as there is no actual danger in her bite. However, there is pain, and she needs real feedback for her action without drama but with clarity so that she can become a human being who is pleasant to be with.

Of course, there is no need to be angry with the child once the action is over. She didn't know. You can be authentic. In the case of running into a busy street, you can say, "I was so scared. I am so relieved that you are in my arms now," "You could have gotten hurt," or, hugging and kissing her, "Oh my, I am so happy that you are safe." And obviously, you learned that a toddler cannot be close to a street without you holding her hand or carrying her on your body.

Back to the biting: Indeed, biting is not life-threatening, but if you don't want your toddler to conclude that "biting works" to create an effect (a sense of power and of having an impact), then the response must be final and clear. This does not mean be punitive or angry. Clarity is not about anger but about reality—like gravity: *When the child falls, the ground is not always gentle, but the message is clear.*

That first bite, when you respond strongly, will be the last: "Ouch, NO! Never." Remove the child off you and offer something safe to bite on. "Do you need to eat something? To test your teeth? Here is something you can use." Give the toddler a toy, or something rubbery and safe to chew on. Later you can play other power games that meet her obvious need to have an impact. (See page 310 for power games examples.)

If your child is scared and cries, you can follow with a validation and in-arms affection. "Mommy scared you. You are safe, no worry. I screamed because it hurts when you closed your teeth on Mommy." Then offer things she may bite.

If your baby bites your breast, do the same thing—words and action. "Ouch, no!" In this case, interrupt her bite by opening her mouth with your fingers and remove her off your body or off the breast. You may have to do so a few times, not with anger, just clarity and promptness to help her make the connection. Then resume breastfeeding.

The thoughts that get in the way of such clarity and authenticity can be inquired into. Write down yours and inquire, as demonstrated repeatedly through the book. Some other thoughts that I have often heard from mothers and fathers are:

Her feelings will be hurt.

She should not experience hurt feelings.

I will scare her.

It doesn't hurt.

She won't like me.

She is too little to understand.

She will grow out of it on her own.

It's cute.

Whichever is your thought, it stops you from being authentic, and your toddler assumes biting is fine. Little ones want us to lead the way and to give them feedback about their experiments. They are asking, in essence, "Is it okay to do this?" Give one clear answer, and usually there won't be a second time.

New Magic Words

It is common in society to teach children the magic words—"please," "I'm sorry," and "thank you." These aren't really magical when imposed. To the child who is embarrassed and not at all having these feelings, the words have no meaning. She feels shamed to say what she does not feel. She learns to impress, to be phony, and even to be dishonest.

I offer different words that do have power and create connection. Words of gratitude and of apology develop naturally by immersion, in their own time. But there are words that can create connection in tough moments. There is magic in opening the door to self-expression. When a child says something we don't like, instead of saying, "That's not nice," or "Say you are sorry," we can show interest and use words that, in my experience, are truly magical: *"Tell me more."*

"My toddler said, 'I hate you, Daddy!'"

If your child says, "I hate you," or they say it to a sibling or a friend, be interested and caring. Just like when a child calls you or another "stupid" or "ugly," the drive to stop it is not helpful. It teaches to fear words and to believe that feeling hate is bad. We all feel hate sometimes. Your child will feel shame and guilt if you react in the old way of canceling and apologizing. Feeling regret is natural and fine. Feeling shame is taking it personally into "I am a bad person."

It is much better to listen with an open heart and connect with the child.

Joyce didn't know how to react when her four-year-old said that he hates her. "That just such a strong dig in my heart. Why would he say that? Why would he feel such a bad emotion?" She told him not to speak this way and that we all love each other. But did her child feel love in that moment? Here is Joyce's inquiry:

Joyce: "Ethan should not say 'I hate you.'"

Naomi: Is that true?

Joyce: Yes. It's hurtful.

Naomi: Can you absolutely know that he shouldn't express hate when he does?

Joyce: No. I cannot know that. He is expressing it.

Naomi: How do you react when you believe the thought that he should not say "I hate you" in the moment that he does (to you, a sibling, or anyone)?

Joyce: I am very upset and anxious, and I tell him to stop it.

Naomi: Who would you be without this thought in the moment your child expresses hate?

Joyce: I would feel fine. Perhaps curious and interested. I would ask questions and I would listen.

Naomi: Turn the thought around.

Joyce: My child should express hate when he needs to. Yes, that is more true and kinder. He is feeling it and is too young to know to hold it back . . . (pondering), or actually more candid than adults.

Naomi: And another true turnaround?

Joyce: "I shouldn't express hate to my child," which is true, and I don't.

Naomi: Power is not running away from negative words or emotions but being able to let them in and find gratitude. Holding space for your child to be real with you is the essence of love.

The insight is clear: With the thought, you are disconnected from your child, waging war on the way he feels and on his valid need to express himself. Without it, you are connected, saying, "Yes, continue, I am listening." After all, the child trusted that you indeed are his loving listener. It's about his communication; not about you. (And yes, take it to heart too; you are most likely to learn something important about yourself.)

How wonderful that children carry their emotions on their sleeves. Telling a child not to express hate not only shuts him down but also teaches him, from your modeling, to fear words, to suppress emotions, and, worst of all, to control other people and tell them how to speak.

When you are interested, as in your turnaround, the magic words that I teach come in handy: "Tell me more." To which you can show true interest by adding, "What do you hate the most about Mommy?" Then listen and ask more questions as long as your child seems to be emotional and engaged.

The feeling your child has does not go away by not uttering it; it stays stuck, causing emotional toxicity inside. He is being vulnerable and honest while relying on your open heart and ability to listen with unconditional love. Be the safe listener that he expects you to be.

In the case of hate toward another child or a sibling, respond the same as when your child expresses hate toward you (perhaps not always in the presence of the other child). With this attitude, your child will learn that truth sets her free and that love does not restrict.

Shutting down a child's emotional honesty is a loss on both sides: The parent is losing a chance to learn whatever issue is going on for the child, and the child is losing an opportunity for healing and for learning to express himself from a place of trust of himself and of others.

"Tell me more" is opening the door and saying, "Yes, I hear you, and I am listening." Whatever the child says in response, listen attentively and ask for more based on the details he tells you. If he says, "I hate when you yell," you can ask, "Do you mean when I yelled to be quiet?" And after the "Yes," ask, "Can you tell me more examples that I yell? It will help me," and so on.

Hate is very painful. No child wants to hate anyone, most of all Mommy and Daddy. Yes, any child may feel this way at times. The feeling will dissipate easily when the child expresses it and you listen with an open heart.

Toddler "Play" at Day Care and Moms' Groups

In day care settings, toddlers are expected to do what they cannot: Play with peers. Being guarded and corrected constantly by teachers is not a kind or effective way to learn social skills. Earlier in the book you learned why pushing a baby or toddler to progress ahead of himself is counterproductive. This applies to social skills. When with peers and managed by teachers, the toddler may end up learning, "I fail at playing with others," "I am not good enough," and "I must have an authority figure to be able to relate." In addition, due to lack of skill and language, toddlers tend to fall back on physical solutions such as grabbing, biting, and hitting. These come from helplessness in the face of a situation they cannot handle. We are setting them up for social failure and for being dependent on authority.

Because the grabbing, frustration, and hitting cannot be prevented without constant control, the toddler may end up learning either to hit, grab, and bite or to be the victim of such acts as part of his self-identity. He also learns to need someone to control him and others and to obey authority and be dependent. There are never enough teachers, and so the toddler experiences scarcity of love and care and often develops competitive social strategies to get attention. These are all antisocial skills.

In a small group workshop, Todd raised his hand and said that sometimes toddlers do get along and make friends, which is true—though not common—typically when they interact one-on-one, have compatible personalities, and an adult is present. But Todd was convinced that toddlers also learn social skills if they are put together in groups and that it just takes longer. Here is his inquiry:

Todd: *"Toddlers should play with peers."*

Naomi: Is that true?

Todd: It's not working well. So, no.

Naomi: That was a fast realization. How do you react when you believe this thought?

Todd: I go out of my way to get my toddler to be with other toddlers. Then I get frustrated when they can't play and instead get themselves in trouble all the time.

Naomi: Who would you be without this thought?

Todd: A happy father doing what works socially for my young child.

Naomi: Turn the thought around.

Todd: *"Toddlers and young children should not play with peers because they can't."*

Naomi: Is that as true or truer?

Todd: Yes. Truer and simpler.

Naomi: Can you find another turnaround?

Todd: *"Toddlers and young children should play with those who can make the experience peaceful and enjoyable and who model social skills the toddler can learn from."*

Naomi: Isn't truth amazingly liberating?

Todd: I have another one: *"I can play with peers."* That is true for me as an adult.

Healthy social skills are learned from socially skillful people. The child learns from the way he is treated. Being with same-age toddlers or young children and dependent on adult control is not a good social model to follow. The child learns to hit, to exert control, to rely on control, and to seek authority rather than develop authentic skills.

If you must leave your toddler part of the day, do your best to find a solution that is not a peer group, but one where your child can get one-on-one care by an adult or an older mature kid. This way the toddler learns mature and caring social skills from the way he is cared for. Obviously this is not always possible for everyone, but when you understand the benefits, you can make the best compromises possible.

"My toddler is aggressive with friends. What should I do?"

This proves the ideas of the previous section. Putting toddlers with toddlers is like expecting a blind person to lead their blind companion down a busy street without walking sticks or guide dogs. With rare exceptions, a toddler cannot manage a relationship with another child who has the same limitations.

A toddler needs to be with someone who can care for him, not with someone who is equally needing of care.

This means that you must plan your and your toddler's social activities in a way that your toddler is cared for by an older child (three times his age or older) or by an adult. Or adults should be present with the toddlers (just two or three toddlers) as they play side by side.

The toddler's social experience is "I am with my daddy while playing next to or with this other toddler." If you have to intervene all the time to keep the peace, it is probably best to have an adult for each toddler.

I often hear in sessions from frustrated mothers who hope to have some social time while their toddlers play. Mothers and toddler groups, however, are often very stressful for the mothers unless some of the children are older and can care for the toddlers. The reason this is rarely enjoyable for moms is because each toddler needs her mother most of the time.

To have a mom-to-mom visit, I suggest doing so when your partner, a babysitter, or a friend can stay home to care for your toddler or young child—or come with you and take care of the child wherever you are. In this way, you don't have the stress of being torn between your own social engagement and caring for your little angel. For some, this may not be easily available. However, when a mother tells me that she can never get any such help, after discussing possibilities at her session, she always finds a way. She makes a conscious effort to find a big brother or volunteer helper, or does an exchange of care with another family, and this often results in unexpected friendships and support.

"How do I teach my child to be polite when he gets a gift he already has or doesn't like?"

Politeness is fake, and toddlers and young children are never fake. We should learn from them and develop the skill of facing truth without feeling threatened or shamed. Why can't an adult handle a child who dislikes a gift they brought? Why is the child required to be the therapist to the adult's fragile emotions? Why does the child have to learn to be fake?

Perhaps adults can learn to be at peace with truth and free of ego reactions. Why rescue the gift giver from the direct and candid interaction with the child? Maybe next time they will inquire with you about what this child likes and do a better job of bringing something exciting. If I brought something to a wee one and the child pushed it away and didn't want it, I would use humor to alleviate the phony discomfort of the adults. "Whoops, I brought a silly thing," and make a face and laugh at myself. I would then offer to take it back and ask the child what she really wishes to get.

Sometimes a young child rejects gifts because they don't like the giver or both the giver and the gift, or they don't like the awkward ceremonial behavior with everyone looking at them and waiting for the "polite" dictated lines. It is our job to avoid putting the child on the spot in this manner, which is shaming and would not be tolerated by anyone, at any age.

I am not suggesting rejecting human civil social codes of

interactions, but these should include avoiding shaming and telling others what to say. Part of this code must be to know how toddlers and children are and treat them in response to their capacity and point of view. They will learn the rules all too soon. Meanwhile, an honest and lighthearted response would model to them how to be accepting, flexible, and kind.

Here's the thought to inquire: *My child should say "thank you" and pretend to like the gift.* No client of mine has ever needed to do the actual inquiry once this thought is written down. It is one of those that bring prompt laughter, and the turnaround is right in front of their face: *Of course, the child should not be phony and obey a fake adult ceremony that he has no sense of at all.*

It is clearly impolite to dictate specific words to the child or to anyone—words that contradict their true experience. Learning to lie and to pretend is not a lesson the child benefits from. As the child matures and is able to distinguish such codes of behavior from his own real feelings, he will learn with delight and join social norms with no shame or confusion.

So, what can you do if your child doesn't like a gift? There is nothing to do. Sometimes a gift isn't liked. Question your drive to do something about it. The child doesn't want the gift. That's a valid response to receiving an unwanted item.

You can model to your child kind politeness that is not about imposing any words on him. Be the kind model, saying to the giver, "Thank you for your generous gift. It seems Johnny isn't currently interested. I am sorry." Depending on how well you know your child, you may add, "I can keep it. He may end up liking it later," or ask, "Would you like to take it back and exchange or return it?" This way, you model the polite skills you want your child to learn without being phony or dishonest. When not put on the spot, the child feels peaceful and able to observe and learn.

The Case Against Punishment, Time-Outs, Threats, and "Natural" Consequences

Punishment is the greatest mistake humans have invented. It is rooted in a need for revenge and a belief that imposed pain teaches good behavior. It doesn't! On the contrary, it teaches cruelty, fear, control, avoidance, and emotional isolation. Punishment cannot occur on its own by nature. It is a human design to hurt on purpose, and therefore it models intentional cruelty.

The child cannot fathom pain imposed by the one who loves and cares for him. He will therefore twist himself internally to justify and explain the parent's behavior away, or even explain it as loving. Therefore, the child will most often blame himself and create a negative self-image. He cannot see his parents as bad; that is too painful and scary. He therefore must believe that he is bad and worthless.

Imposing suffering on anyone is morally wrong, and, for children, it is extremely harmful.

No child sits by himself and thinks, *Oh, I get it. What I did was wrong. I should have been considerate of my sister. I will not do that again.* No one! Even if the child is trained by parents to say such words, it is not his truth but his obedience. It is not human, not possible, and just doesn't happen to a child. He only berates himself and feels despair in failing to be "good."

"I punish with a kind heart."

Many of us grew up with punishment, which is why we may be desensitized and not feel ourselves being cruel when we are. We are numb and say, "I don't do it in anger" or "It is for the good of the child, so I feel good when I do it," and other delusional thoughts that are the results of an emotional disconnection. Have compassion for yourself but work to give your child a kinder upbringing.

I invite you to do deep work on yourself to reawaken your own ability to feel and to be aware of causing pain to another. Hurting people of all ages is an archaic, immoral, and useless strategy. The child has no frame of reference from which he can make any sense of it.

I am not saying that there are no criminals who must not be isolated for public safety, only that the concept of "punishment" is barbaric and useless at best. Unsafe people can be housed in isolation and treated for their obvious mental issues so they can heal if possible. The goal is not to hurt them or to get revenge; the goal is public safety and rehabilitation. Famed psychiatrist Dr. Alice Miller demonstrates in her book *For Your Own Good: Hidden Cruelty in Child Rearing and the Roots of Violence* that most criminals come from abusive homes and have lost their ability to feel and to care about others.

A parent is a leader, not a police officer. Discipline is something one can do only for oneself in the context of feeling autonomous. Self-discipline develops with time and with emotional freedom and safe human connections.

"A time-out isn't really punishment, right?"

Imposing isolation is inflicting pain. It is punishment under a different name, just like spanking is hitting under a delusional different name. Both are concepts conjured by the human mind to give oneself permission to do harm. The child only experiences the pain and is hurt and harmed by it.

Some thoughts to inquire in this regard are the following (and there are many more):

It doesn't hurt for a child to sit in isolation against his will.

It is natural and helps the child to think about what he did.

He won't learn any other way.

It's effective in making the child understand his wrong behavior.

None of the above are true, and their opposite shows their harm. If you still believe these or other similar thoughts, write them down and question them with the four questions and turnaround as you have read in the many examples in this book. If it doesn't wake you up, book a session with a friend or a professional who can facilitate your inquiry. There is nothing healthy or natural about being able to apply pain to your child, and it only does harm. Fear-based "good" behavior is not a caring or responsible behavior.

If you want your child to want to act with care and inner peace of her own free will, hurting her is not the way.

It is well-known and demonstrated in many studies published in journals indexed in the National Library of Medicine (PubMed) that emotional and physical hurts in childhood have negative outcomes. In the long term, the children who are punished most often, or repeatedly put in time-out, are often the ones who end up behaving the worst. Many—though certainly not all—are the bullies in school and on the playground and, as adults, lawbreakers or drug and alcohol addicts. Others, however, are so oppressed by fear that they always behave timidly and are more likely to behave very well while silently suffering inside. They may end up with more anxiety and depression or other fear-based and insecurity issues. There are also humans who, despite being hurt by parents, sense the love due to their own nature, through observing other people in their lives, and from having an unusual ability to not lose sight of a sense of rightness and love. Such people often seek therapy as teens and adults and work on recovery and are able to heal and to forgive their parents.

What Happens During Time-Out?

The isolated child feels upset that you rejected and isolated him, resentful of you, misunderstood, confused, and unable to connect the dots. His conclusion can be something like "I am a failure; I am bad." He feels unheard, thwarted, angry, or desperate that he isn't getting your approval or care for some real need because, often, the punishing parent isn't aware of the valid need behind the child's behavior, or they would have handled the need and not punished the child for the expression.

For children, no isolation makes sense. Taking connection and love away as a tool to hurt a child only teaches cruelty. Some people say that hitting is less painful than isolation. I don't recommend inflicting pain on your child in any way, shape, or form at any age. Threats, yelling, deprivation, and consequences are intended to hurt. Connection, communication, and finding solutions together are the way of love. I elaborate on how to do so in my first book, *Raising Our Children, Raising Ourselves.*

A Note About "Natural" Consequences

Even so-to-speak "natural" consequences are systems of control, manipulation, and ways to punish and hurt under a nicer-looking name. This is because if consequences are real, they occur on their own. If the toys are all over the place, not going to the playground as planned is not "natural" but imposed. The natural consequence of toys all over the floor is toys all over the floor. It may also mean not finding things, no place to walk in the room, and so on. There are no other consequences. Even having to clear the toys is not a consequence; it is just what is useful to do to have a better play area.

For toddlers, these ideas are hardly relevant. They learn about order from you, not from your sermons, but from your kind actions. A toddler couldn't care less about order until he notices you putting things away and making the world "pretty" and user-friendly. They are usually happy to join you in your efforts, and it is best to *accept the help but never demand it.* Keep the natural goodwill alive by not correcting or judging, and make sure you model joy in any action you take. In organizing the toys, you model not only the benefits of order but also kindness, generosity, and doing things for others.

Wendy was exasperated by her daughter's mess. "I can't get through to her. Roana won't cooperate and won't put anything away." The following is Wendy's inquiry:

Wendy: *"My child will learn order and cleanliness (or whatever else) by being made to clean and organize."*

Naomi: Is that true?

Wendy: Yes.

Naomi: Can you absolutely know that it's true?

Wendy: No. I cannot know that for sure.

Naomi: How do you react when you believe this thought?

Wendy: I become stressed and controlling, and I struggle with Roana.

Naomi: How would you be without this thought?

Wendy: I would be fine. Perhaps less stressed about Roana's learning to organize. So I will do it myself, which is actually less work, without feeling a need to push her.

Naomi: That's a relief. Let's see what else we learn from you; turn the thought around.

Wendy: *"The child will not learn to clean by doing it against her will."*

Naomi: Can you prove how this is more true?

Wendy: I guess the experience of hating to do something while doing it is more likely to cause the child to avoid doing it in the future.

Naomi: Indeed, makes sense. Now, turn it around to yourself.

Wendy: *"I will learn cleanliness when I clean. And Roana will learn to clean with joy when she observes me cleaning and organizing generously and happily."*

Naomi: Isn't that fascinating? And in my experience, toddlers often want to do the chores. If we don't force it later, this trend may stay, or return naturally at a later time.

CONCLUSION

There are no difficult toddlers and no terrible twos. There are only innocently confused parents who struggle against the reality of who a toddler and a young child is. Inquiry into the thoughts that hijack your love away is a wonderful tool to bring you back to seeing your toddler with clarity. You can then respond to what is possible and not to an expectation that is not available.

We must set things up to enable the child's success in her behavior and relating skills. Take a toddler to a location or social setting he can handle without undue stress. Give her a playmate who is old enough to care for her rather than fight with her. Use the manners you wish to teach, and care for your child based on her ability rather than on your expectations. Trust your senses and trust your child while always asking yourself: "What is my child needing? And what is the most loving way to respond or guide her if needed at all?" Be a loving listener, and in tough moments, open the door with the magic words, "Tell me more."

Chapter 11

Your Child's Development

Every stage in a child's life exists for a purpose. If we can respect and respond to her needs fully during each stage of her life, she can complete that stage and move on of her own free will and with joy.

As we saw earlier in the book, the physical unfolding of the baby cannot be pushed. In this chapter, we will look at other physical and emotional developmental aspects of a baby and young child. The question is how to allow, enable, and nurture the unfolding of a new human being, without getting in the way of her autonomy and self-actualization.

How Seeking Your Approval Hinders Your Baby and Child's Development

When a baby or child is permitted to move naturally through the stages of development, she benefits from each phase fully and does not yearn to go back, because she is not left with a sense of not enough or of feeling dependent on authority to tell her what to do. If she returns to a previous way of being, she needs it in her progress and it is part of her development. A child can move easily away from each stage after she has completed it fully (including some back-and-forth stages); therefore, her timing is perfect. You can sense it and dance with it such that there is no pressure or stress.

From breastfeeding to using the toilet and sleep time, babies and toddlers do best when they are protected and respected to follow their inner guidance. When this occurs, their development typically goes peacefully and smoothly. In contrast, if we try to push the child out of one stage of development into the next, she is unable to complete that stage and yearns for more; the authentic inner process is disrupted and slowed by her resistance or compliance.

Even if the child looks happy to be doing what we expect, her joy is about pleasing us and not about her own self-generated accomplishment. The sense of incompletion turns into resistance, defiance, or a dependency on someone else's authority; she loses confidence in herself because she is learning not to trust her own inner guidance but follow others, even when it feels wrong. Later we are dismayed when the child dismisses her own sense and follows peers or puts up with abusive treatment.

Living up to others' expectations often becomes a pattern that can get in the way of emotional independence.

The child may appear to be advancing, but she is merely acting to please you and is actually pulled away from her authentic process.

Her apparent accomplishment is external and has a high cost to her long-term development, happiness, and self-confidence. By trying to please you and meet expectations, she is learning to ignore her inner signals and seek external approval instead. There are no advantages to such externally driven accomplishments.

Seeking approval is one of the main aspects of insecurity. A child who is used to following authorities is more likely to follow peers and not stand up to abuse. It is the child who trusts herself who has the confidence to be aware of and resist peer pressure, and more likely to speak up in case of attempted or actual sexual or other abuse. Propelling a child to develop faster creates dependency on the adult.

To understand this phenomenon fully, look at your own experiences. Have you ever tried to learn a new skill (perhaps play a musical instrument or sport) and someone pushed you to learn faster and move up to the next level before you mastered the one before? How did you like it, and how well did you do? Did you justify it because you succeeded to overcome the damage and to learn well anyway? Did you then conclude that it was good to push children ahead of themselves? Did you lose your trust in your own knowing about your own pace? Did you become more dependent on what others say, calling it "support" even when it contradicted your inner wisdom?

Challenge is a healthy component of life when one chooses it for oneself. We can enable the opportunity for challenge, but the choice must be the child's. Therefore, when older kids and adults hire a coach or a teacher, they have chosen to also be challenged. This is very different from prompting a child to go against her inner guidance.

It doesn't matter how fast the baby moves on—unless there is an obvious physiological issue that requires intervention, but even then, guidance must be provided without pushing. As a parent, you can set up suitable opportunities for your child, and then what matters is that your little one becomes the author of her own path. When directed from within, in each and every moment, she is doing what is best for her and not distracted by external expectations or comparisons.

The baby or toddler is learning the most important lesson: "I know myself, and I trust myself to know how and when to take the next step." She learns not to be dependent on external approval and not to be seduced by the delusion of commercials or coercion; she learns the amazing power of self-trust and self-reliance. We expose the child to age-appropriate opportunities and then allow her to choose her direction freely.

One common example is talking. In an incredibly magical way, toddlers teach themselves to speak. It seems incomprehensible that they figure out how to move the inside of their mouth to form the sounds and connect them to things, actions, and eventually concepts. Yet, many parents expect speaking to occur at a certain age or even correct the toddler and try to teach her to speak.

A few less typical examples can help you trust your child. For instance, consider Albert Einstein, who didn't speak till almost three. When he finally spoke, it was a full, clear sentence. When his newborn baby sister was presented to him, he exclaimed, "Yes, but where are its wheels?" There are numerous such stories of toddlers speaking relatively late. One of my children also didn't speak till almost three and similarly started with a full sentence with clear and accurate pronunciation.

Through my child I can more easily understand the process of learning to speak in a child who starts late. At an earlier age, this child would try a single word only once or twice total. He could tell that the pronunciation was not accurate. He didn't speak again. He communicated with hands, eyes, and body. He responded to us, and it was clear that he understood us, in two languages. A couple of months before his third birthday, out of the blue, he said to his daddy, "Let's get in the van and go to the beach." He simply didn't try words on gradually; he figured it out in the brain, and when he was sure that he could speak correctly, he burst out speaking two languages with no baby talk—that is, as clear as a bell.

Likewise, parents might get concerned about lisping and wrong pronunciations and sometimes hire speech therapists at young ages. Yet, if allowed to unfold over the years, most children self-correct. In the process, they learn to be aware of themselves and to figure out and solve problems. In a couple of cases where clients of mine had children who still lisped at ten or eleven, drawing their attention to it just once solved the issue. Both were boys. One figured it out by himself; the other asked to show him where the tongue should be, and one time did the job.

Development is built in. Respond to it to nurture the child's expressed direction. Offer opportunities and expose her to what is available and possible, and your child will choose and thrive.

Of course, there are other speech issues that are caused by fear. For example, stuttering is related to severe anxiety in the parent-child relationship and should be treated by working with a therapist. The parents should also take sessions themselves to change their parenting ways. Treat your child with the kind of skill you are learning in this book, and your child will thrive and speak well on her own timetable.

Offer Opportunities, Not Overstimulation

Especially with the firstborn, parents are often tempted to constantly engage and offer fun stimulations. Obviously, some of it is very healthy and helps with the child's brain development. Wooden toys, books, blocks, drums, simple musical instruments, and later on art, crayons, and balls are part of the modern child's life that can enhance intellectual development. Some tricky toys make the toddler curious to figure it out. The best is to give toys the child can manipulate on her own, even if not in the intended way.

However, toys that have push buttons and passive entertainment are more likely to make the child passive and dependent on being entertained. Provide items the child can make something with, or explore in her own way, and your child's brain development will be stimulated and actively engaged. Entertaining toys may produce temporary joy and excitement but aren't the best long-term. Therefore, television, tablets, computers, and even some overstimulating toys and experiences may elicit an immediate "I want it" response, but the toddler can easily get addicted to these unhealthy experiences and become dependent on overstimulation of his senses.

The same is true for food. While eating is a natural and nurturing experience, giving sweets or strongly flavored foods to little kids isn't helpful. While giving a toddler a sugary treat may elicit a temporary positive response, this is not an indication that it is good for her. Wanting sugary treats is not a primal need but a trained addiction. Of course, at older ages, children eventually encounter human-made sweet treats and passive entertainment, but if habituated healthfully at home, they often are motivated to avoid those and accept parental guidance on balance, health, and creativity. In my experience with thousands of parents, babies and toddlers who are not constantly overstimulated mentally or physically are much more likely to become children who can sit quietly and daydream, play by themselves, or just be with no agenda and without seeking sweets or external passive entertainment.

At the end of my oldest's first dance class, at age four, the teacher offered ice cream bars to all the children. When I arrived to pick him up, the teacher came over to me and apologized for the fact that my son was the only one not holding an ice cream bar in his hand. She said, "I did offer it to him, but he asked if it had sugar, and when I said that it did, he said, 'No, thank you.'" I was actually astonished as we never spoke to my child about such a situation. Obviously, he heard us talking about avoiding sugar, and we had no sugar at home. I also saw one of my children sitting with other kids who were passing around a bag of cookies. My son passed it on but took none. (I wasn't there; another parent told me.)

Not all children respond to parental guidance in this way, so sometimes, we have to be flexible—balancing a relationship of trust with the exposure to unwanted toys or foods the child encounters away from home. Yes, I spoke to my children about the fact that we had no sugar at home because it is unhealthy, that we had no TV, and no push-button-type toys. Of course as they got older, they tried everything, but the young ages are formative of who they are and of their health. By the time they were exposed, they were already relying on their creative minds for excitement and choices. Their frame of reference for such choices was a healthy one.

Parents often feel desperate because their toddler demands constant attention and cannot be content without ongoing parental involvement. Obviously, toddlers need a lot of care and presence. Be with your toddler, and offer affection, care, holding, reading, and play. And also provide time of just being there without offering anything to do. Let your toddler experience the joy of doing nothing or of engaging herself without your help while you watch or while you do your own activity. This way she can develop self-reliance and the ability to daydream, imagine, listen to sounds, and watch, as well as generate her own play and exploration. Therefore, when I speak of trusting the actual need and cues from the baby or toddler, I mean as long as we are not introducing addictive unhealthy substances or items.

Respond, Don't Direct

There is nothing we can do to alter the baby's development other than not get in the way and support the toddler's practice and exploration by making it safe and available. It all happens on its own, and any attempt to teach or push only gets in the way. Therefore, the way to respond to a child's developmental stages is moment by moment. Notice what's coming and remove the obstacles to make it safe; get out of the way while holding safe space.

The following are a few examples of questions parents grapple with, such as diapering a baby, swimming, biking, and walking barefoot. In all, the principle is the same; trust the child and respond to the cues and not to your mind's complex analysis and desire to control. Parenting is letting go of control while staying in charge.

"How can I keep my baby from squirming on the changing table?"

Obviously, if using a changing table and diapers for your toddler is joyful and the toddler is comfortable, there is no need for change. But if this setup is not in harmony with the little one's sense of herself and you struggle against her will, you may wish to reconsider.

Let's go back to the basics by inquiring into the unconscious assumptions: We are assuming that babies must have diapers and that changing that diaper must be convenient for the parent and must occur on a special table for that purpose.

- When believing these thoughts, you disconnect with reality and with your baby, and instead of trying to understand and meet her need, you create stress for you and for her.
- Without this thought, a better location and way to make it pleasant for the baby can show up easily.
- Turn it around to: *My baby should not stay on the changing table.*

Now you are engaged in finding what would make it easier on your baby.

Why should the baby stay on the changing table? She hates being trapped on her back while her body is handled. Understanding the baby is step one to finding kinder solutions.

Once you understand your baby's bodily autonomy need, your mind will shift the question: Instead of asking, "How can I keep her on the changing table (for my convenience)?" you may alter the question to "How do I change my baby's diaper without disturbing her comfort?"

What does the baby need?

Most likely, to stay naked.

Why do we put her in a diaper?

Actually, if the truth be told, for our own convenience, which is fine, but this is good to know in terms of understanding the experience of the baby/toddler.

How about changing the diaper on a bed or on the floor (on a blanket)? Or on your body, or when they walk, even standing, at least when the diaper isn't soiled. Have you considered elimination communication? Are you using cloth all-in-one diapers? These are much easier to put on a moving baby, better for her skin, and likely feel more comfortable for her as well.

As much as possible, let your baby be naked. In my experience with thousands of parents, it seems typical that babies prefer to be naked, and it is best for them both physically and emotionally. It also prevents diaper rash and discomfort.

The baby is not motivated to be trapped on her back in a high place to enable you to do something she doesn't even want. She has no idea why on Earth you are doing this to her. Once you realize that you are the one imposing on the baby for your own convenience, you will find it easier to accommodate her needs. I used to change diapers while the baby was on his tummy with a toy, on a blanket on the floor, on the bed, and so on.

If you use elimination communication (the no-diaper, native way), your baby is likely to use the potty by age one or sometimes earlier. I am not saying you should do this with the goal of rushing the toilet habits; I'm just mentioning it as a different option and solution to the diapering difficulties.

I recommend cloth diapers that are all-in-one if you can afford it or receive hand-me-downs. Long term, this is *much* cheaper than disposable diapers. It is also better for the baby and for the environment, and the baby will be out of diapers much sooner, around one year or one year and a half. I used all-in-one cloth diapers. They were much easier to put on. I even found an easy way to put the diaper on when the toddler was standing and even while he was on the move. I put it on backward with the Velcro or snaps on the back and kept walking with the toddler. I even managed to change wet (unsoiled) diapers while wearing the baby in a carrier.

Elimination communication is another option; it became known in the West after my children were grown. But looking back, in many ways, I did the communication part. Combined with cotton diapers—which let the baby feel the wetness and discomfort—my children got out of diapers on their own around age one to one-and-a-half years, and at night around two-and-a-half to three years.

Babies learn whatever they experience. With disposable diapers and lack of communication, they simply learn to go dressed. They have no reason to do otherwise. Disposable diapers absorb so well that the baby gets no feedback. The baby has no reason to want anything different. She assumes that's how we do it—in the pants. These children often are in diapers for much longer.

Caring for a Baby Without Diapers

Some mothers today opt to mostly avoid diapers altogether. In many tribal and older societies, babies have been raised without diapers. By carrying the baby on their body and being tuned in, the mother knows when the baby needs to go. The mother then takes the baby to a sink when indoors, or by a tree outdoors, and enables her to eliminate. The baby learns easily what elimination is.

This gets tricky when the baby starts to crawl and walk and is not on a parent's body some of the time. The parent cannot always recognize the need in time, and parents report wet floors and couches. Some use cloth diapers part-time as needed but still communicate and often take the baby to eliminate.

Parents report that a combination of communication and part-time cloth, all-in-one diapers (in car, in public, and so on) is most

> peaceful and easy and, by a year or a year and a half or so, the toddler mostly uses the potty.
>
> The communication part is simply speaking about the elimination as it occurs—"You are peeing" and "You are pooping"—and, if it occurs in a diaper, still saying the words and changing the diaper right away.

"My child asks me to dress her even though she can do it herself."

In the early years, we do just about everything for the children. We change their diaper, breastfeed them, serve them food, hold them, dress them, rock them, take them around, and on and on. These are services of basic needs. These do not take away the child's opportunity to do things by himself and develop confidence. There is no rush to have him do it by himself.

As the child becomes able to do things for himself, we forget the joy of giving and lose trust in the cues of the little one.

Nicole was impatient with her four-year-old daughter for asking her to dress her. She was almost four and was able to dress herself. At her session, Nicole said to me, "I know she can get dressed; why is she asking me to do it?" I asked her how she responded, to which she said, "I told her she can dress herself and that she is good at it. She had a tantrum."

I suggested to Nicole to write down her thought and do an inquiry:

Nicole: *"If my child can dress herself, she shouldn't ask me to dress her."*

Naomi: Is that true? What is she saying?

Nicole: It's not true. She is asking me to dress her.

Naomi: How do you react when you believe this thought?

Nicole: I refuse to dress her, and when she insists, I get angry. She ends up upset. I force her to dress herself, and then she pinches me.

Naomi: How would you react without this thought?

Nicole: I would dress her. But I would feel resentful.

Naomi: That is *with* the thought. How would you react *without* believing this thought?

Nicole: I see. Yes. Without the thought, I would be just fine dressing her. Oh, that's so much more fun, easier, and faster, and she would be so happy.

Naomi: Turn the thought around.

Nicole: *"If my child can dress herself, she can ask me to dress her when she wants to."*

Naomi: Is that as true or truer?

Nicole: Oh, yes. And much kinder. But why is she doing that?

Naomi: Look and see if you can find three valid reasons why she would want you to dress her.

Nicole: She enjoys being cared for in this manner. She misses being my baby as she has a little brother. And it goes faster and easier.

Naomi: Welcome to your own wisdom about your daughter. Turn it around to yourself and find an example.

Nicole: *"If I am capable of doing something . . ."* Oh I see. I, too, like things done for me that I can do for myself. There are plenty of examples: I love when my husband makes me breakfast or does other special things for me that I can do too.

Naomi: With that clarity, you follow the instruction with ease. We are not talking here about giving a child whatever she wants and creating a wanting addiction. It's about responding to a real need for connection. Your child is still needing the touchy care. Lucky you! You get a little more of it! It won't last, and you will miss it.

When it comes to basic physical and emotional needs, you can calmly follow the manual that is your child and her valid and credible communication. Basic needs are the need for connection, love, touch, food, listening, and so on.

Should I Teach My Baby to Swim?

Babies don't have a drive to swim. Just because it is possible for a baby to swim does not mean it is a good idea. There are many mesmerizing tricks babies and young children can be trained to do while going against their will—often while they cry.

However, there are kind ways to keep babies safe and engage them in age-fitting activities that they yearn for. Life is full of dangers. We keep babies off the road, away from fire, bodies of water, extreme cold and heat, and electricity—their safety is in our hands. They don't need to be able to protect themselves; they rely on their parents for protection. Therefore, they don't need to know how to swim or even float.

For safety:

- Don't *ever* take your hands and eyes off a little one next to or in water, no matter how shallow.
- Always have a floatation vest or other device secure on the

child, and always have your eyes on him at all times and stay right by him. *Always*. Even once they do know how to float or how to swim a bit, water is not the place for the toddler's "freedom" but for rigid rules of survival.

We raised our children close to a lake where we often spent time. The young ones always had to wear life vests. No life vest, no being near or in the water, not even wading, unless constantly in our arms on the edge of the water.

Due to how dangerous drowning is, the drive to teach babies to swim is well intended, but since the process causes emotional harm, we must secure their safety in the above ways. No baby or child should be pushed—or even gently manipulated—into anything against their will while disregarding their cries or other nuanced signals of non-consent. In addition to trauma, they learn to disregard their own inclinations. The outcome, as they grow older, can be easily falling for power, molestation, peer pressure, media whatever someone stronger tells them to do—as they are trained to not trust and to ignore their own inner voice.

Let's go back to the principles I propose in this book, your baby's manual: Did she cue a desire to learn to swim? She may love to be in the water with you holding or guarding her safety. But she is not driven to learn to float on her own.

Your baby shows you when she wants to sit, turn, stand, and walk. The idea of swimming is not in the calling of a baby. Do you like seeing the baby body motion of terror and the sound of screaming in the YouTube videos that demonstrate teaching babies to swim? I don't think so.

What is the rush? If you live on a boat, put a life vest on your baby and on children at all times and stay with them. In all other circumstances, let the desire to swim come from the child. I have never seen a baby practicing swimming of her own volition, even when put in (safe) water. She practices standing, crawling, and walking. That is your model. The torment isn't worth the possible eventual enjoyment, and learning to swim later is safer and better in every way. Safety is yours to provide.

To be clear: Babies who can swim have been severely manipulated *against* their will or choice, which causes more harm than good. We must be careful not to please ourselves by showing off a baby's tricks. This is true at all ages. Parents' egos get in the way in this and many other ways.

Safety means your child is always with you when near a body of water (with a life vest), on the street, and in all other unsafe circumstances. Your baby counts on you for safety. She does not need rough training in survival at an age when she is not meant to be on her own.

Feet Are Made for Walking the Earth

When he was a child, my son, Yonatan, said, "Why do people wear crutches on their feet? Feet are made for walking." We should all ask ourselves this question and wonder about the likely harm of preventing children from walking on the earth with their bare feet. Shoes deform the feet and have a negative impact on the whole skeleton.

I raised my children barefoot and, when needed, they wore soft leather or fabric "shoes." Our oldest son refused to wear shoes until he was tall enough that it was required in public places. He won every running race in the wild forest; his friends wore running shoes while he ran barefoot through the rough, uneven, thorny, and stony wilderness.

Feet are made for walking and running the earth. Hunters and gatherers ran barefoot or wore thin leather footwear. They developed strong arches and a great posture. The amazing foot is designed not only to carry the human body on the earth but also to align the whole human spine and skeleton.

Shoes are crutches that distort nature's design. They are the cause, not the cure, for many of our structural-related pain and difficulties. Besides not using the feet enough (that is, sitting too much), when we rely on artificial arch and heel support, an elevated heel, and narrow front, our feet become weak and distorted.

Babies are born flat-footed. A heathy arch develops as a result of walking barefoot, which activates all the needed muscles. You can learn more in *Nature's Scientific Report*'s article titled, "Growing-Up (Habitually) Barefoot Influences the Development of Foot and Arch Morphology in Children and Adolescents," www.nature.com/articles/s41598-017-07868-4.

Regular shoes do harm to the whole skeleton in the following ways: The toes are often compressed and slightly lifted, creating misalignment. Their intent is to prevent us from stumbling into things. When barefoot, we acquire attentiveness and use our own muscles to elevate the toes as needed.

- Arch and ankle support prevent the muscles from developing strength and healthy springing shape.

- Shoes create a dependency on artificial support of the foot rather than developing strong muscles.
- Even slightly elevated heels create an unnatural arch in the lower back and misalignment of the whole skeleton, leading to eventual back pain and injuries.
- Narrow shoe fronts create a distortion of the foot, making it impossible to support the body correctly, which, when extreme, can cause pain and lead to bunions and require surgery.

Babies, toddlers, and young children do best walking and running barefoot in natural and safe places (not a city street).

Internationally renowned child development author Rae Pica states, "There is evidence indicating that going barefoot strengthens feet and improves body alignment. Young children feel a natural affinity for the ground that can be enhanced by removing all the barriers between it and the feet."[1] Moreover, Pam Moor's 2019 article provides substantial information and proof of the importance of raising barefoot children to the feet, body, and even brain development.[2]

Before walking, the baby needs nothing other than socks for warmth in cold weather. Even the notion of cold is often overemphasized. Babies' bodies create heat, and overdressing them could not only create unsafe overheating but also makes them into people who become cold easily. How to know? Listen to your baby; when not yet giving clear signals, check her hands and feet and, with time, the signals will be clear.

The body needs to practice its ability to create heat. The same is true for feet. We put little cute "shoes" on babies for our own entertainment. Unless you are outside or your home is especially cold, the baby has no need for them. Even if you cover the feet for warmth, socks are best. The baby will learn to stand and walk most optimally when barefoot and able to use the designated foot muscles to create balance and the grip (no socks) to hold on to the ground or floor.

With a toddler who walks and runs, in nature and at home, barefoot is best. On pavement or other public places that are not clean, it may be best to put on soft, socklike leather or fabric shoes or sandals. Search for "barefoot"-style companies and family-owned producers of soft shoes, such as Soft Star, Xero, and others.

No Training Wheels and No Helping

We can allow children to climb to the tops of mountains they choose to climb. We should make the conditions possible for their persistent, safe efforts. Creating an illusion of success can only harm the child. For example, walkers, training wheels, and other such crutches deprive the child of the real experience and of learning to master her body and the forces of nature. She needs real feedback from real life. Failing is an excellent lesson, and crying about it can be a healthy response—something to connect with, not avoid.

Obviously, we provide the child with activities they seem ready to learn and not premature and discouraging ones. As mentioned earlier, pushing your child to the next stage of development is futile and harmful; it creates struggle, resistance, and difficulties, even when not visible at the time. The child learns to be dependent and to feel like a failure and even shamed. One of the most harmful results is that the child learns to resist effort because of the experience of needing to impress or please parents by doing something she cannot do or is not interested in.

Even providing toys that are too challenging, rather than allowing the child to generate her own agenda, can be overwhelming. If you try an activity that frustrates your child rather than engaging him, heed the feedback. It's a matter of balance and being in tune with your child.

Earlier, I discussed that teaching a baby to swim isn't the baby's achievement but the parents'. The baby isn't aware, is not inventing a method, or is even interested in having this ability. The same is true not only for swimming or academics but also for all physical-skill development. Whether a walker or training wheels on a scooter or a bike, or even helping the toddler to climb where she couldn't, the child is made to do something she did not arrive at on her own in a natural way. The assumed "help" is depriving the child of consciously inventing, creating, and mastering the skill she chooses to learn—on her own.

Falling off the bike scares parents, but the child decides to learn when he is ready to take the risk. Yes, you can hold the back of the bike if the child wants it, but, honestly, when left to ride on his own timing and interest, the child will learn with no or very little help at an older age, which will help her develop confidence and self-reliance.

Only adults are in a rush.
Your child, like all children, follows the instruction manual—the blueprint she was born with.

CONCLUSION

The beauty of guiding a baby to develop as a human is that it is not about you performing magic—it's not your creation. You are, instead, in the privileged position of guarding and nurturing a world in creation and a soul unfolding. It is a spiritual path that requires surrender. Whatever your baby or toddler is ready to do is in the right time. It's not your will that prevails; the forces of nature run this magic show. Question your assumptions about diapers, shoes, and what your baby should accomplish. A silent mind, free of such thoughts, can easily support the child's steps toward body mastery, without getting in the way of his sense of being the author of his experience.

Chapter 12

Growing the Mind

Like physical development, the mind does best when it runs freely from within. To a large extent, optimal self-actualization depends less on IQ and more on the emotional freedom to use one's mind and talents. Just as physical development thrives when children are given opportunities without unsolicited intervention, so too does the growing intellect. With mind development, the temptation for the parent is even stronger but just as futile or more so. For example, we believe we are building self-esteem or confidence with praise while actually eroding it. Likewise, we live in a competitive society, and it is tempting to enter the parenting Olympics through the child by pushing the toddler to master all kinds of mental skills just to impress or get into the most prestigious kindergarten. In this chapter, we will look at a few examples and how to be a nurturer while getting out of the way to protect the child's self-generated learning and growing.

Self-Esteem Versus Being Rooted in the Self

Self-esteem is overrated and has created many self-centered people. Humility with self-awareness and confidence is by far a better outcome of growing up well. Instead of talking about self-esteem, I suggest striving toward raising a child to be confident, humble, and rooted in the self. As discussed earlier, rooted in the self means not seeking external approval and being free to pursue one's own (safe for all) passions. It means that the child is connected to her own inner voice about herself rather than dependent on what others think of her.

In previous chapters, you learned how to protect the child's ability to listen to her inner voice regarding her autonomous body and mind—for example, where to sleep, who she feels safe with, and similar choices. If we balance safety, guidance, and respect, the toddler stays able to make choices about herself and sort her emotions from within and not from a need to impress or please or due to a fear of displeasing.

Being rooted inside is not identical to being focused on the self. It is simply sourcing oneself independently and includes doing so with consideration of the needs of others and learning from others as a free choice. Focus on self creates greed and a state of always wanting more. Focus on other humans and living things is by far more magical. The greatest joy comes from giving and focusing on others. It is anxiety about living up to expectations and looking good that forces the child (and an adult) into self-focus and anxiety. Being rooted in oneself enables the freedom to care for both oneself and others, making authentic choices that reflect that care.

Babies and children are the greatest gift of joy to us because they force us to focus outside ourselves on another human being. In a way, it is a great relief from the endless race for self-satisfaction, while providing the real satisfaction that comes with the focus on another life unfolding.

Modern society worships the ego, and the common narrative is to focus on how to get more for oneself, do more, and be "successful." "How to get what you want," "The law of attraction," "How to get rich," and "How to win . . . "—all these invite self-focus. Most people end up climbing this type of "mountain" on and on without satisfaction, precisely because of yearning for self-gratification. In contrast, true success is the joy of being alive and contributing to others. And the joy of being alive fails to manifest from pampering the ego. There's nothing wrong with achieving success, but you want your child to pursue what brings her joy and a love for this human journey. The ego is not life-loving, as it is narcissistic in nature and never satisfied, precisely because of being focused on self, self-esteem, feeling good, and gratification.

Therefore, raising a human being who will be truly satisfied is not about fostering self-worth or emphasizing being special, unique, or talented but about nurturing someone who has a passion for living, giving, receiving, and contributing whatever she is passionate about in each unfolding moment.

"Should I teach my toddler to read and other academic skills?"

The answer may be obvious in the context of this book, yet to really see how futile this idea is, consider the following myths:

- Having academic skills at a younger age is advantageous.
- The child who is academically ahead will succeed better.
- The child who is ahead of the game will be happier.
- A toddler's choice is to advance herself academically.
- Life is a competition.
- I will look better as a parent if my child is academically ahead.
- There is no harm in getting toddlers and young children to learn things they don't seem to pursue on their own.
- While being taught to read, the child is losing nothing.
- My friends all teach their toddlers; I should do the same.
- My relatives tell me to teach reading and math to my toddler.
- My child should go to the best kindergarten (based on the myths above).

As you read in the section on teaching babies to swim, these aspirations have nothing to do with what is best for the child but are all about the adult's ego and self-image. And keep in mind that we are committed to the child flourishing in all areas, which occurs in freedom. This does not mean being passive as parents but rather being active in ways that support and enable the child's natural unfolding without exerting control.

If you are strongly convinced of the idea of early teaching, I recommend that you put down your thoughts on paper and question each one of them separately. Find what is true when you are free of these thoughts. Thoughts are not yours and cannot be true when they contradict peace and the cue from the child. The thoughts in your head are not your own; they are inherited from external sources, as is the case for everyone.

When Camilla raised her hand in a workshop, she was grappling with the temptation to teach her three-year-old reading, math, and other academics. She believed that would ensure his future success and prosperity and therefore happiness. She wrote her thoughts down and came to the stage to do the inquiry.

Camilla: *"If my child can read and study as a toddler, it would ensure his success and happiness."*

Naomi: Is that true?

Camilla: Yes. It seems like academic preparation is a great advantage.

Naomi: And can you absolutely know that it is advantageous long-term for your child?

Camilla: No. I am betting.

Naomi: How do you react when you believe this thought?

Camilla: I feel stressed about having to get a toddler to do academics, which he isn't really into. But I also feel excited for the prospect of him being skillful at such a young age. It can be magical.

Naomi: Who would you be with your child without this thought?

Camilla: Well, I didn't expect this. But when you ask, I feel a prompt relief, imagining Roy just playing to his heart's desire and not worrying about organizing his learning time. It's a big project, and he would rather play his own way.

Naomi: Turn the thought around.

Camilla: *"If my toddler reads and knows math starting now, he won't be successful and happy."*

Naomi: Can that be as true or even truer?

Camilla: I never thought of it this way. Hmm. In truth I cannot know that.

Naomi: Good to know. Do you see another turnaround?

Camilla: *"If my toddler reads and knows math at a young age, I would be successful and happy?"*

Naomi: Well, look and see if that is a useful truth.

Camilla: I can see that. It is magical for me but perhaps not for him. He feels magical when he builds a tower or goes down a slide at the playground.

Naomi: Indeed. And can you see another way to turn it around fully on yourself?

Camilla: *"If I can read and do math and academics, I will be successful and happy."* Wow. Wait. (Camilla closed her eyes and then opened them.) Actually, I could see that it may be good for me but not for him. But even better, I actually see that it would not make me happier to excel in something I am not passionate about.

Naomi: Isn't that fascinating? Anything else that you can notice?

Camilla: It's clear now. I am making him my project. But Roy is clearly his own person. I can imagine that this could even do him harm, and I cannot know that having these skills in early age makes any positive difference.

In my experience with thousands of families and their children, it has zero benefits to true happiness in life and is more likely to do emotional harm and even turn the child off to learning. By the time they are adults, they all read and have their academics down or they may have other interests and skills. The freedom to play as children, however, can impact their stamina, passion, ability to thrive, and emotional well-being.

Early academic skills do not have an advantage. Whether you learned to walk at nine months, a year, or two years, it makes no difference. Normally, we all eventually walk. The same is true for reading. Many unschooled children learn on their own time. Those who learn to read at age thirteen read as well as those who learned at age four. After a short while, there is no difference in reading level. For children with special learning difficulties in reading, the later the better because mental maturation makes things easier to figure out, and without emotional scars.

Academic focus, and specifically learning to read, does take time away from what the child needs to do: free play, movement, art, imagination, and creativity. Being taken away from play to sit and learn does harm both to learning and to the child's physical well-being, emotional development, free thinking ability, and self-reliance. His brain is designed to know what he should be doing to enable optimal development, which is to play and create freely.

Advanced academic skills do not lead to true success or happiness, because those depend on being self-reliant and on learning to pursue one's own interest on one's own time and by one's own initiative.

Running your child through learning programs may lead to winning spelling competitions and learning to play the school "game" well. But that is not good news. That means being caught in the competitive, ego-based, anxiety-provoking agenda of competition and achievements. It comes with apprehension, loss of connection to the self, an addiction to pleasing others, impressing, fitting in, and other dependencies.

In her book *Prisoners of Childhood: The Drama of the Gifted Child and the Search for the True Self,* psychiatrist Alice Miller explains how the pressure to be the best at school or other achievements weighs heavily on the mental health of youth. It's a rat race they didn't choose and therefore don't even realize they are in. They may become high-achieving students but often develop anxiety and depression due to the pressure to excel and please parents and teachers, and a detachment from their own inner voice.

No toddler cares about being ahead in the (adult's) academic game. Toddlers and young children want to play and explore freely. Watch your toddler when he is free to know what he should be doing and learning. Our current social culture is often competitive and therefore stressful. Raise your child to be rooted in herself and connected to reality from within and not from needing to impress anyone. In the long run, she will become competitive to the degree that fits her inner calling, not yours. She will follow her own passions in her own time.

Learning academics can actually distract the young one from being in touch with her true interests. She may actually not know what she is drawn to. Many children, after years of schooling, say they don't have a real subject of interest. The child ends up a successful adult in a profession that isn't really her heart's calling, feeling unfulfilled.

Looking good as a parent is not a goal worth pursuing at the expense of what is best for the child. Your child is not your possession or a trophy to show who you are. We fall for the parenting Olympics when we ourselves are insecure. And, like most, we forget that all our and our children's amazing qualities and talents are not of our making or theirs. We have been given bodies that run on their own as long as we follow the instructions for sustenance and other needs. Same with the mental and artistic traits; it's a miraculous gift. Johann Sebastian Bach wrote at the end of each of his compositions, "To the Glory of God." Bach was simply acknowledging that his ability to write this incredible music is a gift; he couldn't have created the brain and soul that put it down on paper.

Life springs to being through our bodies (which we didn't make); we are not the creators.

Yes, if you make your child shine by jumping through hoops, you will get a lot of approval from those who do not understand what I've just shared. And what do you really gain from that approval if it comes at the expense of your child's best interest? Those who do understand will feel sorry for the child and for you. That is good news, as you have nothing to lose, not even a delusional approval. The amazing thing is that striving for excellence is enabled when we don't push it and is then authentic and free for each child. Some children grow up to excel in laid-back living while others thrive by striving for ambitious goals—reaching to the moon, so to speak. Watch, provide, and marvel.

Taking a child away from her path—whatever she is doing of her own volition (with no adult intervention)—is a waste of her time. The child's play, creativity, or imagination is always what is best for her development. You can teach a young child geography for an hour and math for another hour, and she has just lost two hours of optimal play that her brain needs. Children learn through free play not organized by adults. I know people whose profession took them away from their true passions due to adult intervention. In addition, when a child follows her own inner direction, she strengthens self-reliance, self-motivation, initiative, and a powerful sense of ownership over herself.

Therefore, when she uses her time following her inner guidance (playing freely, inventing, creating, and exploring), the child learns the most and in the most effective and nurturing way. Her emotional capacity is strengthened as she feels capable of generating her own life moment by moment.

"Reading is so enriching. Why wouldn't I want my child to start young?"

A child who is not taught to read at any time will figure it out when all the needed brain development is ready. Try to stop him; you wouldn't be able to. And the child will not only learn the skill but also invent a way to learn and master it just like he learned to speak. Rather than merely acquiring the ability to repeat what is taught, the child becomes a creator and an inventor of her own methods, experiencing self-reliance.

Taking the child away from her self-directed play and creation is therefore harmful both emotionally and intellectually. It leaves a child more dependent, less creative, less confident, and more anxious. The skill itself will be learned in the best time—not yours, but the child's.

Obviously, what friends do and what relatives say is not relevant to what is optimal for your child. And getting into the kindergarten with the waiting list is obviously not a good goal, as you now understand from the above information. Let your child stay free to play and learn by finding the kind of school or play group that respects her path.

When you look deeply at the previous list of thoughts about a toddler's learning, you realize that it isn't about the child but about the adults' competitive interest. It is the job of the mind/ego to seduce us with such goals and fool us to think it is for the child's sake.

A child wants to play as nature designed.
She wants to engage with her full body and discover in her own way how reality, society, art, and culture work.
All attempts to teach prematurely take the child away from the best learning nature designed for the young: play!

When it comes to reading, if all the brain components aren't ready, the child stays away from it intuitively. She needs strong eyes and the ability to distinguish direction of small symbols and being able to attach a meaning that changes with the symbol and its direction. Many children for whom this eye-brain coordination isn't ready when they are coerced into learning to read end up with glasses, dyslexia, or just not feeling very capable. In his book *Miseducation: Preschoolers at Risk,* David Elkind demonstrates how premature teaching of reading creates learning disabilities, including dyslexia. Like Elkind, the renowned teacher and author John Holt (author of *How Children Learn* and *How Children Fail*) shows the harm of reading too early.

In contrast, when children teach themselves to read, the ability to read is not the main benefit; the greatest brain development comes from the child inventing a method of figuring it out. My three sons each invented a completely different method to learn to read and at different ages. This is true for most children who are allowed to generate their own learning, when parents read to them, tell stories, sit and read books themselves, sing songs while pointing to the words, and so on.

"What about a Pre-K that teaches academics?"

Whether at home or in a group setting, coercing wee ones into building adult academic skills—while they need freedom to play—has only negative consequences and no benefits. While at the start they obviously have skills that those who were not taught academics don't, within a few years the tables turn precisely because these children missed play time, which is what develops the child's brain and ability to learn optimally.

The Tennessee Pre-K study has proven this point. At the beginning, the academically educated Pre-K group performed better than the control group (children who did not attend such Pre-K school) on academics, but the control group soon caught up and, by third grade, the control group performed better on all academic measures than the Pre-K group. Moreover, by third grade, children who attended Pre-K were 74 percent more likely to have been diagnosed with a learning disorder than the control group, and 48 percent more likely to have committed a behavioral offense at school than those in the control group. By sixth grade, the academically pushed kids were found to have reduced performance on all academic achievement tests, a huge increase in learning disorders, and much more rule violation and behavioral offenses than in the control group.[1]

Darling-Hammond and Snyder produced similar results. The initial skills "advantage" (which has no benefit other than to parents' egos) did not last. Children who *play freely* scored higher on reading and math tests in fourth grade and had far fewer emotional and behavioral difficulties.[2] It is even more illuminating when we look at the results by adulthood. A study to age twenty-three makes it clear: In a 1997 study, David Weikart and colleagues found that by age twenty-three, the "Direct Instruction" group had double the felony arrest records compared to the group that played freely.[3]

None of this means that every child who is taught academics too early will be an offender or fail academically, but it shows clearly that there is at best zero advantage to instilling skills and knowledge prematurely, and more likely harm.

Following nature by listening to the toddler is the best way to ensure smooth intellectual and emotional development.

"My toddler is competitive."

This idea of their child being competitive takes most parents by surprise. They often say, "We are not competitive at all. We do things as a team." However, the sense of competition may be so habitual that we may be unaware of the subtle ways in which we and the world around us model competition.

Today's children seem to learn to compete at an early age. They hear us making comparisons, watch our own striving to be the best, and see us upset when we fail and praising those who are the best. They learn from stories that shine light on the dualistic concepts of good and bad and praise and criticism that are practically everywhere. Even the innocent "good job" or "good girl/boy" are just more of the concept of comparing and competing, of good and bad, and better and worse.

When competition occurs within the family, there is also a sibling issue; it compounds and focuses the competition on who gets more attention, who does what better or faster, and, if children are close in age, the big marathon to get more of Mommy and Daddy.

This sounds hopeless, but it isn't. Children will learn to compete in this world. You may say, "Society shouldn't be competitive," and I invite you to inquire with "Is that true?" and notice reality with love. It is part of human evolution that prompted a lot of innovation and excellence. However, you need not propel it at a young age, and, within the family, you can minimize such stress and live more communally.

We do want to make sure a child does not equate her value or lovability with things or achievement. For that purpose, avoid comparisons, praise, rewards, and division. Then make sure to express love and appreciation in moments of failure in both achievements and behavior.

For a child who, despite your effort, is very set on "I am taller," "I can do it better," "I have this and you don't," "Mine is better," and so on, and taking things away from others, you can help with your attitude. Take the wind out of this sail by showing how it has no impact on the child's value, life, wellness, or how much you love her. Say things such as:

- "I love you the same when you don't have that, when you cannot do this, when you have a smaller banana, and so on."
- "Whether you are first or not, your nose is still in the middle of your face, and I love you."
- "With or without this toy, you still have two legs (or ears, arms, eyes, red hair). I love you the same . . . you are the same you."

Indeed, one way we model competition is by giving uneven feedback as though the value of the toddler changes if she ran faster or made it through the maze. I actually recommend to "not care" about your child's achievements and make no fuss about her actions.

A child who knows that his worth has nothing to do with winning anything will more easily win real competitions that are part of life because he will be less invested in or anxious about it.

When one of my sons won a national music competition, he taught me the result of this attitude. On the flight to the third and final phase of the competition, I reminded him, "You know I do not care if you win, right?" His response was music to my ears. He said in an impatient tone, "Yes, Mom, I know, I know." At the hotel before going on the stage in front of the judges and audience, I asked him what his attitude would be when he walked onstage. His answer: "I go on to win, and then whatever happens is fine with me."

Raise your toddler to become a resilient person by placing less emphasis on winning, ensuring she knows your love is unconditional, and modeling enjoyment of the process, regardless of the outcome.

Work also on thoughts as they fit you personally, such as:

I need my child to be successful so I look good as a parent.

My child will benefit from seeing himself as better than others.

My child should know he is unique and special.

This last one was hard on Marina. She asked, "But isn't it helpful for the child to feel that she is special?" I suggested that she inquire into this idea.

Marina: *"My child should feel unique and special."*

Naomi: Is it true and beneficial for your child to believe that she is special somehow?

Marina: Yes. It is good for her confidence.

Naomi: Are you absolutely sure that your child seeing herself as "special" will build confidence?

Marina: No. Not sure at all. Perhaps it can put pressure on her.

Naomi: How do you react when you believe this thought?

Marina: With anxiety to keep staying on top of it in pumping the "unique and special" image.

Naomi: Who would you be without this thought that your child should feel special?

Marina: Free. Less pressure for me too.

Naomi: Turn the thought around.

Marina: Okay. I think I have a few: (1) "My child should not see himself as special." (2) "My child should feel free to be whoever she is." Oh wow, he must feel the same anxiety I feel about her, or more. (3) "I should notice my desire to be special through my child." (4) "My child should be an ordinary, loving, and thriving human being." Every time she fails, we may rush to remind her that she is good at something else, leading to a greater burden of expectations to live up to. I can see now how damaging it is.

Having to be unique, the child learns that being ordinary is not enough, that she is not enough unless she is special. This discovery is a great relief to parents today and a celebration of who we are and who the children are—worlds in creation.

"Should I help my toddler with his play? Climb a rock? Build a puzzle?"

Toddlers learn either "I can do it" or "I can't do it." They learn to be dependent and insecure if we help them in their own experiments and games when they do not ask for it, or when their toys are too difficult and we do it for them.

Like with the dressing example, the child may want your participation for the sense of doing things together. In that case you can do that, carefully so as not to hinder his interest in the project and not doing anything that he cannot do. If you help make what the child cannot make, then the child may lose confidence and conclude, "I cannot."

We are often moved to help a toddler, thinking it is kind and the toddler will be happy. However, with obvious exceptions, being happy to have things fixed or done is not the same as the true inner joy that comes with self-reliance and enjoying the process.

There are psychologists and parenting teachers such as Jean Liedloff, the author of *The Continuum Concept: In Search of Happiness Lost,* who suggest that adults should not play with their wee ones. This idea is rooted in anthropology studies and in trying to recreate the tribe. In the tribe, the toddler has many children and teens who carry her and engage with her. The idea of not playing with a toddler makes little sense in the nuclear family, where there is usually no one else to be with her. However, ideally, the toddler should play mostly with other older children at least two times her age. In the absence of a youth playmate, you have to play with your toddler at least some of the time.

To avoid being overly child centered and to prevent disempowering your toddler by helping, play primarily as an equal rather than as a helper. Avoid building for him, drawing for him, or solving problems for him. Often when I make this suggestion, a parent will protest with "But my little one cannot do it, and he really wants to have it built or drawn." That is exactly the problem. If we give a toddler toys and things he cannot figure out and enjoy on his own, he becomes needy of our "help" and accustomed to seeing himself as incapable and dependent.

This is not an absolute, of course. It's fine to play a musical instrument for your child, make food for him, and solve many problems daily. Of course he can listen to your music, or watch you paint for your own enjoyment, and be inspired or learn from it. But let your child do his own life enjoying the process, with no attachment to outcome and experiencing challenges.

If you have already offered activities that are too advanced for your child's age, just get toys and activities that are a better fit for your child's independent ability and slowly pack out of sight those that are too difficult for her. Let her figure things out. If she says, "I can't," tell her that she will be able to later, and give her something she can do on her own.

Some parents think that challenging activities will make the child smarter and able to overcome obstacles. Perhaps, but only if the challenge isn't so great that she cannot do it on her own and gives up. Otherwise, she is not learning to overcome difficulties but rather to be dependent on help and to see herself as incapable.

Again, to move away from a habit already built, give her activities and toys she can handle on her own easily and build the challenge gradually and without helping her. If, in the process, she comes to ask you again for help, just say, "You can try this, or put it away and do something else." But of course, nothing needs to be rigid; a toddler may have accomplished everything but one little puzzle piece. Look together and yes, if you see it and he cannot, be kind and offer the piece.

At the same time, be aware of the need for togetherness. If the child wants you to participate, do so without being helpful but more like being another child who is doing things at the same level as your child. Or simply watch her attentively.

Outcome Versus Process

Another problem with helping is that it teaches that outcome is more important than process. Children and people who focus on outcome are likely to have little patience for putting effort into the process. They are more likely to give up or depend on others to do things for them.

Play with your toddler, chase, run, read books, dance, and play music. Activities that do not require "help," yet can be played together, are ideal. In addition, do things side by side, like you make lunch while little junior draws or runs a toy train close by, you garden while he digs in the dirt, and so on. It's fine to respond to "Mommy, look!" Give attention (without evaluation) and then resume the side-by-side activities in a peaceful flow.

Do things you authentically enjoy. Many mothers say they play pretend games with a toddler. Most mothers do not enjoy such play. Indeed, this is a game the child should play either by herself or with an older child. Pretending to be the donkey and following your child's instructions is fine if you enjoy it, but realize that the child tends to become dependent on it and expects it for years to come. Many mothers are exhausted of being such playmates. Playing what you like is more sustainable. When a toddler knows which games and activities Mommy does with her, she will expect and ask for those.

*As parents in a modern society,
we have to find suitable playmates for our children.
In the case of toddlers, a child two or three times
their age is a good fit because the older child
is capable of taking care of the toddler.*

Expose, Don't Impose: The Performing Arts and Athletics

When it comes to dance, music, and some athletics, early bodily training can be helpful but even then, not unless the little one initiates it. Expose your child to what is available, but instead of imposing, follow her cues for a desire to delve fully in. My children were exposed to concerts, museums, theater, martial arts, acrobatics, dance, and more. I never imposed lessons. If your child goes to school, obviously learning is imposed. But don't add to it at home. Let the child take the initiative.

Our oldest son, of his own free will, acted in theater for many years until his teen years. The two younger ones played classical music by ear at age three and a half each on their own, as well as composed and sang. I did not ask them to. Each, at times, would spend long periods of time figuring out music by Mozart, Bach, and Beethoven as well as the Beatles. They also did some ballet with videos, and karate classes of their own choice.

There is no need to be rigid about age in either direction. In rare exceptions, toddlers do start training themselves in the arts, sports, or even figuring out science. But it doesn't mean that we jump in and start lessons. Keep exposing, and the child will ask for lessons at the best time for him. Or he may move on to another passion.

It is not a must to start super early with music. There are world-class musicians and dancers, even in the classical tradition, who did not start very early. However, in my experience, the aptitude sometimes shows up early and even a very young child shows passion for practice. See the section on discipline on page 228 for more about supporting a young child in the pursuit of his own passion.

CONCLUSION

Every stage in the baby's, toddler's, and child's life is there for a purpose. Although, because humans are so intelligent, it is extremely tempting to instill skills and knowledge at young ages, at best it makes no difference long-term, and at worst, it can do emotional harm and even thwart the child's desire to acquire the given skill.

Leave the acquisition of basic academic skills to the child's interest and initiative. Keep this phrase in mind: Expose; don't impose. Model excellence and self-discipline, and allow the child to evolve in her own timetable and ways. Reading early or being a math wizard as a four-year-old can only create emotional problems.

Likewise, trust the toddler to acquire the skills she is ready for by not helping and by providing activities she is challenged by but able to do. Live your life with your toddler in a way that she learns to value the process more than the outcome, and the joy of the moment more than comparing or winning accolades.

Chapter 13

Family Dynamics: Siblings and Extended Family

A baby is a world in the process of creation. A family is a galaxy of evolving worlds, with fluctuating "magnetic" pulls made of deep love and care combined with personalities and passions. This makes living with children an extremely beautiful and rich experience. For each member of a family to benefit and thrive, love must be the guide. Difficulties arise from the mind having thoughts that oppose reality in the moment. These show up as expectations, wishes, and illusions in the face of innocent attempts to connect, love, explore, and play.

In this chapter, we will dive into some of the challenging conflicts and struggles with babies and young children, and the way to keep returning to love. From sibling rivalry and jealousy to relatives who oppose your parenting choices—including a mock scenario between a parent and a relative—this section will help you learn how to talk to your extended family in a way that makes them feel appreciated while preserving your freedom to make your own parenting decisions.

Take your time with this chapter. Use the examples as models to do your own inquiry. Remember to always write your thoughts down and question each one. Like exercising physical muscles, the more you do it, the more capacity for love and connection you will have. If you feel angry, annoyed, stressed, and ready to burst, write your thoughts down on paper. Look at them and use the four questions and turnaround as demonstrated through this book to enlighten yourself and return to inner peace and love.

"How many years should I wait between children?"

There is no one answer to something that has so many unknown parts. With an extended family and a supportive community, families could have children close together because there are always enough adults and older youth around to help; the growing child is not needy of only Mother when there is a community. Other factors are the children's and parents' personalities, the number of children already in the family, parents' health and energy, how many children you plan to have, genders, and so on.

If you want to make things easier and peaceful and you don't have an extended family or a community, then a greater age gap is smoother. When the older child is done with being a baby, she will not need to constantly compete for your attention or become aggressive toward the little one. Seven years apart ensures such a shift for most children. It is the difference between joining the baby to get Mom's attention and joining Mom in enjoying the baby.

I was almost seven when my brother was born. One day, my mother was holding him in her arms and kissing him while I was standing by and looking. When my mother noticed my intense gaze, she asked, "Are you jealous?"

"Yes," I responded, "I want to kiss him too." Obviously, I joined the adults in having a baby. Indeed, my memories of my beloved brother are of mothering.

When new teeth come in, the frontal cortex matures too. The seven-year-old joins the parents in having a baby. The younger child joins the baby in seeking Mom's care and attention. A first-born who is too young is likely to be jealous of a baby sibling over time and become aggressive. Middle children need even more time to be done with being the littlest one because the position of the big sister or brother is already taken, and they are therefore more likely to compete with the baby for longer.

Then there is the nature of each child and the nature of the baby. It is impossible to know how each of them will react to the other and how you will react to their conflicts or cooperation.

"Doesn't having children close together ensure that they get along?"

You may believe that because your oldest doesn't remember not having a sister, she accepted her presence with relative ease. Some children do and some don't. Many siblings born close in age have had difficult experiences.

I once counseled a family who was sure that giving birth close together makes for good friends. Coincidentally, this worked with their first and second children. They assumed that it would work this way again. They waited seven years (a smart move) and had two more children close together. They called me when, to their dismay, the younger children were not getting along.

"How will a third child (or more) affect our family?"

Having a third child is very different from having a second. On the one hand it is not as overwhelming because the family is larger and your firstborn is likely to be helpful. The baby is easily engaged with each family member. However, the middle child is in a tough position. A three-year-old will often enjoy the baby in the beginning, but as soon as the baby starts being another person like her, she is likely to have a very hard time.

How difficult it will be depends on your baby's nature and many other factors, such as whether she gets regular attention from other adults, whether she is an attention-getter or she is at peace with being by herself or she enjoys not being the focus. Is she at peace with being less capable than her older sibling? Is she engaged a lot away from the family or is she used to being mostly with you?

Then there are the unknowns about the personality and needs of the new baby. Will she need a lot of attention, or will she be happy in arms as an observer of you all? Will the baby be of the same or a different gender? Two girls followed by a boy (or two boys followed by a girl) is extremely difficult for the middle one while a middle child who ends up the only one of his or her gender can often handle their position with more confidence.

With short age gaps, it is difficult in the early years when both need Mother's care and compete for her attention. In the nuclear family, this is far more difficult than in the extended family. In the nuclear family, there are not enough people to engage with the child. Jealousy is often a huge issue that must be addressed with tender care and awareness.

"My two children fight over who gets to sit on my lap."

A mother, Esther, shared the following scene: The family of four was sitting for dinner. The four-year-old came over to Mommy and sat in her lap, needing affection. The older, eight-year-old brother responded by going over and sitting on one of Mommy's legs.

Esther tried to have them share. But the four-year-old was upset. She needed Mommy all for herself. Mother validated feelings and suggested taking turns. The toddler refused and became more upset. After all, her original idea to sit on Mommy by herself was thwarted.

Esther moved with both children to the living room couch, where there was more room. The toddler started crying and throwing a tantrum, and Mom got angry—unhappy ending.

At her session, I suggested to Esther to question the thoughts that drove her choices, her anger, and that had made her toddler so upset. Here are a few thoughts Esther explored with her conclusion after a short version of inquiry:

Esther: *"My older boy needed time with me at the same time as the toddler."*

Naomi: Is that true?

Esther: No. He just wanted to thwart his sister's time with Mommy.

Naomi: How do you react when you believe this thought that the older needed you?

Esther: I am tense, annoyed, and feel used and overwhelmed. I try to accommodate and be nice, which doesn't work.

Naomi: How would you feel and react without the thought that he needed you at that moment, now that you know it was not even true?

Esther: I would feel calm and confident about letting my toddler sit by herself on my lap. I would have told my older boy that I will spend time with him later and that now I am going to hold his sister. Or even call him out on his real intent, with humor perhaps.

Naomi: Amazing clarity. Turn the thought around.

Esther: *"My son did not need to sit on my lap at the same time as my toddler daughter."*

Naomi: Is that as true or truer?

Esther: Yes. Clearly. He was just fine until his sister came over to my lap.

Naomi: Can you find another turnaround?

Esther: *"My daughter needed time with me by herself. And I needed time with her as well."* (After a moment, Esther added another thought.) *"The toddler should share Mommy with her brother."* That was obviously not true, either, as she wasn't emotionally able to do so. Reality is truth. She wanted Mommy all for herself and "Mommy ruined it all," so she cried.

Another thought this mother worked on was "I cannot say no to my son." Obviously, this is not true. He could handle it. He was not needy for connection but intent on getting in the way of his sister. We later worked on the *root cause of his need to disturb his sister*—usually jealousy and, yes, needing some time alone with Mommy too. He may also have needed a sense of power, which he tried to satisfy by upsetting his sister. I suggested to Esther, in addition to spending time with him one-on-one, to play power games with him and give him opportunities to have responsibilities that help him feel powerful and valuable.

Validating and making plans for one-on-one time would be the peaceful solution of a peaceful mind. "You and I want our own time together too. I would love that. After dinner, Daddy will be with your sister, and you and I can have time together. That would be wonderful."

This applies to an adult too; sometimes we push toddlers away to cater to the need of an adult. Usually, it makes more sense to expect the adult to be able to let go or wait.

Jealousy Is Innocent

"Mommy, why do you need another Yonatan?" asked my firstborn, looking at my growing belly.

I hugged him and said, "I don't need another Yonatan. There is no other Yonatan. You are the only 'you' there will ever be, and I love you so much."

No matter how much we explain and include a young child in welcoming a new sibling, he will not comprehend this concept any more than you would welcome another lover in your spouse's life.

In an extended family, the situation is easier as there are more loving caregivers. In the nuclear family, a seven-year-old would happily welcome a new baby as a wonderful addition, but a toddler or a young child who is still seeing himself as the baby will have a lot of inner turmoil and needs your reassurance that he is still your darling child.

It is not possible to eliminate the toddler or child's experience that comes with a new baby, and there is nothing wrong with it.

Instead, the goal is to help your child be resilient and confident in the face of such a giant transition. You won't be always able to provide everything your child wants, but you can always stay connected, loving, and affirming of her experience and her emotional strength. Go with her on her path as a loving guide climbing a steep and exciting mountain. She can climb it if you believe she can and if she can fully express herself along the way.

Therefore, it is crucial for you to realize that the insecurity that we call jealousy is innocent so that, if your older child is hurting the baby, you respond not with anger but with compassion.

In his session, Don inquired into his anger toward his three-year-old son, who was hurting the baby:

Don: "*He shouldn't hurt the baby.*"

Naomi: Is that true?

Don: No. He does hurt the baby sometimes.

Naomi: How do you feel and how do you treat your child when you believe this thought?

Don: I am angry. I yell. I feel even hate. I try to be patient and gentle and not show my anger. I say gently that it hurts the baby and tell my child not to hurt him.

Naomi: How well does it work?

Don: It doesn't. He seems upset, and then he does it more.

Naomi: How would you be when your child hurts the baby without believing this thought?

Don: I don't know. Perhaps I would notice that he cannot control himself, and I would feel connected instead of angry.

Naomi: Yes. Feel it. Be with this compassion and memorize it.

Don (taking his time): Oh my. It breaks my heart.

Naomi: Yes. That's your true nature, to love. Now turn the thought around to the opposite

Don: *"My child should hurt his baby brother."* (This is an inquiry, *not* an endorsement or a search for solutions; it doesn't mean that we don't help, only that we have no reason to disconnect and be angry. Solutions are clear when we love.)

Naomi: Can you find three reasons why he is driven to hurt his brother?

Don: (1) He feels desperate for the loss of his place with me. (2) He doubts my love. (3) He feels displaced by his brother and may wish to get rid of him.

Naomi: Yes. Very painful indeed. Can you find a turnaround to yourself?

Don: *"I shouldn't hurt my child with my rejection, control, and anger."*

Parents often cry, realizing this truth, and rush to hug and connect with their child. They want to know how to undo the damage and heal the pain—and, of course, how to help prevent the child's drive to hurt the baby.

Playful Healing

The motionless infant is not threatening to the child. As soon he crawls or walks, the real shock settles in: "This is another person who gets in my way, gets Mom's and Dad's attention, and wants what I want."

The child—whose former position as the only one in your arms is gone forever—can either feel anxious and helpless or excited and powerful, depending on your attitude, his nature, and how demanding the baby is. At some point, she is likely to annoy or to try to hurt the baby, either playfully or as an expression of a desire to rid herself of the new invader.

When you notice these budding anxieties, recognize her need and avoid moralizing or giving her the impression that the baby is more important than she is. Telling her not to hurt the baby isn't helpful because what she thinks is: "The baby is important; I am not." Or "It's all about protecting the baby and I am the bad one," and even, "They don't love me anymore," and so on.

Instead, you can validate the child's feelings by saying, "Do you sometimes wish to be with me all alone again, without the baby?" and "I miss my time with you alone too." Listen to your child and make time to be with her and to let her know how much you cherish being with her alone. You can also tell her, "When I hold the baby, I love you. It doesn't matter what and who I hold. I always love you."

Snatching toys from the baby may be harmless and may be enjoyed by the baby as much as by the child. If the baby is frustrated, protect him by providing another way for your child to play the "snatch and cause screaming" game, with you or another adult. For example, try playing power games in which you say, "Don't take the towel off the knob," and then, "Oh no, she took the towel," as you run after her to get the towel back to no avail. Finally, get it, hang it again, and start over repeatedly. Being with an understanding and playful parent, she won't doubt your love or her own value, and she won't need to hurt the baby as much.

Notice When Your Child Heals Herself

Children who feel helpless about their loss will start their own healing games. A father asked my advice about his three-year-old, who—shortly after the baby had mastered crawling—started throwing clothes all over the bedroom. He was also more grumpy than usual and tried to annoy the baby all day long.

The father tried to stop him from throwing the clothes and to explain to him why clothes should be put nicely in drawers, to no avail. After the guiding session with me, his inclination to stop his son's action changed to realizing that the child was doing self-therapy as described in my book *Raising Our Children, Raising Ourselves:*

> This time, when Chris entered the bedroom and gleefully emptied his drawers onto the floor, his father was ready. Seeing his clothes strewn about, he responded with a dramatic, "Oh no!" which seemed to give Chris the sense of power he was looking for—"Aha, I got my daddy!" Then his father folded the clothes and piled them back in the drawers so that Chris could repeat his self-made "therapy" again and again. Each time Chris threw the clothes out, his father responded with a louder and more dramatic, "Oh, no!" The game ended with the clothes all over the room and Dad "giving up" in exhaustion, laying helpless on the floor.
>
> For two months, Chris continued to initiate this game, and for two months his father gasped dramatically and then picked up the clothes, folded

> them, and put them in the drawer to be thrown all over again. All the while, Father trusted his son's need to play this game in order to gain a sense of power and autonomy.
>
> Chris's irritability and disturbing behaviors have gradually diminished. One day, he stopped dumping his clothes on the floor and has never done it again. Not only has he became very organized, but his relationship with his sister flourished.

When playing power games, it is crucial not to take a child's power away. If you are the one to stop the game or to control its direction, the child feels helpless all over again, realizing that he wasn't the one pulling the strings. This cancels most of the emotional benefits of the game.

A child who is aggressive toward the baby is telling you that she doubts your love and her own value. Telling the child things such as "But you love the baby; touch her nicely" is not helpful as it contradicts her inner experience in that moment and shames her into guilt about what she really wants to do. This is not the time for "I love you" either. The young child who fantasizes about hurting the baby will feel very guilty: "If Mom only knew what I am imagining, she would think I am horrible and would not love me."

The greatest relief for the child is to know that you know what is going on inside her. If you know her fantasies and still love her, then—and only then—she can live at peace with herself and feel worthy of your love.

This doesn't mean that you let her hurt the baby; you don't. But say yes to her emotional expression. Take her to another room with a doll and let her show you what she imagines herself doing to the baby and let her know that you know how she feels, that it is fine and normal to have these fantasies, and that you love her.

As my middle child asked me, "You love me even when I try to hurt the baby?"

"Yes," I said. "Nothing you do or imagine can change my love for you."

Your child wants to do well but cannot control herself, even if she covers up her feelings by pretending to not care or by laughing. She has no control over her fantasies, her actions, or her pretense of not caring. She wishes to have control and do well.

Helpful Strategies to Reduce Jealousy

Your child's attachment needs are especially important when they are challenged by the presence of a new baby. Make intentional plans to meet your child's needs:

- Get help. Find an older child, relative, babysitter, or a friend to come over and hold the baby so you can be with your child.
- Plan one-on-one time with your child daily when your spouse or a relative is at home or when the baby is asleep.
- Plan time for your child with both you and your partner whenever possible (for example, Grandma's visit or when baby is asleep). Even a few minutes make a great impact if you point out how special it is.
- If your child wants to be a baby again, embrace his play. But also provide exciting new activities that help your child see the benefits of being older and point out how exciting it is.

"We get to ride the bike, go to the zoo, read a book," and so on.

- Listen and stay connected.
- Give your child outlets to express his fantasies and show you on a doll what he would like to do to the baby. Once fully expressed and validated, the child won't need to hurt the real baby as much, if at all.
- Share your own similar childhood memories of similar behavior and imagination.
- Instead of having a clean house, have happy souls. Instead of making an elaborate dinner, put together something quick and be content spending time with the child who needs attention.
- Get more sleep by keeping the children in your bed and going to sleep at the same time to maximize your rest and, by extension, your ability to be a kind and loving parent.
- If your baby goes to sleep earlier, keep the baby with you while she sleeps and give your older child time with both parents, which he misses so much.
- Avoid telling your child to give up his own needs for the sake of the baby. He hears it as "The baby is important, but you are not as much." Being asked to share, be quiet, not being able to play, and so on will make the child resent the baby more.
- If the baby is falling asleep and your child is noisy, instead of saying, "Be quiet," try, "Oh, good, the baby is falling asleep. Finally, I can be with you." Then whisper, "Let's be quiet so he falls asleep. Go get the books you want me to read you" (or game or whatever he likes).

These strategies will not eradicate jealousy once and for all. It is a maintenance plan that must be sustained with awareness and flexibility.

How to Stay Calm if Your Older Child Hurts the Baby

It is not easy to be calm when your baby is being hurt, even by your own child. It is crucial to do your best to prevent the situations that prompt jealousy and to repeatedly practice the strategies just shared.

Yet, you are a human, and so is your jealous child. You may find yourself losing control. To get yourself back to calm, understanding, and loving connection, inquire into the stressful thoughts that hijack your peace away. What are you believing that causes you to be confused and disconnected from your child's valid emotional needs?

Be specific as you write down the mind's chatter:

He should not be rough with the baby.

She should know by now not to grab toys from the baby.

He should understand that the baby cannot wait and let her go first.

She should not break the baby's toys.

Shanon is a mother of a three-year-old and a baby. She said she had explained to her toddler countless times why she shouldn't hurt the baby or take toys away from her. Yet her older daughter kept at it. Shanon was annoyed.

Shanon: *"She should know by now."*

Naomi: Is the thought true? What is the reality of it?

Shanon: Obviously not true. She is still rough with the baby.

Naomi: How do you react when you believe this thought?

Shanon: Angry and wanting to yell at my child. Very stressed.

Naomi: Where in your body do you sense it?

Shanon: There is a knot in my throat.

Naomi: Negation of reality feels stressful. How would you feel and act without this thought?

Shanon: I would notice that my child either had no idea how her action feels, or she may need to purposely hurt the baby, and I would yearn to help with care.

Naomi: Turn the thought around.

Shanon: "*My child shouldn't know by now.*" The proof is that she does not or cannot control herself, or she would do so.

Naomi: If this brings on the thought, "*She is capable of controlling herself but does it on purpose,*" question that thought too. For now, turn "*She should know by now*" around to yourself.

Shanon: "*I should know by now that my child is doing the best she can.*"

Naomi: Isn't that much more true?

Shanon: Indeed, yes.

There is no final destination to arrive at on this journey. It is a human path of growth toward more connection and grace; it's about not believing thoughts that take you away from peace and allowing yourself to be consistent with love.

When Relatives Try to Intervene

Society used to be cyclical, with each generation repeating their ancestors' parenting ways. This is not the case any longer. Today, each parent is most likely to stray away from previous parenting ideals. The older generation often feels silenced and worried. Some grandparents and relatives are vocal about their disapproval of things such as breastfeeding toddlers, wearing the baby, sleeping with babies and toddlers, and so forth.

When such relatives speak up, they often hope to make an impact and influence their adult kids to follow their parenting ideals. Yet the young generation is set on finding new, often kinder, and more natural ways to rear their young. Hopefully the information you read here will help you shake away the fear of what Granny would say and the need to silence her. You will learn to listen and allow the connection to flourish while keeping yourself free to do the parenting of your choice.

"My relatives are dismayed that we all sleep together. What do I tell them?"

Why tell them anything? Are you raising their child? Is it a school project in which they are your professors or supervisors? The unconscious thought may be, *I need to be accountable to my parents and in-laws.* Instead of believing it, inquire: *Is it true? Really?* Notice how restricted and contracted you feel when you believe this thought. Here you are, alone at home with your baby, and you cannot care for her the way you really want to because you have to please your idea of what someone else wants.

Notice the pain and constriction this thought brings you while you truly want to follow your heart and respond to your baby. If you didn't believe that you have to meet the standards of anyone else, how would you then care for your baby? When freed from all restrictions of the mind, your true nature is love and responsiveness toward your baby.

Parenting is an opportunity for your own maturation toward full self-reliance. Self-reliance does not mean that you don't learn from others but, ultimately, that you choose what to learn and what to apply.

In this section you will learn how to listen to your extended family with appreciation and respect. It is best not to cancel them and shut them off. Listen to them and respond by affirming what they have said and expressing gratitude as demonstrated further in this chapter. Be open to learning from them. And, in the end, make your own decision. Contrary to your unconscious mind's anxiety, your relatives' thoughts, opinions, and feelings are not a threat because you do not have to follow them.

Anita was in the audience at one of my workshops. As I was speaking about relatives, she raised her hand and said, "But if I listen to my relatives, then I have to do what they say. Even if I only show understanding of their point of view, it means that I agree and will change my ways accordingly." I invited Anita to the stage to inquire about her thinking.

Anita: *"If I listen to my relatives and show understanding, I have to do what they say."*

Naomi: Is it true?

Anita: Yes, well it feels this way because I know they expect it.

Naomi: It feels this way when you believe this thought. Can you absolutely know that it's true that if you listen with understanding, you then must do what they say?

Anita: No.

Naomi: How do you react, feel, and behave when you believe this thought?

Anita: I feel insecure and agree. Then I push my relatives away, creating disconnection.

Naomi: How would you be without this thought?

Anita: I would be fine and could listen to them without worry.

Naomi: Turn it around.

Anita: (1) *"If I listen to my relatives, connect, and hear them, I don't have to do what they say."* (2) *"If I hear out my relatives, I can do what I say to myself."* (3) *"If I listen to my relatives, I build a warm connection with them"* (sighs with relief). Wow, so actually listening to them, I am free to do as I wish.

Naomi: The connection of the two is the mind's conjured fantasy. There was never a connection between listening to them and doing what they say—other than in your mind.

Anita: Only that in one way I create connection, and in the other way, I make war with my relatives. That's so freeing and simple.

Realizing that there is no danger in hearing people and loving them is the key to peaceful relationships. If you search for your innermost truth, what you really want is not to please your relatives, but to do the best by your baby. If you wish for your baby to become self-reliant, model it by your own ability to follow your heart and your mission to respond to your baby with trust, regardless of the thoughts of others.

This is your opportunity to build your self-confidence while nurturing a warm relationship with your extended family and friends.

You do not owe it to anyone to raise your child their way. Likewise, their dismay is their business and not yours, and their expectations impose nothing. This does not mean dismissing an opportunity for learning, which any parent can use. Take it when you need it, and choose the source carefully. If the source is relatives, that is wonderful as long as you choose what you see as best for the baby based on your baby's cues.

Your relatives' or friends' reactions to the family bed may surprise you. Many people bring their children to their beds in secrecy and feel relieved when they learn that others do so. Other people may indeed be shocked. These same people may be sleeping with their dogs or cats, yet they believe the bizarre myth that humans should sleep in separate beds and separate rooms.

Your relatives mean well. They listen to their own thoughts that are made of ideas that are not their own either. If you yourself are still struggling to grasp the fact that thoughts are not personal, I suggest you reread the beginning of this book and Byron Katie's books to help yourself feel it fully. Once you do, it would be much easier to relate to your relative with forgiveness while retaining your freedom.

Be kind to your relatives and without defense. Respond to their inquiries, and hear them fully and with gratitude. You can validate with "I understand that you feel uncomfortable knowing about our family bed. It is so different than what you are used to and unlike most in our culture." This tells them that you hear their ideas and understand the concern. You create a sense of connection. *It does not mean that you will do what they say.*

If the relatives persist with comments, you can ask them if they would like some reading material that may assist them in feeling more comfortable around your family. Focus on helping them to feel at ease, not on convincing them of your ideas and not on explaining why you won't change as those are defensive and therefore create disconnection.

There are studies and research behind the conviction that the baby's and young child's wish is correct about co-sleeping as on all other baby-care topics. Anthropological research and books about natural parenting and co-sleeping may be useful. Reading may help your relatives or friends to be more comfortable with your ways—or not. In my experience, most people are not interested in learning or reading about it. That is fine; it is not your goal to change their minds or have control over their feelings; you offer reading only if the person is interested.

Avoid Debating Your Parenting Choices with Relatives

To respond to your dismayed relatives with respect and love, avoid getting into a debate. You can share about your choices but the moment you try to convince them, you are in their court, trying to meet their expectations and justify or defend your ways.

Convincing is the beginning of war. It tells them that they are parenting your child with you, that they have a vote, and that they have to be convinced and included in your parenting choices. In reality, *it is not about whose idea is right but about who is making the decisions*—that's you. Love them where they are while staying rooted in yourself and trusting your child.

However, do listen to them because it will help both them and you feel connected in a loving relationship. Canceling them by saying, “Don’t talk to me about this,” will hurt everyone by creating tension, secrecy, and the withholding of care and feelings. Grandparents are less likely to help and feel welcomed if they have to walk on eggshells. Your fear of hearing them out is unfounded.

Remind yourself that the thought, “If I listen to them or understand them, I have to do what they say,” is simply not true. When you stay rooted in your ways, they will notice your strength, and over time, they are likely to respect you more. They will notice that you follow your path and that they have no vote, yet they feel connected because you don’t dismiss them and you understand their point of view. You may even learn something. Even the most different parenting approaches can offer useful food for thought.

The gift that comes with this generous approach is that you won’t feel threatened by your relatives’ ideas because you know you are not required to follow them. The result is that you will actually listen peacefully and may even learn something occasionally. Your relatives might wish they had the courage to trust themselves as you do.

There is another surprise that may sometimes occur: Don’t assume your relatives will be dismayed. I know grandparents who, upon learning about natural ways of baby care, were moved and inspired. Such relatives will support you with no quarrel; others, if you listen without trying to convince, may actually be interested and, with time, may join your path. Either way, they are more likely to be open when their original thoughts are not negated or blocked. They then feel free to notice, learn, and listen and perhaps even appreciate your ways over time.

The following is a mock dialogue in which a mother played the role of her "very annoying and pushy" mother (Grandma) while I played the mother, who is peaceful, able to listen and connect, and rooted in herself.

Jennifer, as Grandma: I don't get why you sleep with Elliot (a toddler). How will he learn to sleep by himself? You are just ruining him.

Naomi, as Jennifer: Thank you. I love how much you care. I see, you wish that Elliot would have his own bed and room so he learns to sleep alone. Is that it?

Jennifer, as Grandma: Yes, exactly. I am glad you get it and hope you will now do it.

Naomi, as Jennifer: I get how you feel and think. And I am convinced of my way, and I see that you are worried that Elliot will grow up unable to sleep by himself. I am not worried, but I am concerned that you are having a hard time with it.

Jennifer, as Grandma: Oh, I see, so you are stubborn and won't listen. You will ruin the child. You are selfish—that's all.

Naomi, as Jennifer: Oh. That's a painful thought. I can see that this is very worrisome and uncomfortable for you as you have never seen such practice. I would love to make it easier for you. Would you like to see some research on the benefits and safety of sleeping with one's baby or child?

Jennifer, as Grandma: No. I know better. I don't need stupid research. I have real-life experience.

Naomi, as Jennifer: I understand. I love that you are so passionate about Elliot. I love that you care and are so involved with all your heart. I feel frustrated because I am not going to mother my child your way, and I worry that you will suffer and worry a lot. I wish I could make it easier for you, and I respect your confidence about your way.

Jennifer, as Grandma: Why don't you just get a child's bed for Elliot like everyone else?

Naomi, as Jennifer: That is not an option. Other than changing me, which is not going to happen, is there a way I can make it easier on you to be at peace with this issue? Maybe you would like to visit us without staying overnight so you don't even see our sleep arrangement? Will that be easier for you?

Jennifer, as Grandma: Maybe.

Naomi, as Jennifer: Why not try that for a while and see how you feel.

Jennifer, as Grandma: So, no crib or bed? I was going to buy it for you . . .

Naomi, as Jennifer: Oh, Mom, thank you so much for your generosity and care. No, we will not use a separate bed for Elliot. If you want to gift us something, we could use another child carrier. There is one kind I really wish to have, now that Elliot is bigger.

Mother and daughter would likely feel closer and ready to look at a new baby carrier.

Notice that in the role of me being Jennifer, I never engaged Grandma in a debate about the benefits of co-sleeping without her asking. If I had, it would be as though I had told her that she has a say or that she has to change her mind, and it would never end. It would incite her to keep trying to convince me.

By not engaging on the subject matter, I gave a clear message that *my parenting is not up for a vote or a debate.* Such clarity often results in respect and allows for real connection because you can understand each other without the anxiety associated with having to convince and change the other person's thinking. You don't try to convince her, and she, over time, will stop trying to convince you. Instead of explaining, I made it clear, without engaging in the actual subject, that *the issue is simply a matter of who decides and that Grandma is not deciding and therefore needs no explanation.*

Unwittingly, we often give relatives the idea that they have a vote on our parenting choices by engaging them in the subject matter instead of simply making it clear that we are in charge and validating their difficulty about our different ways. We can do so by listening to them kindly, while validating and appreciating the love and care the relative expresses. Not surprisingly, this creates connection and peace and relatives who are more eager to participate, less with advice and more with love.

"My relatives are uncomfortable with my toddler's breastfeeding." (If you bottle-feed, they are usually fine.)

Sometimes we get caught up in our concern for the comfort of other people. We forget who we are committed to care for. And so the child has to give up on what is best for her so that Grandma or some friends would not be uncomfortable.

Parenting is an opportunity to free yourself from taking responsibility for the feelings of other people. I am not talking about being unkind, as you aren't doing anything to them. You simply care for your child first.

You need your relatives' approval. *Is that true?* Ask yourself and find out what is true so you can set yourself free. Without this thought, you wouldn't have any problem listening to their thoughts and staying true to your child.

At each moment that your parenting choices don't fit the limiting majority vote, you have a golden opportunity to put your love and care for the child ahead of catering to the ideas of other people and their comfort. Your heart knows best. When on your child's side, you act in line with your child's best interests.

Your child will learn from you to either bend for the sake of pleasing others or trust himself and stay authentic.

The Difference Between Learning from Others and Obeying Them

The idea is not to become arrogant and learn nothing from the wisdom of other humans. Yes, some people have skills and information that can indeed benefit you. No need to throw the baby out with the bathwater. Listen and learn. And then choose freely by observing your child and reality.

The real problem is the mistrust of oneself to a point of following voices without checking with reality—with the baby, the child, and your own responsive heart. There is no need to silence the voices that come your way. Instead, listen with gratitude. You can benefit from listening to anyone when you don't feel threatened but free to choose your way. Indeed, other people may know something that can assist you. Learning from other people or books is humble and useful.

Humble means that you realize that you too don't know anything for sure. Every child is an unknown riddle unfolding. Listening to relatives can be done with true interest if you realize that, ultimately, you don't know. If you listen just to be nice, there is a chance it would feel patronizing. When you are humble, you can honestly listen with interest in the experience and point of view of another human being.

At the end of the day, the authentic cues from your child are your first guide. If your mind is still and attentive to your baby, you will often know what to do without any other input. At the same time, a wise grandmother who loves your child may have a useful insight to consider.

In other words, we need not silence our family and friends. After considering their ideas, we only need to make our choices freely, based on the reality of who the child is.

The difficulty to stay rooted in the self while listening is that we are often full of self-doubt and feel threatened because of our desire for approval. For all the reasons mentioned in this book, we grew up learning that someone bigger than us knows better; the adults knew better where we should sleep, whether we should be crying and expressing emotions, when we should breastfeed or go to sleep, what we should learn, how we should play, and so on. These common parenting and school practices left us not trusting ourselves and tending to depend on others' opinions.

We learn early on to adjust our behavior and thinking toward the expectations of others. We learn to dismiss our inner guidance, regard external opinions as more valuable than our own, and follow dogma instead of responding to reality from our deep, caring humanity. For example, when we struggle to get the baby to sleep on her own, we literally dismiss our own heartfelt choice and negate the baby's natural and healthy cues.

It is this insecurity that leads to fearing relatives' criticism. At the end of the day, the more you trust your child, the more confident you will feel about parenting. You will naturally make mistakes, which you will learn from and correct while feeling true to being a loving parent above all.

CONCLUSION

Bringing a baby into the family is like bringing home a new, future roommate. Gradually, you find that your home is shared by this new, deeply loved person. It is never as simple as you envisioned, and you must make room for who they are and consider their relationship to existing or future children, to the other parent, and to yourself. This is easier said than done. Don't expect to be perfect, but strive to keep learning and questioning your thoughts as you navigate human relationships.

Whether it's sibling rivalry, jealousy, aggression, feeling torn between caring for a baby and a toddler, or your relatives insisting on their passionate solutions, staying connected requires letting love be your guide and trusting your child as the magnet that draws that love into action.

When your mind is stressed, it is a proof that you are listening to thoughts that do not fit with reality. Question the thoughts and find your way back to understanding your child's impulses, needs, and abilities, as well as the intent of your partner or relatives. Bring healing to the jealous child, with kindness and an opportunity for self-expression, and bring connection to all relationships through gratitude.

Chapter 14

Nurturing Yourself and Your Parenting Partnership

To conclude this book, we must address the needs of the mother and father. In this chapter, you will read about feeling isolated, marriage, decision-making as partners, daddy time, mother's need for "me time," and even if and when the time is right for a vacation. Through inquiry and stories, you will learn to balance meeting your own needs with finding joy in the reality of life with children.

Short on "Me Time"

It is common for parents, especially mothers of babies and toddlers, to feel overwhelmed, often saying things such as "I am tired, overworked . . . I can't do it anymore. I need some 'me time.'" The answer to this issue is also the same as for the baby who cries. Meet the need when possible, and if you need to cry, allow yourself to do that. However, as an adult, you have a third and better option than the baby: to inquire and release yourself from the thought about a need that is not possible to meet.

The optimal solution is to find out if there is actually a need. But, just for comfort, let's first look at the possibilities to meet the need, at least partially. Crying about it with a loving listener can be a temporary release but not a real solution.

The best way to take some rest is to notice when you have it and use it consciously. If your child is asleep (when no partner is around), or if you have a partner who is at home and your baby/toddler is calm or with your partner, jump on the opportunity even if for a few minutes. If alone with the baby, just rest; meditate, close your eyes, listen to music, or talk to a friend while the baby is on the breast, asleep, or in your arms but not in need. If your partner is at home, you can take a bath or a walk, do some yoga, or listen to music as you like.

Often, mothers use spontaneous free time to clean, make food, or use the computer. Therefore, the trick is to become aware: "I have twenty minutes now. The dishes can wait. Emails can wait. Almost anything can wait." This is the time to take a deep breath and consciously choose to take time off. It is available a lot more than most of us realize—if we only claimed it rather than filling it up with chores.

These snippets of time present themselves even when alone with your baby. Obviously, it is harder for a single parent if that is all she gets, and if you are one, then the idea is to use the times you can and to seek other single parents, friends, babysitters, mentors, and helpers.

When alone with a baby, seize the moment when she is asleep

on you, and go for a walk. If there is also a toddler, get her in the stroller and go. Of course, this isn't always possible, but we often miss opportunities when it is, and then we feel exhausted.

As some point in the baby's development, you can breastfeed and leave a satisfied baby with a spouse or another loving and safe adult who can stay with your baby/toddler for a short while. Take a walk without going far. With our smartphones today, your helper can text you the moment the baby needs you, or you can make sure to be back in a shorter time than you know the baby is likely to wake up and need you.

It doesn't take long to feel rejuvenated. It is more about becoming aware—"I am having time for myself now"—than the actual length of time. Sometimes just listening to a piece of music or taking a few slow breaths with awareness of oneself fulfills the same sense of refreshment that comes from a break and can be done while breastfeeding or lying down with the baby.

I can hear the single mothers saying, "But I have no one to help me." Keep reading, but also write down that thought. Please realize that this is the exception and not the rule; ultimately, it is not true. No one truly has no one; thinking that way is a victim mindset and signals a need to work on this tendency. But mostly, keep reading to get to the part about letting go of the need altogether as that is the ultimate freedom.

Being resourceful, reaching out to friends, the community, relatives, the school, the local library, the seniors' center, homeschoolers groups, mentoring volunteers, and so on, can be very effective, and you may meet wonderful new people too. Ideally, have backup help in place before giving birth. And when no help is available, find ways to breathe with awareness of the moment.

Anything you do can be done with stress or without, by shifting your state of mind. Therefore, the best strategy is to fall in love with the experience of caring for your child and viewing that as your break from having to do things for yourself, especially when there is no chance for physical time alone. For myself, one of the greatest gifts I found in mothering was that it was not about me at all. Focusing on another is freedom from the nags and wants that occupy the mind so often. A break from the "me, me, me" can be such a relief indeed.

"Can we go on a vacation *without* our toddler?"

That depends on many factors. Is the toddler excited about the idea? That is number one. And, of course, is the toddler still breastfeeding? Has she already experienced being overnight without Mommy? Does your toddler have a few siblings who will stay in the house? Will she stay in her own home? Do you have extended family with whom the toddler feels as good as with you? And, if she is seriously stressed out, can you easily return from your vacation—that is, is it close by?

I also suggest you ask yourself whether you will actually enjoy being away and not end up feeling anxious about your child. Most toddlers are not ready to be without their parents and are likely to feel distressed or even traumatized.

When taking the cues from the toddler, you know the answer to this question. From my many years of experience with thousands of families worldwide, as well as my own, the answer is most often "no." I used to take my toddler with me even on public speaking tours, with my husband too, so he could be with him while I spoke.

The thought to inquire: *"I need time with my spouse (or family or by myself) away from my child(ren)."*

Similar to the illusion that you need "me time," a vacation without the toddler is not a need. Unless the child is with other family members he feels completely relaxed with and is happy to be without you for the duration, being apart would be painful, scary, and entirely unnecessary.

If a time away from your toddler or children is a high priority for you, create the above conditions gradually. Leave them for a few hours with Grandma a few times, then try an overnight with you being close by and able to return if the toddler turns out to not be ready to be without you overnight. But again, inquire into why you would need any of it. Mostly, wait and take your child(ren) with you on vacation. You can take a babysitter with you. Most parents don't even enjoy separating overnight from their toddler. Trust that.

Questioning "Me Time" Thoughts with Humor

Talking to yourself out loud while changing a diaper or breast-feeding can bring relief, laughter, and humor. You can even sing it: "I am changing a diaper. I haven't dressed yet or eaten yet, my toddler is pulling on my leg, and the baby has pooped three times in a row and can't get off my boob. . . ." You may chuckle. Or you may speak to an actual person, telling the story in the spirit of a comedian, and both of you will laugh. Isn't that mothering? Your self-talk can be, "This is hell," or you can say, "What a heavenly joy!" It is a choice in each moment.

However, in my experience with parents, including myself, the greatest relief comes from inquiry into the "me time" idea. Even though it's best to do it in writing, if your hands are full with the baby, just visualize writing your thoughts.

Before the inquiry, let's define what is actually a need. What proves that something is a need? You have it! If you don't have it and you are alive, that proves that you don't need it. You may want it, but the word "need" creates stress, urgency, and panic.

Maria, a mother of one baby, felt the need for "me time." Here is her inquiry:

Maria: *"I need 'me time.'"*

Naomi: Is that true?

Maria: Yes.

Naomi: Can you absolutely know that it is true?

Maria: No. I am alive without having it.

Naomi: While caring for your baby for hours, how do you feel when you believe this thought that you need "me time"?

Maria: I feel resentful toward the baby, exhausted, and irritated.

Naomi: Where do you feel it in your body?

Maria: In my tummy. I'm feeling sick, and my eyes feel heavy.

Naomi: How would you feel and be without this thought?

Maria: Fine. Just focused on the baby and enjoying her.

Naomi: Turn the thought around.

Maria: *"I do not need 'me time.'"* Yes, that's more true. I am fine.

Naomi: Can you find another turnaround?

Maria: *"I need a 'be with the baby' time."* For sure more true.

Naomi: And another turnaround?

Maria (thinking quietly): *"My baby needs a 'me time.'"*

Naomi: Oh, yeah, it's her turn to be focused on. She is the baby.

Maria: Wow, this is so helpful.

Naomi: I have another one for you if you wish.

Maria: Yes, please.

Naomi: *"I need time to focus away from myself."*

Maria: Oh, yes, I kind of get it. Can you say more?

Naomi: Why did you decide to have a baby?

Maria: To give myself an amazing experience of raising a human being. Oh, I see. So being with the baby is my "me time." Me doing what I want to do: Be a mother (laughs with a sense of relief).

Yes. And that is true freedom and a path to becoming mature. We spend our youth focused on ourselves. Then we mature and focus on others. Giving is the greatest joy. Focusing on others—in this case, on your beloved child—is a dream come true and, in my life, the best part of being human. This is easy if one surrenders to the joy of giving and lets go of focusing on oneself. Focusing on one's own wants and likes pales in comparison to nurturing another life.

This does not mean you can never have time for yourself—only that it will be less frequent and that it will require more planning. The real freedom comes from realizing you don't depend on it, which allows you to plan without stress. Then, when you have it, you really relax, and often, you may just find you miss your baby and can't wait to get back to her.

Here is another inquiry:

Brigette: *"It's more than I can handle. I need a break now."*

Naomi: Is that true?

Brigette: Well, no. Obviously I am handling it.

Naomi: How do you react when you believe this thought?

Brigette: I feel exhausted and irritable.

Naomi: And how would you be without this thought?

Brigette: I would just do what I do. I will be fine.

Naomi: Clearly, it's not the baby, or the time, but your thought. No thought, no pain.

Brigette: Yes.

Naomi: Good to know. Turn this thought around.

Brigette: *"It's not more than I can handle, and I don't need a break."*

Naomi: Is that as true or truer?

Brigette: Well, duh, obviously I care for the baby and my toddler too, and I am fine and handling it without a break right now.

Naomi: Yes. Other than in thoughts, you are fine.

Indeed, believing that you need a break when you cannot have it is self-torture. Keep the big picture in mind, as I point out in the first inquiry. You chose to have a child for your own joy. Even if your baby was unplanned, this is your life to celebrate with the surprise gift you have received. Therefore, your deepest need, passion, and desire are to spend your time caring for your baby. It is the path you signed up for, your journey to cherish and find ways to fulfill. You are having the time of your life. And, by the way, you will miss it terribly in just a few years.

The big bang turnaround is: Finding joy and contentment in each moment of caring for your little one(s) transforms that time into "me time." Whether you chose it or received it by surprise, it's your journey to escort another human into existence and nurture, guide, and love her into becoming who she is meant to be.

Staying Home with Your Baby

Some mothers, and even fathers, naturally gravitate toward making raising a family their full-time career, and when finances allow, they may share that time at home between the two of them. If you can and love to do that, enjoy. And if you do, make sure your baby has close human connection with extended family and friends as well.

Ideally, the baby will have full-time care from the mother or another primary, consistent, loving caregiver; this is crucial in the early years. The baby needs to be in arms and to breastfeed freely. Bonding is the process that builds the ground for human relationships, self-confidence, emotional health, and physical well-being.

In addition, a stress-free baby who takes for granted the constancy of care and closeness develops well in all ways and is healthier.

Separation from Mother that causes stress can distract the baby from engaging in her developmental steps. Therefore, I do recommend that you make the baby's needs your priority. However, humans are pliable, and finding other loving setups of care is a matter of creative solutions that meet the baby's needs.

If you can take the time to be with your baby full-time, that's optimal. If you are convinced that you cannot, before finding another solution, give yourself a chance to reconsider and look for ways to reduce your absence and stay full-time or most of the time. There is almost never an absolute impossibility. With the goal of being able to give the baby full-time maternal care, I have seen families move from a house to a tent/yurt or to more modest living arrangements, rent out an extra room if they have one, or move in with grandparents, and so on, in order to afford for the mother (or father) to stay with the children. Having Mom is by far more important than what the walls are made of.

All this having been said, there is no need to feel guilty if your ability or even choice is different. If you absolutely must work for emotional or financial reasons, do your best to work from home or to work where you can bring your baby with you. If you must leave the house without your baby, have a wonderful care person who will bond and hopefully offer your breast milk in a bottle while you are away and keep the baby in arms and in constant, loving contentment.

Mothers Who Feel Isolated

Many stay-at-home mothers complain that they are isolated. Ideally, your baby needs an opportunity to connect with a community of loving people. After the first few months, if the baby's world consists mainly of Mommy alone for most of the day, and then just Mommy and Daddy for a couple of hours, the baby may develop anxiety around other people and face social difficulties later. The baby thrives best with an extended family or a community.

That said, if you are isolated, it is still best to give your baby the constancy of Mom, the breast, and in-arms body contact, which allows healthy bonding and development. Humans can grow up in many different ways and conditions. These experiences shape how they develop, and that diversity is something to cherish. Here, I am simply addressing the optimal ways of child-rearing that support a peaceful, harmonious family life.

Isolated mothers call me often feeling anxious and lonely. It is best to plan in advance for communal connections, even when doing so isn't easy. Again, spending less money on rent or a mortgage, renting out a room, cohabitating with other families, getting a regular babysitter, and engaging the help of relatives can be supremely helpful for both mother and baby.

Nurture the Baby's Connection to Daddy

A father is a very important figure in a child's life, and we therefore want to nurture a healthy bond between the baby/child and his father. When I ask mothers how they create Daddy time, they often say that they give the baby to Daddy and leave the room, hoping for the best. In such a case, this elicits a negative conditioning response: "When I am with Daddy, I lose Mommy." After a while, when Daddy (or a grandparent or other helper) gets close, the baby clings to Mommy and turns away from him. This literally trains the baby or toddler not to want to be with his father.

Early on, and over time as needed, let Daddy be with the baby while you stay with them, visible to the baby. Be right there with baby and Daddy. Babies love being with Mommy and Daddy together. You can go on a walk right next to Daddy while he carries the baby. Or you can hold the baby and let Daddy connect with her while she is in your arms. Respond to the baby's signals to know which is best.

When the experience of being with Daddy is not associated with losing Mommy, a loving and healthy bond can be created. In parenting, like in gardening, we often have to take small steps and actions in the present to further a future goal.

Sharing Child Care and Housekeeping Between Partners

Now that we don't live by gender-assigned housekeeping and childcare roles, it seems there is often more confusion than resolution. Many women are still, automatically and unconsciously, moved to do everything in the home, even when they also work professionally. Many men are more willing than women realize to be partners, but as the woman takes more responsibilities at home, some men respond by not participating as much.

Although some men are still coming home from work expecting to be served, this is unusual today in progressive societies. I have seen couples who truly share equally, as my husband and I did. When the man earns the money away from home, he knows, when he returns home, that his wife worked as hard or harder than he did at work. She may have been busy with the children, and he finds a full sink or plates on the table. He comes in delighted to see his wife and children and asks what is most needed or notices and starts handling the needed chores. If Mother is breastfeeding or otherwise needed by a child, he clears the kitchen or the toys. Perhaps he shopped for dinner on the way home and will start preparing food. On another day, he might take the kids out to play, wrap the baby on his back and go for a walk with the five-year-old on a tricycle, and so on, so Mommy can clean up and make dinner.

Cleaning after the meal is done similarly, with an intent to work together and to lighten the load of the other person. I recall a home I have been to as a counselor that inspired me because both partners kept saying, "You rest now, I will do it." And rest was not always possible, but the point is that they competed not for doing the least and not for expecting the other one to do it; they tried hard to ease it for the other and do more themselves, giving rather than getting. Not surprisingly, years later these parents told me that their teenagers were extremely generous and helpful of their own free will.

"My partner helps with the baby and around the house."

When a woman says, "My husband/partner *helps*," I know she is the one taking responsibility for household chores. For some, that is fine, and that is what they want and how they share as a couple. I am not here to assign fixed duties. Any choice you are at peace with and in clear agreement about is perfectly wonderful. But if you want an equal partnering in home care, then no one is a helper. Yes, there are specific projects that are wholly done by one person or the other, and a partner may help sometimes. But the daily running of the house is a "together" responsibility.

Decision-Making as Partners

As a couple, you are equal people, but you are not the same. Each of you has a set of skills, knowledge, and experience, and each of you has passions, interests, and focuses on different aspects of living. Gender-specific differences are a root of some of these differences (the capacity for pregnancy and breastfeeding, for example) but as children grow, some chores are and some aren't about gender at all.

Most peaceful partners decide together who should be in charge of what, at least for some of the major areas that require skills. You can share and take turns cleaning up, shopping, and doing the laundry. But some major decisions require specific skills or knowledge. One person is clearly better at doing the bills while the other loves and is skilled at gardening. One may have practical skills, such as fixing cars or cooking while the other brings knowledge about nutrition and lifestyle.

Couples often argue over where the baby should sleep, or whether the toddler should be in a day care, and other baby/toddler-related issues including to relatives, education, the arts, friends, influences, food, and more.

The difficulty comes from not deciding who is in charge. We trust partners with issues over which we don't need to have a say, but for some reason, parents fail to notice that parenting or specific parenting issues can also be decided by whoever of the two parents is more fit for the subject at hand. This does not mean that the other person has no say. It only means that the person in charge ends up making the final decision with full trust and support of her/his partner.

In most families, a child's early years seem to be mostly the domain of the mother (or the stay-at-home parent). Breastfeeding, sleeping arrangements, choice of diapers, and so on are mostly decided naturally by the mother. The father contributes by participating, holding, diapering, and washing, as well as adding ideas, concerns, wisdom, and points of view. The mother is the deciding one because, at the early stages, she has a biological hormonal connection that no one else has and spends the most time with the little one.

The mother is often also the one who reads parenting books, consults with other parents and professionals, and devotes herself fully to the subject. I must say, though, that today, I see more and more men—strong and supportive men—who read books, schedule sessions with me, and are just as engaged as the mothers. Therefore, to the mother, I suggest you don't reject a supportive father, even if he is "wrong" by your thinking. And to the father, with rare exceptions, in the end, trust the mother.

As children grow, men are often more involved, and families grow to decide things more as a unit and don't have a problem coming to agreements. The difficulty only presents itself when one parent does not do any of the study and yet wishes to make the decisions. In such situations, I always invite that parent to study the books and other sources his or her partner learned from, before forming an opinion. It is fine not to be interested, and then to trust the other to come up with the best possible direction, but it creates friction when one has not acquired the knowledge and yet wishes to make or participate in the decision.

Mistakes are unavoidable; that's life. There are no guarantees for anything, and changes evolve along the way as needed. Whoever makes a certain choice that seems to need change is not at fault. We should always reframe mistakes as experiences to learn from and move forward to the next choice.

When our firstborn was six months old, my husband, who was not in charge of this subject, thought that perhaps sleeping together was not the best for our baby anymore. His strong opinion was not educated, but I didn't just shut him down. My response was to listen to him with genuine care for his concerns. I suggested that we try and see how the baby responds. We got a little playpen and used it as a crib next to our bed. The baby, of course, cried. My husband asked me to wait a bit and see whether he would fall asleep.

A minute later, he agreed with me, and we brought the baby to our bed and never tried it again. This example isn't perfect either; my attempt to let my husband have his experiment was at the expense of the baby. On the other hand, it made it completely clear, and we raised three children without my hubby ever asking to remove a child from the family bed. In fact, he made bedtime into a slumber party that never ceased to be the most fun part of the day.

What the experiment showed both of us is that he could trust me completely. Again, it's not that I never made a mistake, obviously, but trusting and empowering the parent who is likely to know more is going to optimize the children's development and maintain a peaceful home. On the other side is the example of one partner having passionate opinions based in their own childhood or common influences. It is not that he may never have a good idea; of course he will. But sometimes strong opinion and passion does not constitute the best or the right choice. That's where deciding who is in charge of a specific subject becomes helpful and brings peace.

However, the parent who is not in charge of a given issue could sometimes have a thought that can bring on viable solutions worth pursuing. By working as a team, the parent in charge can be open-minded and consider new possibilities. This way the couple is a real team that pulls together rather than apart.

When there is no clarity about who decides, there is often struggle and arbitrary control that cause resentment and marital strife. Such an outcome in the relationship is more harmful to the child than any "wrong" decision can be. This is why I stress that it is most important to empower one parent to be in charge of certain decisions in the child's life. I also recommend that the parent who is less skilled in a particular subject takes the initiative to educate themselves, especially if they wish to be more involved. Read, listen, attend guiding sessions or classes, and let go of the way you were raised and the opinions you inherited by inquiring into your thoughts.

Having one person in charge is, in my view, the way a couple works together. It is the kind of togetherness that is inclusive while ensuring the best outcome based on mutual respect and self-knowledge.

Children benefit the most from a peaceful flow. Parents who get along and empower each other make the greatest positive impact on their children's development, regardless of the specific choices made.

CONCLUSION

Parenting is a lifelong path. Once you are on it, embrace it. Any resistance is painful. At the beginning, having a baby may seem overwhelming. This is the time for grasping the power of true surrender to the beauty of creation, by flowing with it and falling in love with the experience.

Like jumping from a plane with a parachute, if you don't surrender, you suffer. There is no way back and no other path. The view is incredible—so why waste time wishing you were on the ground? The same is true with your baby, toddler, or young child—you are already on the path, and there is no way back. Longing for what is not brings only pain; embracing what you have is the essence of life and of love.

Conclusion

You cannot know the inner world of your child. All you can do is read the cues the best you can. Your perceptions of your wee one are interpreted by your mind as she grows. Your baby's self-expression is also a mirror of you and your perception. This creates a closed mirroring loop. Therefore, it is best to love unconditionally and respond to Mother Nature's creation with reverence. Here are some helpful principles to keep in mind:

- Stay neutral and respond with trust to primal, authentic needs.
- Avoid—or at least minimize—introducing the habit of seeking constant stimulation.
- Avoid—or at least minimize—teaching your toddler to seek and rely on external stimulation.
- Allow your toddler to explore while you guard her safety.
- Support emotional expression—whether rage, tears, or upsets—but not as a substitute for meeting a real need.

- Work on yourself by inquiring into the thoughts that bring on stress and disconnection and obstruct your ability to observe your baby or young child's authentic being.
- Strive to model being the human being you wish for your baby and toddler to learn from. Being peaceful, secure in oneself, and kind is the best way to ensure raising a child who is at peace with herself, confident, and caring.
- Respect your young new being as you would an adult while knowing her obvious limitations.

Life is like a dance; in each moment, the choice is to dance *with* reality or *against* it. Babies and toddlers provide a constant invitation to dance with reality.

Our culture has evolved to struggle against reality, including opposing nature when it comes to raising children. The fear of nature—and the anxious narrative of how to escape it—permeates our lives. We avoid both cold and heat, the outdoors, the sun, soil, dirt, pathogens, rain, and snow. We recoil from even the simple feeling of soil and stones under our feet, and we minimize walking and running. We fear nature more and more, in a vicious cycle, and the result is less endurance. The avoidance of discomfort weakens our bodies, our immune system, and our physical strength. With such an attitude, instead of dancing with nature and being strong, we create injections for fear of diseases and suppressive medicine to cover up the body's lifestyle-induced ailments.

We bring babies into the world mostly with the same kind of fear-based attitude of avoidance and control. Most women in the West give birth in a hospital that is set up for total control, computer screens, lying on the back, ready to suppress pain, far from nature, no squatting, and far from trusting the body to give birth. The home of the newborn is often filled with gadgets that the infant has zero need for. In the first six months, the baby only wants to be in arms, sleep, and breastfeed as needed—very little else is truly needed for the baby's care. Later, the baby gives clear cues on expanding her needs and we can respond without overstimulating.

Having stuff does no harm by itself. Many attachment parenting mothers hardly use any of the gadgets in real life. Yet the parental attitude of finding a product for every issue spills into how some parents handle the challenges of simply having a little squirmy infant whose needs are constant. As the baby moves from the initial coma-like state to awakening, parenting becomes a choice between fighting reality by getting the baby to bend to our comfort or surrendering to the forces of nature and flowing with the baby's instruction manual.

The opposition to the instruction can manifest in separate sleeping, paper diapers, strollers, cribs, control of sleep time, overuse of pacifiers, and so on. It is the way of shaping the newcomer to fit the adults' preconceptions and belief system. Surrender, in this powerful sense of the word, is riding the waves and swimming with the river. It means becoming mature and turning into the giver who reads the cues and responds by trusting nature's design. Babies are not mistaken to need what they need.

By questioning your thoughts as you have learned to do in this book, you can wake up to your child's reality. Free from delusional thoughts, you won't react to the baby or try to shape your child. You will respond with only one consistency: love. Every thought that feels stressful or confusing is therefore an invitation to inquire and bring yourself back to your child.

I hope this book has woken you up to the possibility of celebrating surrender to reality by questioning what is not real—your thoughts—because that is what makes life and being with your baby and child the miracle that it is. By embracing truth, you free yourself to return to love.

With love,

Naomi Aldort

Recommended Reading and Viewing

Books About Parenting and Self-Development

Naomi Aldort—*Raising Our Children, Raising Ourselves: Transforming Parent-Child Relationships from Reaction and Struggle to Freedom, Power and Joy*

A compassionate guide to parenting that emphasizes connection, empathy, and mutual respect, helping parents respond without control or coercion.

Byron Katie—*Loving What Is: A Transformative Approach to (Questioning) Freeing Oneself from Stressful Thoughts*

A transformative approach to questioning stressful thoughts and beliefs, offering tools for cultivating clarity, peace, and presence in everyday family life.

James J. McKenna, PhD—*Safe Infant Sleep: Expert Answers to Your Cosleeping Questions*

Evidence-based guidance from a leading researcher on infant sleep and co-sleeping, helping parents make informed, safe choices for nighttime care.

David Elkind—*Miseducation: Preschoolers at Risk*

A classic warning against pushing academics too early, highlighting the importance of play, curiosity, and developmentally appropriate learning.

Katie Allison Granju—*Attachment Parenting: Instinctive Care for Your Baby and Young Child*

A modern introduction to attachment-based parenting, offering practical ways to build strong emotional bonds through responsiveness, closeness, and trust.

Aletha Solter, PhD—*The Aware Baby*

Grounded in developmental psychology, this book explores how to understand babies' signals, emotions, and needs without suppression, laying foundations for secure attachment.

Jean Liedloff—*The Continuum Concept: In Search of Happiness Lost*

A groundbreaking account inspired by Liedloff's time with Indigenous communities, advocating for a return to instinctual caregiving practices such as constant physical closeness and trust in natural development.

Pam Leo—*Connection Parenting: Parenting Through Connection Instead of Coercion, Through Love Instead of Fear*

Practical tools for creating deep emotional bonds and resolving conflicts without punishment, rooted in the belief that strong relationships are the foundation of peaceful and caring behavior.

Thomas Cowan, MD—*Commonsense Childrearing: Unconventional Wisdom for a Nourished Childhood*

Encourages parents to trust intuition and natural development, offering a holistic perspective on raising resilient children.

Books About Your Baby's and Child's Health

Barbara Reed Stitt—*Food and Behavior: A Natural Connection*

Explores the deep connection between diet and mood, showing how nutrition can impact mental health, learning, and behavior.

Natasha Campbell-McBride, MD—*Gut and Psychology Syndrome (GAPS): Natural Treatment for Allergies, Autoimmune Illness, Arthritis, Gut Problems, Fatigue, Hormonal Problems, Neurological Disease and More*
Presents the GAPS nutritional protocol, linking gut health to neurological and psychological conditions such as autism, ADHD, and depression.

Robert Mendelsohn, MD—*How to Raise a Healthy Child in Spite of Your Doctor: One of America's Leading Pediatricians Puts Parents Back in Control of Their Children's Health*
A classic in alternative pediatric care, encouraging parents to trust their instincts and use medical care wisely rather than reflexively.

Shawn Baker, MD—*The Carnivore Diet*
A case for an all-meat diet as a means of improving health and reversing chronic illness, written by a leading advocate of the carnivore approach.

Judy Cho, NTP—*The Carnivore Cure: The Ultimate Elimination Diet to Attain Optimal Health and Heal Your Body*
A practical and accessible guide to implementing the carnivore diet, with troubleshooting, nutrient insights, and real-life applications.

Paul Thomas, MD—*Vax Facts: What to Consider Before Vaccinating at All Ages & Stages of Life*
A pediatrician's perspective on vaccines, presenting risk–benefit discussions intended to help parents make informed decisions.

Suzanne Humphries, MD, and Roman Bystrianyk—*Dissolving Illusions: Disease, Vaccines, and the Forgotten History*
Examines historical data on infectious diseases and vaccines, offering a critical reinterpretation of mainstream narratives.

Books and Resources About Childhood Nutrition

William Duffy—*Sugar Blues*
A classic exploration of sugar's impact on health, mood, and disease,

raising awareness about the hidden costs of refined sugar in the modern diet.

Katherine Erlich, MD, and Kelly Genzlinger, CNC—*Super Nutrition for Babies, Revised Edition: The Best Way to Nourish Your Baby from Birth to 24 Months*

A practical, research-based guide to nourishing infants and toddlers with whole, nutrient-dense foods from the very beginning.

Eva Iliana and Betty Johnston—*Keto Kids*

Focuses on using ketogenic dietary principles to support children's health, with recipes and strategies for families.

Kristie Sullivan—*Growing Up Keto: A Practical Guide for Kids and Parents with Over 110 Recipes the Whole Family Will Love*

A family-oriented guide to maintaining a ketogenic lifestyle, including tips, recipes, and insights for raising kids on low-carb nutrition.

Nicole Au Yeung and Theo Henusse—*Our Species Appropriate Diet: Tiger's Mystery in Lionland*

An exploration of diet through an evolutionary lens, advocating for approaches that align with human biology and development.

My Little Eater—*"Beef for Babies"*

Online resource discussing the role of beef and nutrient-dense animal foods in infant feeding, mylittleeater.com

Multimedia Resources

YouTube: "Plants Are Trying to Kill You!"

Challenges conventional views about plant foods, emphasizing that plants may be harmful or less "natural" than typically portrayed, especially from the perspective of proponents of animal-based eating. https://www.youtube.com/watch?v=d3iXJAJaZp8

YouTube: "The Carnivore Diet for Children."

This video discusses how to start a carnivore diet for kids—providing tips, tricks, and common pitfalls in applying a carnivore approach to children's nutrition. https://www.youtube.com/watch?v=Oi5qI_P8qUs

Dr. Ken Berry, MD—YouTube
"Red Meat Should be Baby's First Food," https://www.youtube.com/watch?v=cM1fRxeqAnk&ab_channel=KenDBerryMD.

Dr. Paul Saladino, MD—YouTube
"Using an Animal Based Diet to Optimize Fertility and Pregnancy with Lindsey Meehleis" Discusses ancestral, carnivore-based nutrition, lifestyle interventions, and metabolic health. https://www.youtube.com/watch?v=g6wlcKzZLMA

Books and Written Guides About Healthy Pregnancy and Birth

Dr. Robert Mendelsohn, MD—*Mal(e) Practice: How Doctors Manipulate Women*
Argues that condescending attitudes towards women have become institutionalized in modern medicine and result in unnecessary, degrading, and dangerous practices

Gloria Lemay—*Wise Woman Way of Birth*
A resource on natural, empowering birth practices, emphasizing informed choice, connection, and holistic maternal care. wisewomanwayofbirth.com.

Additional Multimedia Resources

Dr. Robert Lustig—"Sugar: The Bitter Truth"
Explores sugar's effects on metabolism and chronic disease.

Brian Sanders—"Food Lies"
Challenges mainstream nutrition advice and advocates for nutrient-dense, ancestral diets.

Resources

The following organizations and experts offer caring, practical support for parents who want to nurture strong, loving connections with their children. Each provides trustworthy guidance rooted in respect, empathy, and understanding.

Attachment Parenting International (API)

A nonprofit organization dedicated to supporting strong, nurturing parent-child relationships through principles of attachment parenting, an approach to childrearing that focuses on building a secure attachment bond between parents and their children. API provides education and support to families worldwide, advocating for a family-centered approach that values empathy, responsiveness, and physical interaction. Visit attachmentparenting.org

La Leche League International (LLL)

Founded in 1956 by a group of seven mothers in Illinois, LLL aimed to promote breastfeeding through mother-to-mother support and education. Today, it is a global organization that is dedicated to providing support, education, and advocacy for mothers and families about breastfeeding, chestfeeding, and human milk feeding. The organization operates in over eighty countries. Visit llli.org.

Dr. James J. McKenna, PhD, and the Mother-Baby Behavioral Sleep Laboratory

Dr. McKenna is a leading researcher and director of the University of Notre Dame Mother-Baby Behavioral Sleep Laboratory. He is known for his groundbreaking studies on co-sleeping and infant sleep safety. Dr. McKenna is recognized as the world's leading authority on mother-infant co-sleeping in relationship to breastfeeding and SIDS. The website features articles, Q&As, and videos. Visit cosleeping.nd.edu.

NaomiAldort.com

The official website of parenting author and speaker Naomi Aldort, offering resources, Zoom sessions, and guidance for parents seeking to raise emotionally resilient and content children with respect, empathy, and awareness.

Endnotes

Chapter 2

1. "Breast Cancer and Breastfeeding: Collaborative Reanalysis of Individual Data from 47 Epidemiological Studies in 30 Countries, Including 50,302 Women with Breast Cancer and 96,973 Women Without the Disease," *Lancet* 360, no. 9328 (July 20, 2002): 187–95, https://doi.org/10.1016/S0140-6736(02)09454-0.

Chapter 3

1. Mandy B. Belfort, Sheryl L. Rifas-Shiman, and Ken P. Kleinman, "Infant Feeding and Childhood Cognition at Ages 3 and 7 Years: Effects of Breastfeeding Duration and Exclusivity," *JAMA Pediatrics* 167, no. 9 (September 2013): 836–44, https://doi.org/10.1001/jamapediatrics.2013.455.
2. YouTube, *Carnivore Diet for Children and Toddlers [Why the Controversy?],* video, 1:05:02, uploaded by Ken Berry, MD, June 15, 2025, https://www.youtube.com/watch?v=I8oYe6OLNnw.
3. Kristie Sullivan, *Growing Up Keto: A Practical Guide for Kids and Parents with Over 110 Recipes the Whole Family Will Love* (Las Vegas: Victory Belt Publishing, 2020).

4. Inbound Pursuit, "Carnivore Diet for Kids: Help Your Children Reach Their Full Potential with This Dietary Regimen," *Carnivore Snax,* September 26, 2024, https://carnivoresnax.com/blogs/articles/carnivore-diet-for-kids.
5. Nina Teicholz, *The Big Fat Surprise: Why Butter, Meat, and Cheese Belong in a Healthy Diet* (New York: Simon & Schuster, 2015).
6. Catherine Shanahan, *Dark Calories: How Vegetable Oils Destroy Our Health and How We Can Get It Back* (New York: Balance, 2024).
7. "Vegetable Oil Was Initially Created to Be Machine Lubricant, Not Cooking Oil," *Noble Origins* (blog), March 31, 2023, https://nobleorigins.com/blogs/articles/vegetable-oils-lubricant.

Chapter 11

1. Rae Pica, "Shed Those Shoes: Being Barefoot Benefits Brain Development and More!," *Rae Pica* (blog), September 2017, https://www.raepica.com/2017/09/barefoot-benefits-brain-development-2018/.
2. Pam Moor, "It's Science: Being Barefoot Boosts Your Kid's Development," *Motherly,* accessed September 16, 2025, https://www.mother.ly/health-wellness/its-science/benefits-of-being-barefoot-for-children/.

Chapter 12

1. Kelley Durkin, Mark W. Lipsey, Dale C. Farran, and Sarah E. Wiesen, "Effects of a Statewide Pre-Kindergarten Program on Children's Achievement and Behavior Through Sixth Grade," *Developmental Psychology* 58, no. 3 (March 2022): 470–84, https://doi.org/10.1037/dev0001301.
2. Linda Darling-Hammond and Jon Snyder, "Curriculum Studies and the Traditions of Inquiry: The Scientific Tradition," in *Handbook of Research on Curriculum,* ed. Philip W. Jackson (New York: Macmillan, 1992), 41–78, https://stars.library.ucf.edu/cirs/2228/.
3. Lawrence J. Schweinhart and David P. Weikart, "The High/Scope Preschool Curriculum Comparison Study Through Age 23," *Early Childhood Research Quarterly* 12, no. 2 (1997): 117–43, https://doi.org/10.1016/S0885-2006(97)90009-0.

About the Author

Naomi Aldort is the author of the bestseller *Raising Our Children, Raising Ourselves,* which has been published in twenty languages. She has spoken at parenting conferences, universities, and other events worldwide, and her parenting advice columns and articles have been published internationally in widely distributed magazines, including *Mothering, Nurture, Pathways, Natural Parent, Juno, Natural Life, Life Learning, The Attached Family* (of Attachment Parenting International), among many others.

Naomi brings peace, self-realization, and deep connection to families, children, individuals, couples, and audiences worldwide through her compassionate communication approach and The Work of Byron Katie. She is a mother of three adult children and currently has three grandchildren.

For interviews, articles, and to book sessions and workshops, visit AuthenticParent.com or NaomiAldort.com.